Thomas Sheridan is an author, artist and filmmaker from Dublin, Ireland who came to international recognition in 2011 with the book *Puzzling People: the Labyrinth of the Psychopath*. In the years since, he has written several more books, and has made films on topics such as social engineering, political and corporate pathology, and on to the occult foundations surrounding the emerging years of the *Third Reich*. In recent times, his work has been featured in some of the world's largest media outlets and he is a highly sought-after public speaker around the world.

Sheridan offers a holistic approach to all the topics he covers, believing that by re-examining everything from art, mythology, the occult and on to social engineering, that this can equip all of us with what he terms a 'consciousness firewall' in the face of pathological forces.

www.streetdruid.net

Published by Thomas Sheridan Arts
First Edition
thomassheridanarts.com

ISBN: 978-1-326-73580-7

Includes Original Artwork and Photos by Thomas Sheridan
(where indicated)

Cover Photo and Back Photo: Connor Clements

Cover Design: Justin Jezewski

Raven Artwork: 'Odin's Spy' by Amy Malone

Copyright 2016

All Rights Reserved. No part of this publication may be reproduced, stored in a retrieval system, or transmitted in any form or by any means, electronic, mechanical, photocopying, recording or otherwise, without the prior permission of the copyright owner.

This is a Never-for-Kindle Book

THE DRUID CODE

MAGIC, MEGALITHS AND MYTHOLOGY

Thomas Sheridan

FIRST EDITION 2016

INTRODUCTION

The primary purpose behind writing this book is to address—within my own philosophical framework—the gaping hole that currently exists between the study of European mythology, megalithic 'sacred sites', Neolithic rock art, and the subject of Druidic 'magic'. In particular, magic in the modern sense; as a specifically purposeful, proactive system of *art* and *science* in accordance with *will*, which is then *charged* in order to bring about desired changes within the material world. Rather than this book being merely a study of primitive 'hunting magic' derived from Mesolithic peoples, it will look at the wider concept of magic and the occult being utilised as a form of early, collective psychoanalysis by druids and other similar European Heathen priesthood traditions and why this came about, as well as how it relates to the megalith builders, lost civilisations and continual changes/challenges for the human experience. The research presented in this book includes the transition from early hunting magic methods to more developed forms of consciousness-enhancing cognitive and cultural processes during the Neolithic age. This is a book specifically about magic and not spirituality as such, and how magic developed along a very different historical tangent as an initial result of seeking tribal psychological stability and security within a volatile material universe.

It is my firm contention that the druids of Ireland, specifically, were the link in the esoteric chain of Western occultism from early proto-shamanic cults of Mesolithic/Neolithic Europe, and on to the post-Christian witch cults, and eventually towards the alchemists and the great occult revivals of the *Enlightenment*. Rather than druids being viewed as some isolated spiritual tradition, I will be presenting them as the guardians of magic in the same way that early Irish Christian monks safeguarded *Classical* literature during the so called Dark Ages.

This application of ritual magic is found within the vast canon of (mainly) Irish mythology, and it is this archive of folklore and epics which will make up the main body of evidence for the arguments put forth in this book. In particular, how and why there is a strong cultural overlay of this mythology with the mysteries and anomalies of the surviving megalithic structures of western Europe. It is my belief that a major cataclysm befell the Northern Hemisphere of the planet some time around 2500BC, and this is the primary origin of Plato's *Atlantis* story. This book will set out to make the case that this "Atlantis" was indeed based on a real civilisation located on the Atlantic shores of western Europe and which extended into the Mediterranean as far as Malta and Sicily. The druids were, I believe, the repositories of an ancient knowledge from before the rise of civilisation in Sumer.

Irish mythology, when examined in tandem with the great stone monoliths of western Europe, was the primary mode of ritual magic that held the memories of past cultures—both traumatic and historical—within the western European psyche. Magic theories and practises were created, and then, were continually developed as a result of this "Atlantis" cataclysm, as humans developed more conceptual modes of cognition and an understanding of the fundamentals of psychology. The adoption of allegory, metaphor, and on towards systems of magic rituals, came out of Neolithic society as a direct result of the trauma created by the natural disaster(s) which consigned huge areas of the Atlantic regions beneath the waves and which ostensibly 'sterilised' Ireland and Orkney of large-scale human habitation for about six hundred years after 2500BC.

This magical tradition created by the survivors was kept alive for thousands of years until the arrival of Christianity in Europe, which in and of itself became something of a psychic cataclysm for the communities—who were previously Heathen and pagan nature-based spiritual traditions—now having to cast off their numerous gods, goddesses and nature deities in order to serve the imported 'one true god' of the Middle East under an increasingly centralised world view. The druids and their magic continued to function in their traditional capacity within Christian Ireland, as well as parts of Britain, Celt-Iberia, Brittany, southern Scandinavia and the Eastern Mediterranean, serving the psychic well-being of their respective tribes and clans by carrying forth the mythology and wisdom from the deep archetypal pagan past, and into the modern Christian age.

Central to this magical approach was the association of these mythologies with certain megalithic 'sacred sites', and this magical inter-connectivity was continued on into the European *Enlightenment* by mainly, Freemansonic antiquarians. I have termed this conduit of magical progression *The Druid Code,* and it is a legacy which is with us to this day in everything from art to philosophy and to religion. The story of *Atlantis* can be seen as something of a trigger within the European psyche in terms of changes in the human cognition —and of the subconscious mind—which was a profoundly traumatic event implemented within European tribal structures. Triggers, which later manifested through following generations, when stories of ancient cataclysmic disasters were spoken of. The disaster story resonates within us even today—as if we are aware that on some deeper, primal level, the story of *Atlantis* has some basis in vital truth.

The "Atlantis" story—under many different names and metaphors—was carried from generation to generation within much of the folklore, culture and mythology of western Europe. Initially by the proto-shamanic Neolithic magicians in the initial aftermath of the great 'surge', this was later carried on through the centuries by druids and other holy men and women. In time, it eventually became the basis of the European magical tradition leading to developments such as modern alchemy, analytical psychology as well as certain artistic movements.

This is the *Druid Code* of the modern polymath which will guide us as part of the narrative to uncover the meaning of the surviving megalithic sites of Europe in order to tell us what earthly tales they speak of, as well as the secrets of the human condition they continue to unleash from our past, and what traumas may be held within that collective subconscious. I have travelled all over Europe in order to unravel this code, and this book represents my own lifelong mythological journey of discovery. It is your story too.

My own personal familiarity is mainly with Irish mythology and megalithic sites, and this will form the majority of the content provided within this book. Even so, when comparative examples with other associated cultures and archaeological evidence presents itself, I have also included these other mythological records and evidence, which will be encapsulated into the overall central theme of this book. In doing so, I hope other researchers and authors—more personally familiar with their own homelands and heritage—in time, will likewise perform their own explorative insights into these other cultures and histories. Likewise, I encourage other researchers to apply similar archetypal interconnectedness with archaeological discovery, as I have with my own ancient Irish code breaking. The evidence, I believe, is there to be found from the semi-Arctic regions of Scandinavia to the warm sunshine of Malta, and everywhere in between the wide sway of the lands of the so-called Atlantic 'megalithic' arc.

Even if this book is rooted in a philosophical approach based on my years of research, *The Druid Code* also functions, by default, as something of a potentially useful field guide and reference source to take readers on a journey through the megalithic and ancient pre-Christian sites of Britain, Ireland, as well as other regions around western and southern Europe. I hope to also provide a valuable resource of the complementary mythologies, insights and history, in tandem with describing the magic, rituals, interpretations and traditions associated with these sacred sites, along with their gods, goddesses and their associated festivals.

The best manner in which to experience the full awesome power of these locations and tales connected to them is for people, if possible, **to visit the megalithic sites of Europe for oneself,** and to soak up their mysteries and partake in their sense of wonder. Hopefully, this book will perform the function of something of an accessible template from which anyone can begin to explore these places and experiences, and from this, open up one's own personal connection to a more holistic understanding and creativity within the context of the journey itself. To draw upon the hidden narratives and encoded meanings within these locations—along with their associated legends—in the hope that it unleashes further insights and exploration for the readers themselves. There is something for all of us in doing this.

It may be a tired old cliché, however, it is a cliché that still holds true, especially with this topic: 'you don't know where you are going, unless you know where you have been'.

The magic continues.

Thomas Sheridan
Sligo, Ireland
Summer Solstice, 2016

CHAPTER ONE

MISSING TIME

According to one telling of the great Norse mythological epic, the world of men begins in the aftermath of the battle of *Ragnarök* in which the gods of *Asgard* are destroyed during an apocalyptic showdown of immense proportions. The Norse gods are doomed to the poignant fate of accepting their own individual demise, so that a new world can arise from the devastation caused by the unleashing of seismic and supernatural forces of destruction and chaos. The gods are fated to die, and this prophetic lamentation of impending destruction—from Odin to Balder and several other gods and goddesses of the Nordic tradition—is a constant within the Norse mythological pantheon. Just as the Ice Giants, whom the gods themselves destroyed, likewise they—the *Æsir* tribe of gods from *Asgard*—are also doomed to die.

Ragnarök has, and continues to conjure up, endless visions of bedlam and chaos within the imagination of people long after the end of Viking age. A powerful narrative which continues to grow in popularity right up to the present day. It is generally forgotten, though, that the story of *Ragnarök* is, in actuality, a powerful restoration myth. Albeit one that comes with a price. That price being the loss of certain powerful crafts and 'magical' abilities which were once the exclusive possession of the pre-*Ragnarök* races and beings. The mayhem and destruction is the not final outcome by any means. Life, and even the gods and goddesses (in somewhat lesser forms), begin again. It is their magic, crafts and supernatural powers that are lost. Or at least, are no longer mentioned (or have taken second place) in being central to the Nordic identity.

The concept of cataclysmic floods, either submerging or unleashing 'monsters' before a new age of restoration and human social/spiritual rejuvenation, is a common thread within European folklore. The Swiss psychoanalyst Carl Jung believed the deep waters of the seas represented the personal and the collective unconscious. "By the sea shore. The sea breaks into the land, flooding everything...The sea is the symbol of the *Collective Unconscious*, because unfathomed depths lie concealed beneath its reflecting surface...The sea is a favourite place for the birth of visions (i.e. invasions by unconscious contents)."

(image: British Library Collection)

A similar motif appears within the telling of the Irish mythological classic *The Children of Lir*, when the old world of magic and the supernatural are slowly tormented into oblivion by nine hundred years of a cruel watery fate—as the result of a wicked curse—which ends in an Ireland where the old Heathen ways and sacred places have vanished into the stuff of lore. This is an idea which is common in many magical traditions; the concept of making corporeal and incorporeal sacrifices in order to exchange one set of powers for another. Sometimes the sacrifice is in the form of a racial memory, tradition or trauma preserved within the subconscious of the tribe as an allegory-filled fairytale or mythology. Other times, it can be a material hoard of gold, jewellery and other precious and valuable objects buried in the ground at significant locations. In both examples, the intention is the same. They are magical spells sent forth into the future in order to alter, expand or transform the consciousness of the individuals and societies which rediscover them.

A votive hoard represents a powerful example of a ritual burial of gold and other treasures so as to acquire the blessings of the 'gods'. This can also extend to spiritual, cultural and even psychological sacrifices to the future gods in the guise of an older way of living and worship being buried within the culture of a society as a kind of votive hoard of the subconscious mind of the tribe. In many ways, this is the most powerful votive hoard of all, as it exists not buried in an obscure field somewhere, but rather, it is buried, or 'charged' into the psyche of every member of the tribe waiting to be restored within the collective consciousness of the whole.

THE GOLDEN GRIMOIRE OF THE *BROIGHTER HOARD*

In 1896, the *Broighter Hoard* was found in a field adjacent to Lough Foyle in County Derry, Ireland (now Northern Ireland) which included the ritual burial of a delicate golden boat as a gift to the Irish and Manx sea god Manannán mac Lir. The initial finding of the *Broighter Hoard* resulted in a major diplomatic to and fro between Dublin and London as to which of their respective national museums would keep this stunningly beautiful artefact. In the end, Dublin won, and the *Broighter Hoard* now sits in the *National Museum of Ireland*. However, it was the sensation and diplomatic tensions surrounding the ownership of the golden boat—creating something of a psychic 'charge'—which unearthed the most powerful treasure of all: the return to the public consciousness of an old pre-Christian god. The *Broighter Hoard* had performed its main task when the druids buried it on the shores of Lough Foyle thousands of years previously; Manannán mac Lir was once again the pagan sea god of the Gaels.

Today, a large sculpture of Manannán mac Lir—along with his magical boat controlled by his thoughts which guide the god between this world and the otherworld—now sit atop of Binevenagh mountain looking down on both Lough Foyle and also across the sea to the west of Scotland. At one point in 2015, the statue had been removed from its plinth and hurled off the side of the mountain by fanatical Christians. The damage was minimal. Even so, this act demonstrated to remind us all how Christianity actually became a force in the Heathen world as a violent and vindictive crusade against indigenous Europeans. During 2016, the reinstalled statue of Manannán mac Lir was featured in many photographs silhouetted against the *Aurora Borealis*. The god had returned 'back home' in more ways than one. The votive hoard within the Irish psyche had been restored as a living and popular pagan god once again, sailing his magical boat between this world and the otherworld.

Both the stories of *Ragnarök* and *The Children of Lir* have two very significant commonalities; the transistion—or painfully traumatic tranformation of one version of reality into another—by acts of fate and/or wickedness ultimately involving an unleashing of the power of water, along with temporary submergence, and, in both cases, Christian scribes wrote down these tales having broken the long line of the previous, orally-transmitted traditions from which they came. At which point, some creative editing placed biblical entities and timelines into the native mythology as if to imply, somehow, that the shift to Christianity was in and of itself a traumatic event which required tapping into the same mythological traditions of traumatic transformation and eventual restoration which produced earlier disaster and survivial myths.

Ragnarök itself is a series of 'future' (or possibly, cyclical?) events which culminate in an enormous battle in which many of the supreme deities of Norse mythological pantheon are killed; including Odin, Thor and Loki, along with many humans who are destroyed upon the plain of *Vigrid* (the 'place of the surge'). The descriptions of the actual battle of *Ragnarök* within the Norse *Eddas* tell of fire giants burning bridges to cinders, giant serpents splashing toxic liquids upon opposing armies, along with several mentions of weather warfare, including mighty winds and targeted tidal waves. Such is the fury of the battle, along with the other turbulent events surrounding *Ragnarök*, that it allows Fenrir the giant wolf to break forth from his cage, and then, following his death by Odin's vengeful son, all the other giant beasts tear one another asunder until the entire world sinks to the bottom of the sea among waters that have been turned into a boiling cauldron by the intensity of the battle. In the mythological aftermath of the battle of *Ragnarök*, the world eventually floats back up from the depths to be reborn and renewed as a fertile land of new opportunity and tranquillity.

The gods who survived the chaos of *Ragnarök* then hold a council and decide to repopulate the earth with a male and female human—who have both managed to survive—along with the lesser gods who were not killed in the cataclysm. These two people will find shelter in the still standing *Yggdrasil* 'world tree' under the protection of Odin's sons Vidar and Vali, and their uncle Honir, along with Thor's sons Modi and Magni, who still retain possession of their father's hammer *Mjölnir*. These gods then emigrate to the unscorched land of *Idavoll* (the fields of fertility). A new world will then be constructed and the age of men shall begin in earnest.

THE MYSTERY OF THE MATA

The Irish mythological tradition, on the other hand, has not revealed any such creation-apocalyptic myths to date. The legends speak of waves of successive invasions from across the sea who changed the nature of Ireland with every new culture that arrived. This could also denote a shift in consciousness as much as real races from other countries invading Eire. However, there is one extremely tantalising mention of an entity referred to as the *Mata*, which, according to the translation by Lady Gregory, was a four-headed, many-legged sea turtle-like creature, and the idea of this being an Irish creation myth has been recently brought back into focus by Anthony Murphy of the *Mythical Ireland* website:

> *"And the Valley of the Mata was there, the Sea-Turtle that could suck down a man in armour."*

The *Mata* is eventually slain by the Dagda (the 'good god'), and the *Stone of Benn* was then erected on the spot where the monster was cut down, somewhere in the *Brú na Bóinne* area around Newgrange. The location of the *Valley of Mata* itself has still not been fully determined, although this 'valley' may well be an allegorical idea as much as a real place. As we shall see with the *Midgard Serpent* of Norse mythology later on in the text, the most incredibly startling synchronicities exist between tangible reality and mythology that goes way beyond the concept of coincidence.

The reading and understanding of the Irish mythological record in terms of it being something of a psychological archive of the Irish ancient psyche has been generally lacking. This is unfortunate, as such an approach can reveal more about the lives of the ancient Irish than by just merely looking for proof that the individuals mentioned in the text might be based on real historical figures (which itself is still plausible). The *Mata* story would appear to be far more significant in terms of its meaning than the attention it has been given to date. The concept that some monster(s) from the deep emerging to be slain by the 'good god' harkens towards an almost Lovecraftian concept of subconscious fears bubbling up from the depths of the psychic abyss. These are the dangers that inevitably come with a shift in consciousness, either personally or collectively.

Even the term '*Mata*' itself speaks of a primordial linguistic archetype as in the 'mother' aspect of the initial maternal godhead. The 'Ma' sound is a universal constant within early human language and may well be a linguistic version of a neurological form constant (phosphene), in that it is derived from inside the human mind—independently without an external source—similar to how basic shapes such as spirals and crosses are generated deep inside the brains of people who are kept in absolute darkness for long periods of time. The process is still unexplained by neuroscience, although it can be induced by the triggering of electrical or magnetic stimulation of the retina and/or visual cortex, and the effect is also known as the *prisoner's cinema*. The same archetypal shapes are also experienced by people using psychedelic substances. The phrase 'seeing stars' also comes from this experience.

The term for 'Mother' sounds very similar all over the world—in dozens of unconnected linguistic traditions—and may well be the term that came to denote measurement and calendric cycles based on the human female menstrual cycle: "Ma"..."Mater"..."Mother"..."Parameter"... and so on. Women kept out of sunlight for long periods of time stop menstruating, and perhaps this was even discovered by our ancient ancestors. Did these women—while sequestered inside a cave, passage cairn or long barrow—also speak of tales surrounding magical dancing spirals and other shapes eventually appearing in the darkness around them?

Imagine the psychological effect of these tales recounted by women, and how it would have impacted upon the entire tribe when their experiences were told... The witches had arrived! Only for the men to then also spend time inside these 'wombs' or absolute darkness to witness the same dancing shapes and forms appearing within their own minds... The magicians had arrived! Are some of the shapes we see carved inside Irish passage chambers from Knowth to Newgrange to Loughcrew the artistic representations of neurologically generated phosphenes beheld by our ancestors while in their magical state of absolute darkness? When a culture develops not only an understanding of the menstrual cycle itself, along with its relationship to the moon, and coupled with this, the ability to stop menstruation in places of darkness among the triggering of dancing forms and shapes within the visual void of the enviornment, then we have the beginning of ritual magic.

The female cycle then becomes the sacred scale of measurement which can be predicted and controlled according to its direct relationship to the cosmos. The ancient magi through their *Mata magic* could create, or prevent, the creation of life by their **art** (caves, underground chambers) and **science** (lunar and menstrual cycles) in accordance with their **will** (birth control) in order to change **consciousness** (phosphenes). The basic fundamentals of ritual magic are born.

We also can't discount that the 'monster' nature of the *Mata* was a much later degradation process similar to how Christians also changed 'Lugh' to 'Leprechaun'. The four headed aspect of the *Mata* is numerically also highly significant within the overall Irish mythological pantheon. The very idea that the ancient Irish based their early cycles on the menstrual-lunar effect would have been represented as an affront to the imported religion of the Middle East when one considered their own attituted towards women and the menstrual cycle... The 'curse' was born.

Therefore, we have to consider that the possibility that the universal mother of the Irish, "the *Mata*", was transformed by Christian scribes into a monster from the deep which had to be slain and be replaced with a psycho-phallus in the form of a standing stone. Again, this example serves to demonstrate that we cannot always take the translations of Irish mythology as honest uneditorialised accounts. What was hidden or changed by early Christian monks tells us a great deal indeed if we read between the lines. Such editorialisation may also have been compromises created, or rather, altered by druids within the early Irish church to keep on the 'good side' of Rome by not appearing to be too nostalgic for the old gods. The *Mata* story presents us with a humbling indication of just what an immense task deciphering the *Druid Code* is, and always will be.

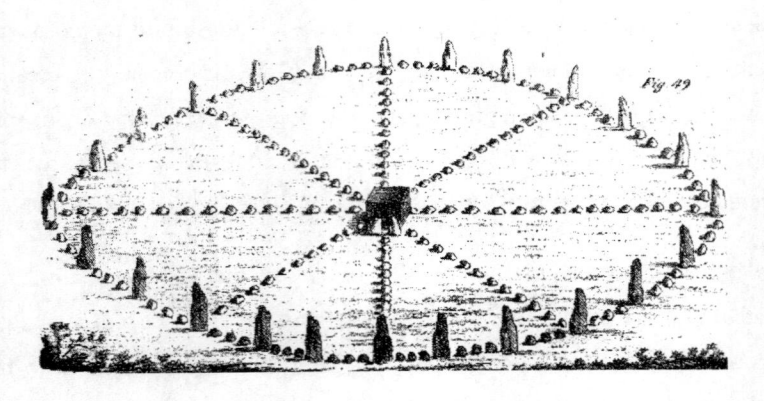

Perhaps the most northerly megalithic stone circle in Europe is the *Domsteinane* site in western Norway near the city of Sola. Looking more akin to a magical symbol laid out in stone, than a traditional Neolithic stone circle, the complex suggests a more 'ritualistic' arrangement when compared to the stone circles we see in Britain and Ireland. However, *Domsteinane* may actually be a better preserved complex than say, Beltany circle in County Donegal, Ireland which contains large numbers of random and scattered smaller stones within its circle and which may has been laid out originally in a more segmented, geometric design.

As *Domsteinane* currently remains a mystery as to its actual antiquity, we can only speculate upon its original purpose. In 1822, the Swedish archaeologist and folklorist, Nils Henrik Sjöborg theorised that it was a royal chamber, with the king seated on the throne at the centre. However, this is unlikely as such a scenario is more commonly applied to ritual magic circles whereby the magi, or elder priest, is the focal point of energetic focus and protection during the performance of the ritual. *Domsteinane* suggests a highly developed degree of sophistication and cultural elegance by its original builders.

(illustration: Nils Henrik Sjöborg)

BRITAIN'S 'ATLANTIS'

At the time of the publication of this book, there is a growing interest and awareness among the general public of the once huge areas of land which once had connected Ireland and Britain to mainland Europe, along with the now submerged vast regions of the western Mediterranean; where islands such as Malta were once tall mountains which stood in the middle of fertile plains protected by the *Straits of Gibraltar*, which acted as a giant natural dam holding the remorseless power of the Atlantic ocean at bay. The nearby island of Sicily was, likewise, a tall mountainous region covering a much more expansive landmass than is the case at present. In recent times, what appears to be a large menhir (standing stone)—with distinct signs of having been worked by humans—was discovered sixty kilometres off the coast of Sicily (which is part of the overall European megalithic arc from Malta/Sicily to Scandinavia). The menhir is located at forty metres (over one hundred feet) below the surface on a now submerged island known as Pantelleria Vecchia. I predict that more menhirs, dolmens and other man-made megalithic structures will be discovered on the seabed specifically from Orkney to Malta—including the most likely 'place of the surge' itself, Doggerland—in the years to come.

Effectively, if one chose to do so—and perhaps as recently as five to eight thousand years ago—a healthy person could walk all the way from Norway, across the presently submerged Doggerland on to Britain and Ireland, continue south to Brittany, around the western coast of Iberia and across into Malta perhaps without needing to make a single sea journey. Or at the very most, perhaps only a short crossing by boat. In effect, the landmass of western and southern Europe currently available for human habitation is significantly smaller today than what was habitable during the age of the megalith builders before 2500BC and earlier.

One can only imagine how the social, cultural and psychological impact this loss of land must have affected the humans who once lived there. Especially if the rise in sea level was more sudden and catastrophic than is presently accepted. Such an event would have left a profound and lasting legacy unpon the psyche of the people who survived, as well as that of later generations.

The Druid Code:
Magic, Megaliths and Mythology

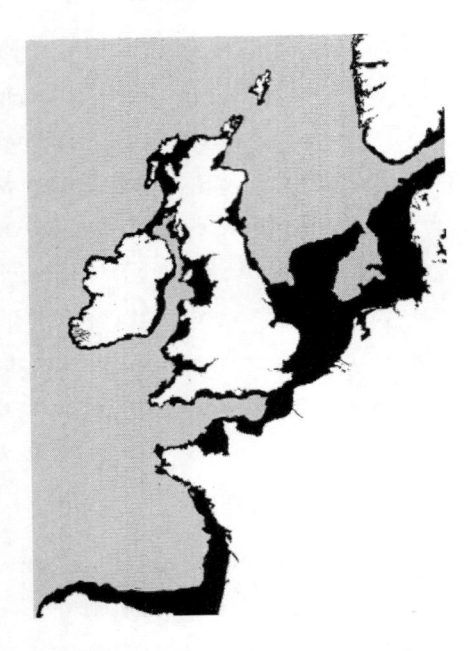

Regions of western Europe which became submerged leading up to and during the loss of Doggerland; the entire black region of this map represents a conservative approximation of the total amount of land once available for human habitation and settlement. The complexity of the human societies which settled in these now submerged regions are to date, unknown. However, recent discoveries of submerged structures found off the coast of Orkney, along with the famous 'Seahenge' site off Norfolk, England, give tantalising insights of what is yet to be found under the sea further out from the present coastline. This Doggerland landmass now beneath the North Sea has long been known to fishermen who would occasionally pull up mammoth tusks and large deer anthers while trawling the seabed. No serious investigation has yet been undertaken to locate any possible megaliths which may be located within the black regions of this map.

(image: The Triskele and the Dragon Website)

In allegorical terms, the battle of *Ragnarök* fits in well within this initial European climatic catastrophe, as does the numerous surviving tales from around western and southern Europe which speak of lands and ancestors doomed to be imprisoned under the seas as a result of some apocalyptic event. If the epic of *Ragnarök* were to be the only apocalyptic legend to survive, that would be a coincidence. As there are many others which bear the same narrative—albeit using different gods and monsters to describe similar events—we are then dealing with a detective story. A code to be unravelled in the form of comparative mythological archetypes and distinct naratives which are brought into manifestation when reciting them within the repository of one's own subconscious mind among the ancient stone ruins and megalithic sites.

The evidence is both tangible and psychological, and only a polymath-like approach (from the Greek *polymathēs*, "having learned much", or gathering evidence from several disciplines so a body of cohesive evidence can reveal a more complete picture) will present us with a plausible—if not wonderfully liberating and exciting—presentation. A 'lost', and very distinct society which represented a highly developed culture spanning most of western Europe and which was destroyed (and perhaps not for the first time) in a monumental event somewhere around 2500BC.

The rise and loss of this civilisation thus became the lore of *Ragnarök* and *The Children of Lir*, along with the stories of the lost lands and races from *Hy Brasil* to *Tir Na Nog* and even Plato's *Atlantis*. These events were so traumatic to the peoples who survived them that they sequestered them within a compensatory mythology, and this was then passed down from generation to generation by various priest classes to the ordinary people who heard them, and who kept the stories alive until the arrival of Christianity. This represented an on going development of magic and the occult (meaning hidden) being entrusted to an elite class of select individuals who were the primary guardians of the message. Following the arrival of the new faith from the Middle East (by way of Babylon and Rome), along with it came the mandate to create a concensus which stated that the development of the *Occidental* was an exclusive by-product of spiritual, agricultural, technological and social-engineering innovations which arose originally in the Middle East some time during the Bronze Age.

The Temple of Ġgantija ('Giants Tower') on the island of Gozo. Given this name due to the colossal boulders stacked neatly upon its huge walls, the building is clearly from a time of great antiquity if the weathering of the stones is compared to a nearby Roman aqueduct. Maltese folklore states that the islands of Malta and Gozo were inhabited by a race of giants before the first people arrived from Sicily. This mythology is common with other European tales of giants; in that the new arrivals deceive, murder, rob/starve the giants out of existence. Why are these folk tales so common and so similar, while also being often intrinsically connected to the megalithic structures of particular regions? Why have these legends of giants been kept alive over the centuries?

(photo: Thomas Sheridan)

Eventually, this Sumerian trajectory 'humanised' the savages of the west and north with the coming of the Roman Empire and then later, Christianity. In time, this 'East to West' migration theory became the origin of all European societies, ethnic groups and cultures and it has remained steadfast ever since. There can be no escaping the fact that all Indo-European historical research, along with linguistic, cultural and genetic investigations, have only one agenda: and that is to copperfasten the 'Out of Babylon' consensus. All the other contradictory data and anomalies are dismissed, ridiculed and ignored by the academics. Yet, there still remains profound linguistic, archaeological and other large scale cultural and startlingly puzzling anomolies which fly in the face of this almost dogmatic theory.

THE SIGILS ON THE STONES - THE MESSAGE IN THE MIND

Why is it that the complexity of Neolithic structures on the fringes of Europe—such as the *Brú na Bóinne* region in Ireland, and at Orkney to the north of Scotland—portray a degree of artistic and design complexity which is often superior to anything on mainland Europe from the same historic era? Sites such as Knowth and Skara Brae suggest being at the centre of a culture, rather than one lost on the extreme margins of a civilisation. The level of design at both locations is significant, and with most of the other major megalithic sites in Ireland and Britain, they tell us much about the kind of people who lived there in Neolithic times.

In 1980, the maverick Irish megalithic rock art and astro-alignment pioneers Martin Brennan and Jack Roberts (both artists, incidentally) identified that on August 1, the setting sun rested on the back stone of *Cairn F* at the Loughcrew complex where the Neolithic artists had carved a circle with radial lines and a crescent. The sunset at that time of year had effectively been 'sigilised' by the ancient artists who used the setting sun on a specific date to 'charge' the symbol. Thereby not only infusing it with a practical connection between earth, sun and the cycles of the season, but also applying abstractive and quantitative attributes to the simplicity of the symbol itself.

This was a sigil (a magical symbol or seal) and not just a simple drawing locating the fall of light from the sun on a particular day of the year. Neolithic people understood the power of their own emerging conscious minds through this magic. They knew *how to get inside their own heads*. This represents a quantum leap in human understanding and a million miles away from the stereotype of grunting, knuckle-scraping primitives that is generally applied to these people.

The idea of compacting a sophisticated level of data into a very simple shape, not to mention all the scientific, psychological and magical qualities associated with the shape itself, demonstrates a high level of cognitive processing. There was no need to create a complex narrative of images and words composed of highly accurate drawings of animals, humans as well as other elements, such as we see in the caves at Lascaux in France. The simple shape containing a myriad of information, emotions and ideas, which today we know as a logo, was already understood by our ancient ancestors. All the same amount of information could be retained—by translation and recognition—within a simplified graphic. Today we see this in the logos of corporations. However, it began in the Neolithic. The McDonalds logo, for example, tells us that a particular style and range of fast food is available below the arches and so on. The early artists of the Mesolithic age had no choice but to create remarkably accurate and beautiful images of animals, people and places on their cave walls as they lacked the language of logos. The Neolithic artists had come to understand that they could compact all the same levels of information and data into lines, circles and other shapes. In both cases, the obvious levels of cognitive sophistication, emotional and psychological communication was already apparent. It was as if the early artists and magi of Europe had arrived 'ready made'.

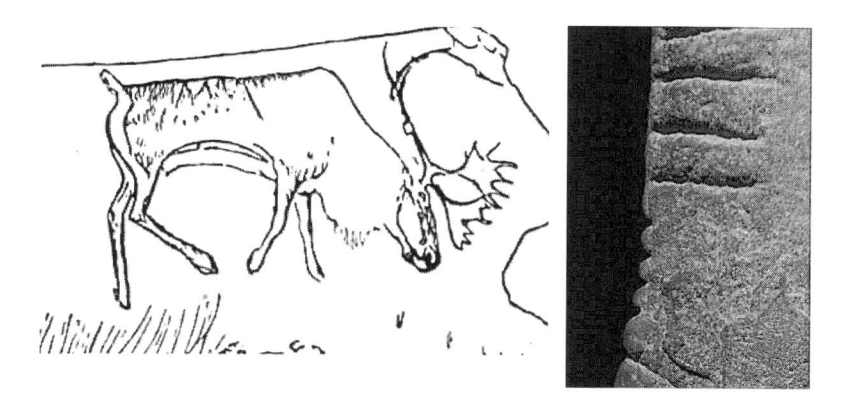

The complex and highly accurate cave art of the Mesolithic era (left) compared to the simplified and basic pictographs of the Ogham script (right) which was developed thousands of years later. Yet both are equally complex, with the Ogham 'sigil' containing as much, and even more complex information within the simplified forms which is then assembled into a completed message within the mind of those who can read the markings. Similar to how a corporate logo we are familiar with conveys to us the range and nature of their products. This transition from visual complexity to basic graphical shapes in order to convey a concept or complex message was highly developed among Neolithic rock artists with simplified circles, dots and wavy lines often 'charged' by alignments with astronomical cycles and seasonal events.

(illustration: British Library Collection, photo: Thomas Sheridan)

The complex imagery of the animals, people and places being bound within specific symbols was within the level of cognition of the Neolithic people themselves, and not just on the walls of their underground chambers. All that was required to compress the same level of complexity of data contained within a simplified shape, and also to generate an emotionality relating to the actual shape was to 'charge' it: to infuse the rock art or 'sigil' with a high level of cultural and emotional symbolic meaning into the consciousness of the community by illuminating it with the rays of the setting sun on a certain 'magical' date. Ritual magic, by means of practice and theory, had been born.

The Druid Code:
Magic, Megaliths and Mythology

This in time would lead to the complexity of new forms of linguistic communication, and along with this, not only the birth of allegory and metaphor, but also the ability to 'charge' these occult narratives within a mythology or legend. The magic was moving from the cave walls to the rock art petroglyphs, and eventually into the human mind. Complexity was turning inwards, towards the subconscious.

It also appears that humans became quickly mindful to the danger of everyone in a tribe or community being aware of this ability to create occult magic, and this led to the development of a class of initiates—along with an elite priesthood class—who would eventually congregate at geographically and spiriutally stategic locations such as Uisneach in Ireland. Uisneach became the supernatural 'navel' where the old kingdoms of Leinster, Munster, Connacht, Ulster and Meath met at a single point. The first *Bealtaine* fire was lit there by the Nemedian druid named Mide—which was visible as far away as the *Hill of Tara*—signifying the purification ritual of the island of Ireland. Geoffrey of Monmouth stated that the stones of Stonehenge were brought to England from Uisneach by Merlin using the magical sciences of the Irish druids. The still remaining large stone at Uisneach is the *Stone of the Divisions* and is considered to be a gateway to the otherworld. By then, a group of, or even just a single standing stone told stories that were epic in proportion, as the landscape had been painted like a giant canvas from one part of Europe to the next, with megaliths and 'sacred sites'.

Uisneach itself is located on top of a long, sloping hill surrounded by lowlands extending all the way to the river Shannon to the west, and the coastal mountains and hills to the east. In a time before light pollution, a single fire lit at Uisneach would have been visible at night across a vast region of Ireland. One can only imagine how psychologically powerful the first sighting of this *Bealtaine* fire must have been to communities at that time, who would then light their own ritual corridor of fires for their livestock to be driven between the walls of flame so as to purify them as part of a chain-reaction of *Bealtaine* fires, which would be lit all over Ireland literally within minutes of the first fire at Uisneach.

THE FOUR TREASURES OF IRELAND

In terms of the general absence of magic and esoteric knowledge being applied to any serious study into Irish mythology to date—and what this might reveal in the broader context—we can compare symbolism and tropes across comparative cultures and later historical timelines as a useful pointer in this regard. As this is a book which utilises both the framework of philosophy and magic in order to work our way through this remarkable detective story, we can begin with the magical and archetypal significance of the *Four Treasures of Ireland*. I believe that this generally misunderstood story is a vital clue to not only to how the Druidic supernatural world view was expressed in Ireland and beyond, but also how this very ancient idea connected to the significance of the number four—in both magic and symbolism—offers up some very insightful information. Applying common 'magical' ideas brings forth insights that would otherwise be lost in the miasma of more conservative speculation. Comparing symbolism brings us right back to the consciousness of the very ancient past, while also demonstrating a continuum from ancient Druidism and into the later Western magical tradition.

According to *Lebor Gabála Érenn* (*The Book of the Taking of Ireland*) the *Four*

Treasures of Ireland were brought to Tara by the Tuatha Dé Danann—or the people of the goddess Danu—which they had collected from their four destroyed cities in the Atlantic to the north beyond Ireland named Falias, Gorias, Findias and Murias. Incidentally, the Tuatha Dé Danann used a magical mist to hide themselves as they arrived, and this notion of a magical mist, or hidden mysteries is found extensively within Irish Heathen and early Christian stories.

These four treasures, or jewels, included:

(1) **The Cauldron of the Dagda**. The Dagda being the 'good god' or the 'father of all things' or the *Eochaid Ollathair*. He is considered the nourisher of the people as his cauldron was never emptied.

(2) **The Spear of Lugh**. Lugh being the extremely dynamic god who was known as the *Samhildánach*, which means "equally skilled in many arts." He is the god of dexterity and craft.

(3) **The Sword of Nuada**. Nuada was the king of the Tuatha (tribe), and once his sword was unsheathed, then death was certain for any adversary who gazed upon its blade.

(4) **The Stone of Fál** (*Lia Fáil*). Pictured on the cover of this book, this club-shaped stone would cry out beneath the king who took the sovereignty of Ireland and is located on the *Hill of Tara* in County Meath at the centre of what is a ritual landscape or magic circle.

Any student of the *Tarot* will be immediately struck by the passing similarity between the *Four Treasures of Ireland* and the four suits of the *Lesser Arcana*.

The similarity does not end there. The stories of the *Holy Grail* which were written down and published by Geoffrey of Monmouth from around 1130, also speak of four sacred objects, or *Grail Hallows,* as he termed them.

When we connect this knowledge of four magical objects to Geoffrey's legend of Merlin being in contact with druids in Ireland, this then begins to reveal Geoffrey of Monmouth as a far more interesting historical character than had been previously assumed.

The unique attributes of his *Grail Hallows* are as follows:

(1) **The Holy Grail**. Identified as the cup used by Jesus Christ at the Last Supper.

(2) **The Sword of the Spirit**. Which belonged to King David in the *Old Testament.*

(3) **The Holy Lance**. A remarkable object in terms of its significance to both European Christianity and *Häxan* magic. This was the lance said to have been used by a Roman soldier to pierce the side of Christ.

(4) **The Holy Platter**. From which Christ and his disciples feasted on their last supper of lamb.

These four symbols are clearly pre-Christian motifs and almost certainly represent a reworking of the *Four Treasures of Ireland* in a later guise. We can see how powerful the Irish mythology was in terms of its usefulness towards legitimising Christianity within the so-called 'celtic' world. According to the British occultist Alfred Douglas, this may have been a result of the Norman conquest of Britain reaching into Wales in the second half of the twelfth century. Eventually, the legends, which were orally spoken in Welsh, were then translated into French as the *Conte del Graal*. As incredible as it seems, there is no doubt that the *Four Treasures of Ireland* not only played a major part in the development of, and cultural acceptance of Christianity in Europe, but how they also came to be central to the suit marks used on European playing cards—and that of the *Lesser Arcana* of the *Tarot*—presents a profound mystery indeed.

Why four, and not five or six or twenty? The *Grail Stories* were an on going development of the Gnostic religion's concern for man's quest for wisdom, psychological growth and supreme methods of spiritual emancipation. As we have a good understanding of these particular symbols within both Christianity and European esoteric knowledge, we can safely—both culturally and socially—back-engineer these understandings towards the original druids and maybe even as far back as the megalith builders. The fundamentals of magic are basically the same everywhere, and all throughout history.

When we hold a tarot deck in our hands today, are we also holding—within its seventy eight cards—the symbolic representation of the *Four Treasures of Ireland* brought by the Tuatha Dé Danann from their mysterious and lost land beyond the waves thousands of years ago? I believe we are. At least in the sense of the 'treasure' being the underlying symbolism with the archetypes on the cards. Add to this the mystery surrounding the origin of *Tarot*—which has never been fully resolved—and we are left with something more than just idle speculation on the matter: that druids of Ireland weaved a far more complex and far reaching web throughout European history than they are credited with.

Taking this one step further, the question must then be asked: how much of an influence did the druids have on the development of European spiritual and occult ideas long after the *Classical* period ended? We can safely determine that

Irish druids played an immense part in developing Christianity in Ireland. Did they do the same in Europe later on? We know for a fact that Irish druids existed as the powerful group known as the *filid*, and were central to Irish life until September 14, 1607, when they departed Ireland for Europe along with the exiled old Irish Gaelic nobility and taking with them an unnamed "treasure" on their way to Rome.

The object(s) vanished down a ravine below the *Devil's Bridge* (*Teufelsbrücke*), near Andermatt, on St Patrick's Day in 1608 (of all days!). It has never been recovered and is known as the *Lost Treasure of the St Gotthard Pass*. This is a very cryptic story and filled with dates, locations and circumstances that would make an enjoyable fantasy novel if it was not also true. As far as I have determined, the last official mention of the Irish druids, then known as the *filid*, also happened around this time.

We have located a strand in a cable of knowledge, and from this, we can work our way backwards and forwards along this central core to reveal more clues to the ancient past. What were the Gaelic lords and their entourage bringing to Rome? Why all the symbolism if it was just an accident, or something 'lost'? The legend of the *Devil's Bridge* itself is that the Devil constantly sabotaged the initial construction of the bridge. After the bridge was completed, the Devil became a kind of spiritual toll collector from the first man to cross the bridge by demanding his soul as payment. The people instead sent a dog across the bridge which attacked the Devil. This *sleight-of-hand* so enraged the Devil that he picked up a huge boulder to destroy the bridge with. However, a 'holy man' used magic on the Devil, and the rock was dropped from the bridge and can still be seen there to this day. This was at the precise same location where the unnamed "treasure" of the last of the Gaelic lords was 'lost' on Saint Patrick's Day 1608, denying the Pope in Rome possible ownership of the mysterious object.

Along with T*he Four Treasure of Ireland*, there are the four mythological epics of Ireland; the *Mythological Cycle*, the *Ulster Cycle*, the *Fenian Cycle* and the *Historical Cycle*. Ireland is still divided into four provinces based on their respective ancient kingdoms; Ulster, Munster, Leinster and Connacht. The *Muintir Partholóin* ('People of Partholón') is said to have brought with them four oxen—which were the first cattle in Ireland—and they then cleared four plains on which to graze them. Nemed, derived from Old Irish meaning means "noble" or "holy" and his wife Macha, came to Ireland with his four sons. There are also four quadrants in an Irish *High (celtic) Cross*. The number four within ancient Irish society allows us something of an insight into that world view when we consider the significance of this number in terms of its properties and symbolism.

THE FOUR ROYAL SITES OF ANCIENT IRELAND

All of the following sites have no defensive properties, and even modern academics have had to come to accept that they are dealing with are 'symbolic' circular formations and not defensive structures. It was the Christians who first built defensive walls around holy sites in Ireland, and until recent years, the same assumption has been made of the early Heathen sites of similar importance. These pre-Christian enclosures can be seen as very real magic circles representing the very heart of the tribe as both a sanctified and charged circular space. The are energetic power points from which all the dynamic forces are both focused and distributed from. In many cases, these enclosures are multi-ringed structures and are not unlike how Plato described the ground plan of *Atlantis*, with the high priests and royalty at the very core of the complex which radiated outwards as concentric rings. Ireland and Britain are unique in Europe in that these are structures being of such prominence on the landscape, and existing in such large numbers.

The four generally agreed upon ancient capital sites of Ireland are:

(1) **Dún Ailinne**. Located in present-day County Kildare. Enclosed within a circular site—of thirty two acres in area—ringed by an earth bank and ditch (or "henge" as they are known in Britain). The ditch is located on the inside of the circle and would have been pointless for defensive purposes.

(2) **Emain Macha** (Navan Fort). The most significant Druidic site in the north of Ireland and is associated with the goddess Macha (representing war, horses and freedom) and the Ulaid, from which the province of Ulster derived its name. Emain Macha was one of the great royal sites of pre-Christian Ireland. Located in present-day County Armagh, it is one of the most puzzling locations in Ireland and one which Saint Patrick took a special interest in, eventually turning it into the ecclesiastical capital of Ireland. It consists of a circular enclosure two hundred and fifty metres in diameter, and formed by a bank and non-defensive ditch, which is again, located on the inside of the circumference.

(3) **Rathcroghan-Cruachán**, in present-day County Roscommon, and is associated with Queen Meabh and the mythological epic of the *Táin Bó Cúailnge*. It was also from here that Saint Ciarán of Clonmacnoise began his powerfully ritualistic and literal transformation from Heathenism to Christianity

while in the presence of a sacred cow—which he ritually slaughtered in the Druidic manner—whose hide provided the vellum on which the extremely important *Book of Dun Cow* was later written. Perhaps the most mystical, and at times, somewhat unsettling, of the four ancient capitals of Ireland, Rathcroghan-Cruachán abounds in mythology and legends, and this may explain why the site was mothballed by the Christians who looked upon the location with a sense of dread and loathing. This enormous site—in and around the present day village of Tulsk—contains over two hundred sites with several circular enclosures, including the spectacular multi-ringed site at Rathra which is over one hundred and fifty metres in diameter.

(4) **Teamhair** (*The Hill of Tara*) The only ancient 'royal' site well known outside of Ireland and among the most important archaeological sites in the country. As with Rathcroghan-Cruachán, the location contains a selection of ancient monuments. This includes the seat of *Árd Rí na hÉireann*, or the High Kings of Ireland. The hilltop complex measures three hundred metres north to south, by two hundred by sixty metres from east to west, and again, with an internal ditch, surrounded by an external bank, known as *Ráith na Ríogh* (the Fort of the Kings)

There are other sites of lesser (or later) importance around Ireland; however, the four listed above are the ones that have all have an ancient historical and mythological footprint which accounts for their overall significance within the Irish psyche. Aside from Rathcroghan-Cruachán (replaced, to a degree by Cashel as the forth Christian site), the other three locations became active centres of early Christianity in Ireland, either on the sites themselves, or were superceded by ecclesiastical infrastructure built adjacent to them. The four great Druidic centres of Ireland were replaced by four great Christian centres. Demonstrating just how powerful the old gods and goddessess were in Irish society.

FOUR POINTS OF THE CROSS

The original symbol for the number four was +, and this was later stylised into the modified version of the 4 we see today. As the cross is among the oldest human symbols on earth—predating Christianity by many thousands of years—it is hardly surprising that it also appears on Irish rock art such as the *Bohea Stone* in County Mayo, where it has been mistaken for being an early Christian cross, even though it is clearly contemporary to the Neolithic rock art surrounding it. The ancient Irish (and other Neolithic peoples) were also clearly interested in the idea of 'four', as many passageways such as the example at *Cairn T* at the Loughcrew complex in County Meath, Ireland, which has a floor plan identical to a classic Irish *High Cross* design laying flat on the ground. There are three chambers and a passageway radiating from the central chamber.

When Christians first arrived in Ireland, it was only a matter of taking this design and erecting it vertically—like a sanding stone—to create the classic 'celtic cross' we know today, with its four quadrants allegedly representing the cardinal points of *North, South, East* and *West*. At the centre of the Irish *High Cross*—as with the central chamber area of cruciform Neolithic passage chambers—is the focus of symbol. The charged core. The magical circle. This sacred space represents the portal between this world and the next. It is a part of the otherworld or the fifth province of the unseen world. The four worlds of material reality representing the here and now, with the central fifth space outside of this reality. Once again, similar to the *Four Treasures of Ireland,* we can see this same idea adopted beyond the confines of early Irish proto-shamanic holy men and women of the Neolithic era, or indeed, by the later druids.

A COSMOLOGY OF FOURS

The human heart consists of four chambers. There are four seasons. The totem animal of the ancient Irish and Neolithic era, the cow, has four stomachs. There are four basic states of matter: solid, liquid, gas, and plasma (or *aether*). There are four winds (*Boreas, Eurus, Notus, Zephyrus*), We have four seasons during the year. There are four limbs on the human body. In ancient geographic allegory, there are four corners to the world. In later religious traditions, the number four is very significant. Four Christian *Gospels* of *Matthew, Mark, Luke,* and *John*. The Jewish *Tetragrammaton* is the four-letter name of God. In Hinduism, there are four Vedas: *Rigveda, Samaveda, Yajurveda* and *Atharvaveda*. There are four books in Islam: *Torah, Zaboor, Injeel, Quran* and so on.

The significance of the number four would appear to have its origins well back into the Neolithic, and the Irish mythological record—as well as the Vedic system of fours—also points to this. It is worth noting that another possible clue in the *Tarot* is the *Magician* card in the *Major Arcana* which is the first numerical card (the *Fool* card is 0 and represents the unconscious mind). The Swiss occultist, artist and author Oswald Wirth evolved the card's image into that of a magus.

The curves of the *Magician's* hat brim is stylised into symbol for *infinity* and on the table in front of the *Magician*, Wirth placed the four (treasures) Cups, Coins, Swords (as a knife). The fourth item, the Baton, the Magician holds in his hand as his wand. Although English language translations of his work are difficult to come by, Oswald Wirth was one of the foremost occult historians in Europe who wrote several highly regarded books on the origins and rituals of Freemasonry.

Was he also aware of the *Four Treasures of Ireland*—and like Geoffrey of Monmouth—somehow aware of the concept and carried it forward by transforming the original jester of the *Magician* card, and thus giving the world back the druid?

THE 'CELTIC CROSS' AS THE MANDALA OF THE GAELS

During his work on the significance of the Tibetan mandala, the Swiss psychoanalyst Carl Jung developed his theory of the *Four Functions of the Psyche*: *Sensing, Thinking, Feeling,* and *Intuition* with which he had also made their connection to the four suits of the *Tarot*. According to Jung, the purpose of *Sensing* is to establish that something exists (and not always objectively within the material universe), *Thinking* gives the experience of the sensation meaning(s), *Feeling* applies a value or measurement to the sensation, and finally, the *Intuition* function contemplates the origin and outcome of the 'thing' which was initially detected by the primary sensation.

Jung further proposed that *Thinking* and *Feeling* were rational functions, while *Intuition* and *Sensation* were irrational (but not in the pejorative, materialist sense) functions. Then Jung took the *Four Functions of the Psyche* one step further, and visualised them as a type of 'celtic cross' graphic. In the foreword to *The Portable Jung*, the American mythologist Joseph Campbell describes the concept beautifully, but yet failed to see the full significance of Jung's *Four Function of the Psyche* in relationship to the actual real celtic crosses of Ireland —known as *High Crosses*—or indeed, with the cruciform chambers of the Neolithic age.

So, for the sake of inclusion within the objectives of this book—by demonstrating the level of sophistication of the pre-*Classical* mind of Western Europe—I will present an overlay of the theories thus:

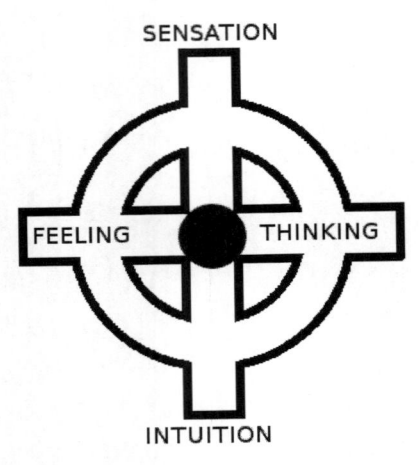

```
              SENSATION

FEELING          ●          THINKING

              INTUITION
```

The black circle in the centre of the cross represents what Joseph Campbell termed 'the inconceivable "God"...'

Along with Jung's revelations concerning the cosmological, symbolic and spiritual interrelationship between the number four and the psyche, he noted that mandalas created by most people often contained symbols or images also relating to the number four. Jung termed this phenomena the *quaternity*, as being something of an instinctual expression within mediaeval alchemical manuscripts as the process known as "squaring the circle", or the *quadratura circuli*. Jung believed that "squaring the circle" represented the combining of the four elements into the wholeness at the centre of the four quadrants, or paths, at the focal point of their meeting.

The magic circle at the centre where man becomes one with the godhead and all aspects of existence are resolved from the multitudes of fours meeting at their own centres. This expression of totality via the merging of the four is found at the centre of a 'celtic cross', as well as in middle of the central chamber at *Cairn T* at the Loughcrew and other cruciform Neolithic sites. In every case, the underlying, instinctual thrust is the same human phenomena of the psyche in action being expressed from early ancient rock art and cave paintings and developed throughout the trajectory of human history.

While Jung's discoveries, along with his revival of the western alchemical tradition, was both ground-breaking and vital towards developing his theories of the unconscious, it was, as we have seen, the legacy of something that began off in the far distant past of Irish pre-history, and even the very cultural fabric upon which Ireland was continually developed by the druids. Within the ring enclosures of the Irish Neolithic and later sacred sites, the magic circle had already been squared into a cosmology of fours which was to repeat itself all through history. From the four ancient and lost cities of the Tuatha Dé Danann, to Jung's *Four Functions of the Psyche,* the instinctual desire to 'square the circle' was derived from the same expression of the unconscious.

FREEMASONRY AND DRUIDISM

Before we look at the links between Druidism and Freemasonry, first let's consider how freemasons viewed the druids compared to how Christians looked upon them. None other than Thomas Paine—the English-American political activist, philosopher, political theorist, and revolutionary—made the following statements about the druids in his essay *Origin of Freemasonry*:

> *"...when the Christian religion over-ran the religion of the Druids in Italy, ancient Gaul, Britain, and Ireland, the Druids became the subject of persecution.*
>
> *This would naturally and necessarily oblige such of them as remained attached to their original religion to meet in secret, and under the strongest injunctions of secrecy. Their safety depended upon it. A false brother might expose the lives of many of them to destruction; and from the remains of the religion of the Druids, thus preserved, arose the institution which, to avoid the name of Druid, took that of Mason, and practice under this new name the rites and ceremonies of Druids."*

Here, Thomas Paine—the man who coined the term 'United States of America'—is not merely making speculative connections between Freemasonry and Druidism, but he is openly stating that the **freemasons are the druids in their modern form**, and are likewise, locked into the same battle with the Christian power structures.

The following document was cited in the *Masonic Annals of the Grand Lodge* at York, England

> *"In 1717 a Grand Lodge was organised at London, England, and soon afterwards the old Grand Lodge at York was revived, and its members took the name of Free and Accepted Ancient York Masons, from which emanated the charter of the Grand Lodge in the United States, which was organised in Boston in 1733. In 1813 the rivalry between the Grand Lodges of York and London was*

compromised, and the supremacy of the former was conceded.

From church history we learn that in the year 596 of our era Pope Gregory I. dispatched Augustin, and forty other monks of the order of St. Andrew, from Rome to Britain, to convert the natives to Christianity; but, while the Anglo-Saxons embraced the new faith, the Britons rejected it, and, being persecuted by the Christians, retired to the fastnesses of the country known as Wales, where, for a long period, they maintained the observance of the Druidical form of worship; and although that country has long since become Christianised, the society of the Ancient Order of Druids has existed with an uninterrupted succession at Pout-y-prid, where the Arch-Druid resides, and from, whence emanated the charter of the Grand Lodge of the order in this country."

So we can see from their own writings that the some British lodges claim direct lineage from the druids of the pre-Christian era. We know that there was at least one Irish Freemasonic lodge—mentioned by Thomas Paine himself—which was located in Dublin and also claimed to be part of an unbroken line back to the ancient past and not merely a Freemasonic druid revivalist sect. It would appear that the highly influential *York Rite* of masonry makes no bones about its codes, along with the organisational elements of its structure that is based, in part, on ancient Druidic practice. This is not the same thing as being 'connected' directly to ancient Druidism; it is indicating a continuum. In other words, the original 'masonry' of Irish and British (and possibly French lodges, such as *The Grand Orient*) freemasonry is not exclusively rooted inside the temples of Egypt and Jerusalem, but among the megaliths of Stonehenge, Avebury, Carnac, Évora and Newgrange.

The specific mention of the town of "Pout-y-prid", or Pontypridd as it is known today, is worth noting too, as it was where the Welsh nationalist William Price (1800–1893) became a member of a secretive group known as the *Society of the Rocking Stone*, a lodge which held meetings and rituals at the *Y Maen Chwyf* stone circle in Pontypridd. Price's involvement in Druidism came about as a direct result of being exiled in France following a failed uprising against British rule when he chanced upon a stone in the *Louvre* museum which depicted a druid invoking the moon. Not much is known about the specific rites of the *Society of the Rocking Stone*, except that William Price was renowned in his day for claiming that all the knowledge of the ancient Greeks and *Classical* world had been stolen from the European druids.

Can we determine specific rites and beliefs within Freemasonry which might present us with clearer insights into the specific rites of the ancient druids themselves? The answer, apparently, is a resounding 'yes', and freemasons themselves—within their own writings—make this direct connectivity very clear indeed. As we are ultimately dealing with a secretive society, we have to accept that such information is difficult to come by. I am personally in possession of some impressive and rare, original Irish Freemasonic texts, which state that the there are two branches of Freemasonry in operation today. The first and most popular branch is Egyptian Freemasonry which is based on *Hermetic* principles and rites. The other branch of Freemasonry, on the surface, presents itself as a pseudo-Christian form of mysticism—which was originally derived from ancient Druidism—and which considers itself as being a direct lineage back to ancient druids of Ireland and Britain without interruption, or coming about as a later revivalist or NeoDruidic philosophy. The Irish freemasons (and some British lodges) claim to be a continuation of the same Druidical tangent that curves off into the far distant past. They state this without reservation along with some very interesting commentaries on the uniqueness of the ancient Irish and their connection to the lost continent of Atlantis. These descriptions and theories are closely related to the descriptions outlined within *The Secret Doctrine, the Synthesis of Science, Religion and Philosophy*, written in 1888 by the Russian occultist Helena Blavatsky suggesting a common source for both.

Is this the face of a real druid looking back at us from the far distant past? One of the strangest, and little known ancient artefacts of pre-Christian Ireland is the *Tanderagee Idol*, which, along with some other very interesting ancient stone artwork, is practically hidden away inside *St. Patrick's Church of Ireland Cathedral* in Armagh, not far from Navan Fort. Its origins are vague and contradictory, and we can only confirm that it came into possession of the *Church of Ireland* about a century ago, and is similar in style to the other Heathen statues found in and around the Lough Erne region of Ulster.

The stone is heavily weathered to the same degree as other known pagan idols from the pre-Christian era, so its actual antiquity is certain. The *Tanderagee idol* is around sixty centimetres tall and appears to be clothed in a robe with short sleeves reaching to the elbows. One theory claims it is an effigy of the Tuatha Dé Danann king *Nuada and his Silver Arm*. However, this is pure speculation based on little or no actual evidence. More likely, we are looking at a representation of an ancient druid still being held captive (in a symbolic manner) by Saint Patrick. This important artefact needs to be displayed in a museum and not hidden away inside a church. How this situation came about is as mysterious as the object itself.

(illustration: Thomas Sheridan)

ENTERING THE MAGIC CIRCLE

The concept of the magic circle—as a charged, psychically-secure space contained within a round enclosure—may well have been the first ritualistic structures which humans built, even before they built housing or shelter. In 2016, French archaeologists alerted the world to an "extraordinary discovery" following a find of several Neanderthals-made circular structures dating back one hundred and seventy thousand years. These ritualistic formations were constructed out of stalagmites from the *Bruniquel Cave* in southern France and were composed of four hundred stalagmites that had been removed from the cave ceiling and arranged in two circles; one larger one and a smaller one.

Magical ideas, even in their most primitive form, and the charging and altering of consciousness, has been around as long as humans have walked this earth. The primal states of duality and humanity's relationship to both—being inside and outside of the magical circle—creates a very powerful psychological sense of termination between diferent states of psychological awareness. This then leads to the idea that being inside the circumference of the circle, one is in a very different place than the material world, beyond its orbital demarcation line. A sense of exclusivity and power then results from specific conventions and attributes which then arise both within and outside the magical circle.

The negative space inside the circle of stalagmites arranged by the Neanderthals inside the cave in *Bruniquel Cave* became, for them, a portal to other states of consciousness. An idea that has not left humans since. From the stone circles of megalithic Europe, to the huge sports stadiums of the world, the results are the same: altered states of human consciouness and heightened senses of awareness within a 'hallowed' space. As with all ritualistic structures from barrows to cairns to passage temples and sacred groves deep in the ancient woodlands, it is the 'empty' negative space that is enclosed within the boundary of stones, earth and trees which is sacred, and not the nature of the perimeter itself. The stones, trees and fence posts are the demarcation lines of the magic circle, and the terminator between different states of consciousness. What is inside the circle and what is outside the circle, are connected only by incorporeal and conceptual strands of consciousness and awareness. It is not so much the boundary that is important (visually) it is the invisible otherworld held within the circumference of trees, stones or an earth bank that really matters.

While the technology used to quarry, move and install the great stones of the Neolithic era is well discussed and speculated upon, less effort is given to the mystery of how complex masonry and engineering was performed using—as we are told by the experts—antler horns as tools. The above example, which was originally a multi-chambered structure hewn out of a huge boulder into complex sub-chambers and square decorative openings, would be a major challenge for any modern engineer today. Located at Pranu Mutteddu near the village of Goni, in Sardinia, how Neolithic people managed to hollow out the interior of the boulder with precise right angles remains a great mystery. This is but a single example of many such sites all over this Mediterranean island.

(photo: Thomas Sheridan)

The stone circles and ring enclosures of the Neaderthals, Mesolithic, Neolithic and later periods, were the primal sacred spaces of our ancestors from which the concept of the magic circle is derived. From Stonehenge, to *0* in the *Major Arcana* of the *Tarot*—represented by the *Fool* card—the primal circle is the ultimate and untainted truth on the cusp of transformation. The ovum, the cell, the earth, the sun and the unborn ego stepping into consciousness. From a basic arrangement of boulders as a circle, it became, in time, *Shiva*, the Vedic god of death and lord of the world, who dances at the centre of the earth banging the drum of creation as, no doubt, our Neolithic ancestors did themselves at the centre of their own stone circles in heightened magical states of awareness.

From the Bronze Age stone circle known as *Long Meg and Her Daughters* in Cumbria, England to the *Divine Circle* in the brow of the Buddha, the material circle representing the inner eye peering towards the subconscious mind seeking the answers and guidance by means of dreams and visions. There is no fundamental difference between the people who created the *Cromlech of the Almendres*, in Évora, Portugal and the Tibetan mandala in terms of both being symbolic representations of the concentric conduits into the personal and social cosmology.

From the sacred groves of the druids, to the *Wheel of Fortune* of the *Tarot* beginning and ending its cycle at 0—the *Fool* card, symbolising the unborn ego on the cusp of its own archetypal adventure within the never-ending rotation of of the wheel of creation—as the wholeness of Jung's concept of personal *Individuation* is completed, all have their origins in the boulders and the standing stones our ancient ancestors laid out across the landscape with the same objectives driving them on. The magic circle encompassing the sacred space within the boundary operating as a kind of laboratory of consciousness, created and developed so as to attain a fuller understanding of what lay beyond the perimeter of the stones, the trees, to the chalk marks on the magi's floor by means of forces of concentration and pure streams of psychic energy.

When the later druids used these stone circles to perform their own rituals, they became the amphitheatres for the development of the psychological well-being of the community, and thus became the wombs from which important mythologies were gestated. When the Irish and other druids created these mythologies, they were bound to the limitations of the society for which these stories were developed for. Therefore, the tales had to be sequestered within adventurous, exciting and, most important of all, magical narratives which were easy for the average person of the time to recall and retell to others without any complexities of intellectual examination, nor insightful exploration of any meaningful social undercurrents—negative or otherwise—contained therein.

CHAPTER TWO

THE MEMORY MEN AND WOMEN

The Druid Code:
Magic, Megaliths and Mythology

In Europe, the tale of the more ancient and less primitive continent of the far distant past was kept alive for thousands of years by pre-, and post-Christian Heathen shamanic and other priest class traditions through story-telling and mythology. These tales were assumed to have originated east of the Danube and were carried in the folk memory of migrating tribes moving west. Then, in the twentieth century, when it was discovered that the most complex megalithic structures in Europe appeared to be far older in antiquity the further one goes west and north, it demonstrated that, at the very least, the technological and engineering developments of the Neolithic Atlantic regions were not exclusively dependent upon arrivals from the east. The mythology was not so fanciful afterall. The people of western Europe were capable of a 'magic' of their own.

Another factor resulting from these mythological records is that the past trauma became something of a ladder which allowed later humans the ability to step up one more rung of what Aldous Huxley termed the *Super-Consciousness,* allowing human beings to develop the cognitive tools in order to deal with social catastrophe by developing new types of psychological, spiritual and intellectual survival skillsets. Similar to what occured in ancient Egypt after 2500BC, these societies moved away from being collectively conscious, socially-orientated groups, and the rise of the individual began in earnest. The impressive monuments of the society slowly gave way to the subconscious monoliths of the human mind and individual creativity.

However, as the mythologies tell us, this new stage towards our S*uper-Consciousness* came with a price: the loss of magic in the broadest sense. The same 'magic' which allowed people in ancient times to build the great megalithic structures that would fill the fanatical Puritan 'stone killers' with dread, and the rest of us with wonder and awe. For the further humans move away from the shaman and druid, and even the artist and Natural Philosopher, the closer they come to looking back in fear and suspicion of these ancient megalithic structures. We will probably never fully understand why and how these megaliths were built by utilising a modern approach of materialist reductionism alone. At best, we can collect enough data in order to gain a truer insight and become closer to answering the questions which have baffled generations since the time of the Neolithic era.

THE REDISCOVERY OF NEWGRANGE'S MAGIC

In 1699, during a road building project at the farming estate of the 'New Grange' in County Meath, Ireland, a large boulder with intricate spiral designs was discovered by workers—in the service of the landowner Charles Campbell—

who were collecting stones for a building project. It was the entrance to the now world-famous Newgrange passage mound. Rediscovered and reentered for the first time in hundreds of years, Campbell was convinced that the complex was built by the Vikings. The 'Danish' mound was soon visited by the Welsh antiquarian and naturalist Edward Lhuyd, who arrived to copperfasten its Viking credentials. During Lhuyd's investigation of the 'barbarous mound', he chanced upon talking to a local man named Cormac O'Neill regarding the folklore connected to the Newgrange site. Edward Lhuyd's account of their discussion was to become the most significant revelation concerning the direct connection between megalithic sites and mythology, when Cormac O'Neill had told him of strange beings (whose origins were not fully identified until many years later), associated with the passage mound with names such as 'Elcmar' and 'Aonghus', along with a mysterious tribe of wizards and poets known as the Tuatha Dé Danann.

However, one tantalising account reported by Edward Lhuyd pertained to "a vulgar legend" concerning some "strange operation that took place in the time of Heathenism". It is probably fair to speculate that O'Neill was describing the rising of the midwinter sunrise which illuminates the interior chamber of the passage mound each year. This "vulgar legend" gained traction among many interested people as the centuries progressed, when more and more folklore was discovered which spoke of Newgrange having some very significant solar aspects relating to the *Winter Solstice* illuminating the interior chamber. This event which was not officially recognised until the 1960s, following decades of ridicule by Irish academics. This spectacular event—which has now made Newgrange a world famous location—was rediscovered as a result of a local man recounting the folklore back in 1699. Cormac O'Neill has been proven correct, while the following generations of antiquarians, academics and archaeologists who dismissed the vulgar legend were completely wrong.

Following his investigation, Edward Lhuyd declared Newgrange a tomb and a place of human sacrifice with absolutely no evidence to suggest that it was a cemetery or a human slaughter house—either in terms of archaeological artefacts or folklore—to underpin his assumptions. From that point on—and to this very day—this 'death cult' default position applied to megaliths—not just in Ireland, but all over the world—is the initial baseline for determining the original purpose of these sites. Where bodies have been found in relatively very few instances, there is often little to disprove they were not from later cultures which used the pre-existing sites for their own funerary rites. In many ways, the 'tombs' back story has become the mainstream academics' own 'vulgar legend' and one which has only become increasingly vulgar as more and more spectacular megalithic 'tombs' are discovered.

In 1967, a team lead by Professor George Eogan entered the passage mound at nearby Knowth and became the first person to have entered this spectacular Neolithic art gallery in five thousand years. In his highly entertaining, if not at times thrilling account of the initial entry into the passageway at Knowth, Professor Eogan gives a wonderfully vivid discription of the magical experience of viewing the forms, shapes and simulacrum of the rock art covering the orthostats (large stones or slabs stood upright) leading to the central chamber. Then, following this thoroughly entertaining account of the dig, he declared (in time honoured fashion) Knowth to be a 'tomb'. Yet not one single trace of a human skeleton or bone was found there. Professor Eogan remained convinced that the corpse-less Knowth passage mound was used exclusively for funerary rites taking place at the *Spring* and *Autumnal Equinoxes*. How did he come to this conclusion? He didn't; he had to apply the academic 'death cult' narrative by default.

Yet, what Professor Eogan and his team actually discovered were superb stone carvings, and a rather sublimely carved object described as a 'mace head'; an object which may have served any number of purposes other than a barbarous killing device. Even more fantastic was that the flint used to make the mace head is only found in the Orkney Islands many hundreds of miles away in the Atlantic to the north of Scotland. Here we have hard proof of very ancient people culturally connected across—relative for the time period—vast distances.

Perhaps this beautiful object was just what it is: a piece of handmade art left inside a Neolithic archeo-astronomical art gallery created by a highly cultured people from the distant past. Perhaps it was a magical charm infused with certain powers. Its beautifully stylised twin spirals and perfectly round hole suggest a simulacra of a human head creating a sound with its opened mouth and speaking to us the name of the tribe and a people whom we have a very real name for; the Tuatha Dé Danann (the people of the goddess Danu). Perhaps it is even a representation of the Dagda god himself left there by the a very real Tuatha Dé Danann who, along with the other mounds at the *Brú na Bóinne* complex (Newgrange and Dowth) created, possibly, the largest collection of Neolithic art in Europe amid a beautiful landscape saturated within the legends of the Irish mythological world. The stones, the rock art, the landscape and the mythology connected to them are one and the same, and all this remained within the consciousness of Cormac O'Neill and his friends and family until he spoke of this folklore to a visiting Welsh antiquarian in 1699.

Almost two hundred years later—at the height of the *Gaelic Revival* in Ireland when the bulk of the Irish mythological record finally became common knowledge—Cormac O'Neill's local folklore connected to the 'Mound of Aeongus Og' was finally confirmed. Within the consciousness of ordinary Irish people—as with the mythological records of native peoples everywhere who have a strong folklore tradition and culture—the archives of real history and experiences remained, and, in the majority of the Irish stories, the mythology was directly connected to the megalithic sites themselves.

AN ARCHAEOLOGY OF THE SUBCONSCIOUS MIND

Mythology and folklore survive because they are something far greater than entertaining stories told in order to frighten young children, or to help pass long winter's nights. To the druids of the north and west Europe, as well as the Brahmins and their Hindu *Vedas,* these 'tales' were passed on for thousands of years in orally transmitted form alone (until, as far as we know, the development of Ogham and Runic script). Discoveries of ancient texts written in Sanskrit of the Indian epics such as the *Ramayana* and *Mahabharata* not only testify as to how incredibly old these orally transmitted stories are, but how uncannily accurate the orally transmitted versions remained across an immense human time scale. The ancient magi and priest class of times past realised that these stories could be embedded within the collective subconscious as a kind of living library of the human psyche. Then, by telling and retelling the stories—especially within a dramatic and theatrical (magical) fashion—they somehow became embedded deep within the human condition.

The term 'Heathen' comes from 'the people of the hearth fire' and it was among the flickering firelight and glowing embers that these stories became 'real' to the people who heard them. When a story or mythology is conveyed among a blazing, comforting fire of dancing sparks and glowing embers, or even under the canopy of a light pollution-free night sky below a majestic *Milky Way* augmented by falling meteors, the tale being told is transformed into a blazing stream of psychic energy which plunges deep into the subconscious mind of the listener. There, it is retained as a valuable repository of information. A non-material archive which can hold both the history of the tribe, along with the subconscious allegories and metaphors concerning their own immortality and fate, the stories become ghosts which haunt, not only the psyche of the listener, but also the stone-lined passageways and tunnels below grass-covered hills where the non-material entities wait to be called into our world.

Not only are these stories incredibly ancient, but when transmitted in allegorical form—as we have seen with Cormac O'Neill at Newgrange in 1699—they can be remarkably accurate, too. They stand the test of time within the human condition for as long as the megalithic stones of Ireland, Britain and Europe have stood within the landscape. Perhaps even longer. Together, both the mythology and the megaliths represent the only two conduits pertaining directly to humans —in that they reveal a bi-directional bead of investigation—which eventually triangulates upon a common source in the far distant past. In my opinion, archaeology without mythology is akin to performing a piece of music without instruments. They are inseparable and vitally interwoven in order for us to holistically determine greater insights into the people who created both, and why they did so. Neither the human psyche nor the great stone structures of the ancient past lie to us.

The Druid Code:
Magic, Megaliths and Mythology

Ogham Stones are upright standing stones containing the earliest known indigenous Irish alphabet. Of unknown (fully determinable) antiquity, this alphabet represents the earliest form of the Irish language. While the majority of Ogham stone script is transliterated from Latin, some examples are not, and these have proven near impossible to decipher. Their use continued well into the Christian era (Latin). Today, there are over four hundred surviving Ogham Stones remaining in Ireland, as well as some examples in Britain (mainly in Wales).

The origin of the term 'Ogham' (pronounced 'om') is from the Irish "og-úaim" meaning 'cut with a sharp point'. This is also the same basic origin of the term 'Rune' which suggests something of an emotionality given to the markings as they were made. A kind of a 'magical' charging of the inscription rather than just recording a line of text. The Ogham Stones illustrated here are located at Burnham House in County Kerry.

(illustration: Thomas Sheridan)

OTHER MODES OF MEMORY

In 2016, researchers in Portugal and the UK made a remarkable discovery as to how incredibly ancient European mythologies and folk tales actually are. Not hundreds of years old as previously assumed, but thousands of years old with some extending as far back as the Bronze Age. Dr Jamie Tehrani, an anthropologist at Durham University, determined that the *Jack and the Beanstalk* story was rooted in a very common universal archetypal narrative of tales—surrounding humans deceiving and defeating a race of giants—which go back at least five thousand years. From Scandinavia to Malta, this almost universal story of humans replacing a previous race of 'giants'—often by cunning and stealth—is as common as the ancient stories of the great disasters causing the seas to rise and submerging vast areas of western Europe.

By using techniques employed by evolutionary biologists, the research team in Durham and Lisbon comprised of Dr Tehrani, in tandem with folklorist Sara Graca Da Silva from the New University of Lisbon, discovered several folk tales had prehistoric origins dating back to well before the literary record. *The Smith And The Devil*, for example, tells of a blacksmith selling his soul to a demon, elf, fairy or djinn (depending on the regional culture) so as to acquire supernatural powers, was determined to go right back to the Bronze Age, and is still a commonly told tale to this day from Scandinavia to Persia.

Likewise, it was also determined that both *Beauty And The Beast* and the *Rumpelstiltskin* fairytales are almost as ancient in origin as *Jack and the Beanstalk*. Zoomorphism, fairies and giants appear to be among our oldest concepts and archtetypal companions. Is there really any difference between a Native American or Siberian shamanic ritual of wearing the skin of a 'beast' in order to bring back information from the spirit world which is required in this world, and that of a modern fairy tale whereby a merchant seeking the means to win a lover becomes lost in a deep forest and enters a 'dazzling palace' where a 'beast' is there to provide him with the object which he seeks to win his lover's heart in the outside world?

The findings of the research programme were published in the *Royal Society Open Science Journal*, and were undertaken using the novel methods of applying phylogenetics as a means of identifying correlations within ethnic groupings, along with determining specific cultural criteria.

To the surprise of the researchers, when they applied this methodology to factors such as languages, personal relationships, social constructs, hierarchies and the arts, they discovered that not only were the folktales far more ancient than anyone had previously believed, but they also discovered that the oral method of story-telling retains information with remarkable accuracy over thousands of years. Story-telling is such a powerful cognitive device, because as human beings we ourselves are stories, too.

Stories are timeless links to ancient traditions, legends, archetypes, and necessary symbolic myths. Mythological stories connect us to our own personal monomyth, and to that of the wider universal truths. They communicate to us through our sensations, and reflect our own experiences, hardships and joys. Their charge is highly emotional, and, by extension, magical, as we place our own life experiences within the unfolding narrative.

The underlying allegories then cascade like waterfalls of vital truisms into the deep well of our subconscious lives. The wand of the bard is in his use of language. Every satire is a spell, and every adventure told contains the seeds of the listener's own personal salvation held within. This is what also what made them dangerous to emerging power structures and dogmas, from the Vatican to Disney. Their power was recognised and co-opted.

The Druid Code:
Magic, Megaliths and Mythology

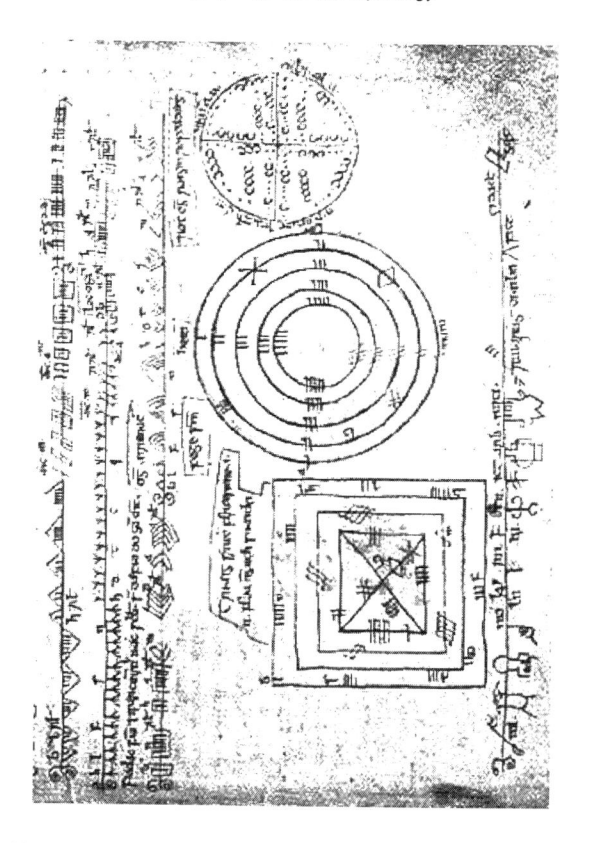

Looking more akin to an alchemical manuscript, or a grimoire of spells, the 1390 *Book of Ballymote* potentially demonstrates the paranoia which some of the Irish Christian fathers still had of Druidism and Heathenism remaining as a force in Ireland, many hundreds of years after the arrival of Saint Patrick. At the time of the *Book of Ballymote's* authorship, everyday Irish society would still have been saturated with Heathen folk customs, as well as the constant celebration of pagan festivals and feast days.

Christian monks observing these cultural manifestations of previous Heathen traditions would have been reminded of just how difficult their task of replacing the old faith of gods and goddesses, with the new faith of the imported 'one true god' from the Middle East. Powerful cosmic gods such as Lugh were to be disregarded and ridiculed to the status of the 'little stooping Leprechaun'. This is a detail from a page of codes and cyphers on how to decode and translate both Irish Ogham script and the Norse Runic Script which the authors of the *Book of Ballymote* referred to as the 'Ogham of the Vikings'.

(image: Royal Irish Academy)

The Druid Code:
Magic, Megaliths and Mythology

When the first Christian scribes wrote down the Irish mythological stories, it was, ironically something of an act of magic on their own part. The placing of Cessair—the granddaughter of Noah—as the first person to arrive in Ireland, tells us so much. Firstly, that a woman had to be the 'creator' of Ireland within a goddess-orientated society, and secondly, rather than rewrite the Irish mythology, they simply added this Middle Eastern element at the very beginning. The Irish mythology was just too powerful and could not be erased. Local folklore and customs were too closely connected to the mythology surrounding the thousands of megalithic and other ancient, sacred sites around Ireland. Particularly, the socially and culturally profound *Holy Wells* of the druids, and this made a complete obliteration of Irish mythology and replacing it with *Bible* stories impossible. It was as if this folk association between the megaliths and the mythology performed the function of something, which I have termed in my other work, as being a *consciousness firewall* within the ancient Irish psyche.

The cyphers in stone and mythology are constantly waiting for us to discover their carefully sequestered transmissions. The druids are still there to guide us and present us with revelations when the time is right, and more importantly, when we are ready to receive them. It is as if we somehow already know their secrets, but we lack the language to communicate with them directly. The secrets within the very stones and landscape of the megaliths reveal new paradigms and wonders constantly and with remarkable regularity. The Stonehenge complex being one of many examples of how such megalithic sites surprise us with new discoveries and ideas. They were designed to be this way. The magical encryption of the megalithic is present in not only their design, but their precise and important geographic locations.

There is still so much more to find in and around the megalithic sites all over western and southern Europe and beyond. Along with the folklore associated with them. We do not go looking for the sacred sites; the sacred sites come looking or us. They call to us.

A rather stereotypical, Victorian view of the elder druid bedazzling the ancient Britons with tales of the heroes, gods and the supernatural. An image which has come to illustrate how druids are perceived within popular culture even to the present era. Even so, this image is probably fairly accurate in terms of the druid being the repository of the racial and cultural memories of the tribe. Often compared to the oak tree, the druid maintains the deepest subconscious roots of the society so that even the mightiest winds of change cannot blow his or her legacy over. Female druids are commonly mentioned within the Irish mythological pantheon.

The tales, satires and sagas were told in a dramatic and symbolic fashion in order to impact deeply upon the consciousness of the listeners so they are retained within the subconscious mind as allegory and archetypes. In Ireland, druids remained central to Gaelic society until the 1600s—as the secular bardic group known as the '*filid*'—who were ostensibly druids in all but name.

(image: British Library Collection)

INTO THE MYTHIC

Perhaps an individual arrived at this place of magic and wonder when, by chance, ended up walking the stones of a Neolithic circle, or visiting the sacred landscapes, or by choosing to avail of a shamanic entheogenic substance, or even descending into a deep cave underground in order to read the markings left on the wall by some individual(s) thousands of years previously. From meditating in the groves of an old lichen-covered woodland—with only birdsong and the rustle of the branches in the wind for company—at the start of a journey which would eventually lead towards the man-made sacred landscapes of the ancient world.

All are equally valid first steps when taking the journey across the frontiers of this reality and into the initial hinterlands of the fifth province of the *Druid Code*. The otherworld of our ancestors and its many gifts of knowledge and insight for us—both as individuals and as communities—has no strict door policy. Once you are inside this world, you're in. You are entering their magic circle and you will instinctually know this when it happens. Our intuition never lies to us. We are drawn to megalithic locations due to the very real magical charge placed into these structures initially by their builders, and then, by the later generations of druids, bards, witches and then right up to the very present with NeoPagan and NeoDruidism practitioners. They are akin to batteries of psychic energy recharged by successive generations using their own magical crafts. The legends and stories connected to these sacred sites are also part of this constant charging and recharging of their power, and explains why we are continually drawn to these places. They charge us, too. They are the proton to our neutron. It is really that simple.

THE KINGFISHERS OF THE PSYCHE

Even during times when Christianity held total and absolute sway over the consciousness of the culture, the continuation of folk traditions and beliefs were

The Druid Code:
Magic, Megaliths and Mythology

the ongoing continuum of the pre-Christian consciousness surviving as 'superstitions' among rural dwellers For the most part, the Christian power structures and even the *Inquisition* itself had to effectively turn a blind eye to these 'pagan' customs, as they were far too numerous, culturally entrenched and widespread to be eradicated by either edicts or crusades.

The *Labby Rock*, located at *Cromlech Lodge* in County Sligo, fuses the magic of the megaliths and mythology perfectly within the shadows of its seventy ton capstone. This impressive dolmen is located in the heart of the 'Plain of Reckoning' where the *Second Battle of Moytura* took place between the Formorians and the Tuatha Dé Danann.

Among the legends connected to the *Labby Rock* is that the famous eloping lovers, Diarmuid and Gráinne, made love and slept upon the capstone while fleeing Fionn mac Cumhaill who was to marry the beautiful princess Gráinne. The dolmen is also the reputed resting place of Nuada *of the Silver Arm*, King of the Tuatha Dé Danann who is said to be is buried here after he was slain by Balor *of the Evil Eye*, the King of the Fomorians in the *Second Battle of Moytura*.

(photo: Thomas Sheridan)

The Druid Code:
Magic, Megaliths and Mythology

Following the *Reformation*, and from this, the later *Enlightenment*, the tone became one of backwardness and ridicule being applied to these "old wives' tales". The fact that such practices lasted for so long serves to demostrate how powerful the Druidic consciousness was retained deeply within the social order of Europe for thousands of years after their official disappearance

Demonstrating the connection between old Druidic magic—and the emerging symbolism of the Western magical tradition—is the Pictish *Picardy Stone* in Aberdeenshire, Scotland from around 600AD. In this 1918 sketch, we can see this evolution in process. The images are more esoteric and sophisticated in their arrangement compared to the previous phosphene-generated spirals, circles, hatch marks and crosses of previous rock art magical symbology. There is a strong sense of 'sigilization', along with a development of design elements which would eventually find their way into alchemy and European witchcraft.

The significance of the serpent image cannot be underestimated, as this is the calling card of the druids who were developing new spells for becoming 'invisible' with the increasing power and spread of Christianity. In the Irish tradition, there are several stories about Saint Patrick and the Irish druids both using the power of becoming 'invisible' in order to 'hide' from one another.

(Illustration: Gray, Louis H. The British Library Collection)

The Druid Code:
Magic, Megaliths and Mythology

One example of this folk magic, which goes right back to ancient times, is the veneration of the kingfisher bird. This powerful animal totem was noted not only for its beautiful, perfectly colour-coordinated plumage, but also its ability to move seamlessly between the elements of both air and water. The kingfisher's tail feathers were considered a powerful charm for attaining the love of another, as a protection against hexes and curses, and even to predict and change the weather. The bird's power was such that it has been dreaded by some and venerated by others.

In the European Heathen tradition, the kingfisher was strongly associated with the period following the *Winter Solstice,* as it was believed that the bird created the initial seven days of peace following the first *Solstice* sunrise. Now consider this in the context of the kingfishers along the banks of the river Boyne just below Newgrange in the wake of the sunrise having illuminated the passageway and inner chamber, and one can clearly grasp the concept of how a 'magical state' of being was unleashed. Perhaps to their ancient eyes, the constellation now known as Cygnus the swan—so prominent in the Irish winter night sky—was to the ancient Irish a kingfisher of the heavens plunging into the depths of the material world?

It is hardly surprising that humans would develop such a special—if not esoterically complex—connection to this species of bird. Like a stage magician, we are beckoned towards the experience as a 'volunteer' from the audience. The subtle stealth and power of the kingfisher means it can also devour the *Salmon of Knowledge* before it has time to reach adulthood. Removing the helpless fry from the depths of the river as the bird emerges from the cold, watery abyss displaying its iridescent plumage all performed with a sleight of speed and dexterity. Then feeding the *Salmon of Knowledge's* magic to its own offspring before the heroes of myth can have a chance to avail of it.

The forty day incubation of the kingfisher's eggs was also seen as significant, as it was believed that spirits of the dead lingered on earth for forty days and nights before moving on to the otherworld. The direction in which a kingfisher's beak pointed was used for divination or 'weather magic' at a time when a change in the weather could be literally life or death for a rural, agrarian community. It was seen as the bird's wand for all intents and purposes. The dazzling wizard by the water's edge.

SINGULAR VISION

To the modern reader, all this may seem absurd, but when viewed in the context of an indigenous European framework—and one connected more closely with the natural cycles than we are today—this 'kingfisher magic', when presented in allegory, represents a very powerful ancient understanding of human consciousness, along with an insight into the dynamics of the human psyche. Providing wisdoms that are just as relevant and potent as the analytical psychology of the modern era. How do we really know—or more precisely—how does one truly begin to grasp what it is like to be inside the mind of another conscious living individual or entity? Should we reasonably believe that our own highly personalised understanding of the everyday consciousness which we experience from the moment we wake in the morning is any different than the consciousness of our sleep which fills our nocturnal hours with dreams and occasionally, nightmares?

Furthermore, can we even then attempt to extrapolate our own customised and often highly prejudiced cognition on towards the consciousness of that which another human being may also be experiencing, both at the present and within the far-off past? Who are these individuals behind the façade of skin and flesh encapsulated everyday lives, along with the fleeting glimpses into their behaviour at any given moment as we observe them? What about our pets, the animals we see on TV nature shows, or the fish in an aquarium frantically making their way to the edge of their glass prison to the sight of their owner approaching them at their regular feeding time? How is life for them—in terms of how they might experience it—beyond their basic needs of their survival? How deep does their cognition go? The druids of the ancient past also grappled with these questions during their heyday.

Can we even fathom the various layers and dynamics of the myriad of mammalian and other forms of consciousness residing on this planet? What happens to our consciousness when we sleep? What was our consciousness like as we lay in the womb waiting to be deposited into this reality? What of people in the distant past who may have produced great artistic wonders and scientific discoveries? Do you really know what was going on inside the mind of Leonardo Da Vinci, for example? Would his version of a *Renaissance*-era Florentine adapted consciousness be considered abnormal, pathological, or even defective when compared to our own liberalised pre-*Enlightenment* mentality? Now let's take this question right back to the time of so-called pre-history.

Is there a baseline of human consciousness? Can there be such a thing as absolute cognitive standardisation, and from this be derived an accepted framework of sanity which can be applied across the board to the entire human experience from the prehistoric to the present? Is a person who has difficulty functioning in a modern capitalist society—but who might well possess incredible artistic ability—still be considered mentally disabled? Perhaps to the banker and the politicians, but not to the lover of beauty, and certainly not to the art collector or gallery owner who may be getting wealthy from such expressed creative eccentricities. Conversely, would the banker and politician be considered insane in a world built on creativity and bereft of global finance, or governmental administration? Is the devoted religious individual a lunatic, and the atheist a paragon of sanity? Context, time and place, along with the necessities of survival determine the answers to these questions.

It is impossible to specifically apply a universally quantifiable system of standardisation when it comes to the phenomena of what constitutes a healthy consciousness (or society), or even a baseline as to what constitutes absolute sanity? As the old adage goes, 'We are all nuts when no one is looking.' Concepts surrounding a healthy consciousness and baselines of sanity are subject to endless variables ranging from cultural to social, and even spiritual. A German with Jewish sympathies in the 1930s would probably be considered a 'nutcase' to his fellow citizens. Many other Germans at that time would not have been able to come to grips with their friend's, or co-worker's Jewish sympathies as their own concept of sanity at the time would have been almost exclusively determined by propaganda, social conditioning and most important of all, the fear of punishment and even death.

Imagine the fear of trying to get inside the head of a fellow German who had rejected the tenets of *National Socialism* due to the possible repercussions of seeing eye-to-eye with this 'nutcase'. The fear of losing their status in German 1930s society as being mentally sound, and therefore with this, requiring the necessity to be highly protective of their situation (sanity) in that particular place and time, of what would be considered in most Western democracies today as basic human decency. That being, the ability to show compassion for a marginalised group. Social status at the time would be survival based on acceptable self-control and maintaining this 'sanity' at any cost with little or no respect for any 'nutcase' who viewed things differently. As O'Brien casually informed Winston Smith in *1984,* it was he alone who 'chose' to become a lunatic.

Such examples serve to illustrate the dynamic range of what is declared sane and insane, and it is entirely due to two things: failure to understand what the experience of how consciousness is experienced from the point of view of another person, and imposing our own version of prejudiced cognition of what it is to be 'normal'—within our own specific social experience—upon another human being. Something that no one, not even the skilled psychoanalysts, brilliant neuroscientists and marketing experts can ever truly fully accomplish.

Only you know what it is like to be you—and once your cognitive complexities are autonomous and neurologically sound—then only you, and you alone, can experience this. 'Sanity' is—in the general sense—conformity with the social consensus of the present era which the 'sane' are living in. Therefore, to the eyes of an atheist, the past is a place filled with superstitious mad men and mad women who danced around stones because they were a bunch of know-nothings. So to apply a modern 'understanding' to the people of the ancient past—in the hopes of figuring them out—is completely pointless. We can only communicate with the people of the ancient past by the narratives of the subconscious alone. This includes their ritual landscapes, their art and their magic.

Essentially, once *Beyond the Pale* of the myriad of personae, social masks, and personalities, we are a complete mystery to one other. The ghost in each of our respective machines can only speculate and evaluate the conscious and cognitive experiences of another human based on our garnishing behavioural, social, intellectual—and to a degree—economic trappings, coupled with applying crude levels of psychoanalysis via making determinations based on causal observations in everyday situations. Deeper insights may be gained from personal conversations and private interactions, but even then, we are only being exposed to the overall road map of another person's consciousness. Until we invent time travel, then the people of the ancient past will always be a code which we will have to unravel by methodologies outside the rules of materialistic engagement.

So who are any of us—in any situation or any period of history—to quantify another person's mental state as being less healthy, or their culture more backward than that of our own? The Romans made an art form of dehumanising cultures they could not incorporate into the Roman imperial model. More importantly, are we missing out on something far more profound which this 'superstitious' person or backward society may be in possession of a hidden wisdom, realisations or vital insights which we can all benefit from?

Bearing all this in mind, let us return to the kingfisher. This bird waits patiently along the water's edge scanning any possible movement below the waterline which may indicate that prey is there for the taking. Once a potential meal is sighted, the kingfisher essentially enters into another form of consciousness—an aquatic adaptation of itself, so to speak—or, a very real magical state. The bird from the riverside branch is now using its wings to swim through the water compensating for the refraction on the surface of the river or stream which gives a false impression from above of the actual location of the target (in space and time) which the kingfisher has sighted from above. The precision, gracefulness and genius of the kingfisher's adaptability is undeniable. However, this marvel of nature which leaves us is awe was a result of an initial 'madness' 'dreamt up' (and this is a very important point that is fundamental to the message of this book) millennia ago.

An illustration from a Victorian religious text on the wicked superstitions of the ancient Britons, complete with images of nudity and nature worship, and also including the displaying of severed heads within a magic circle. Ever present are the druids who are behind all this Christian-imposed vista of primitive wickedness. Even today, this is still the image which people conjure up in their minds when it comes to the ancient rituals of their own ancestors.

(illustration: British Library Collection)

At some point in the evolutionary past, one kingfisher—perhaps in the form of a previous subspecies of the same or similar type of bird—realised that a potential untapped nutritional resource was available under the surface of the water and took a leap of faith, or more likely, 'madness', into order to improve the survival chances of its genetic repository by attempting to exploit protein-rich prey from within the aquatic domains. In other words, this humble colourful little bird had to conceptualise a shift in its own consciousness which required it to make the evolutionary leap to the magnificent, highly-adaptable and efficient creature it has become today. The risk paid off. The 'madness' of the initial 'dive' improved the survival rates of the species as a whole.

Now imagine if it was possible for a kingfisher to communicate with an osprey; a larger bird of prey which pulls larger fish from just beneath the surface of the water, in a conversation with a kingfisher concerning its method of hunting. Yes, that the osprey would be aware that just below the surface there are fish, but has no idea what is down there in among the watery depths. The kingfisher, on the other hand, would know all the advantages of taking the plunge, but would find it difficult (if we were applying this scenario in human terms) to describe the animals, plants and insects it has experience of below the surface in such a way the osprey could comprehend it. The osprey would find it strange, absurd even as it could not place itself into the experiences of consciousness that the kingfisher experiences. Now let's bring a third party into this dialogue; a condor who lives high in the mountains... how could the kingfisher ever begin to explain to the condor that below the surface of a lake or river is a whole other world? Could the osprey act as mediator between the condor and the kingfisher?

Taking this one step further, consider the consciousness of the human of the ancient Druidic mindset, outside what we presently refer to as as 'normal', 'sane' and 'rational'. Are we correctly identifying this person as being lost in a condition of 'superstition', or are we robbing a human kingfisher of their evolutionary risk of experience and potential? Are we also robbing our entire species of the same when we discard other people as being 'away with the fairies'? Perhaps something far more profound is at work and the time has come for humanity as a whole to take the plunge into the realms of consciousness where the artist, shaman, seer, eccentric and druid are already familiar with. We have given the

Abrahamic dogmas, the scientist, the politician and the banker due respect and power within this society; and now have a good look around you: is the world we reside in a place of happiness and security for all? Perhaps it's time for all of us to get a little crazy; we might rediscover something we lost a long time ago and start listening to the kingfisher's song to find our own seven days of peace following the *Winter Solstice*.

EVIL SORCERY?

Often, when I give lectures on this topic, the question invariably gets brought up concerning the magic of the druids and if it was evil? I generally answer the question that there is no such thing in reality as black or white magic; only magic rituals which are a reflection of a particular culture and era. I have personally witnessed *Santeria* rituals myself—which on the surface could well have been termed as being 'black magic'—but then, would this have made me bigoted towards the culture behind the ritual? Like most things in life, magic is always relative. What can cost you your soul in one life, might regain it in another. I have in my personal library *The Great Book of Saint Cyprian*—one of the most forbidden 'black magic' texts—which even some friends of mine have expressed aghast at my ownership of such a book which, just by having a copy of, is considered a pact with the devil in most of the Spanish- and Portuguese-speaking world. However, if I did not purchase a copy of this book, I would not have discovered that Saint Cyprian himself identified the druids as the first magicians. There are answers to questions in everything.

Therefore, we can say there is no such thing as 'white' or 'black' magic. There is only energy and the outcome is determined entirely by the personality, intellectual maturity, along with the compassion (or lack thereof) of the practitioner. It is only either 'black magic' or 'white magic' to the person observing, or on the receiving end of the ritual. From the standpoint of the practitioner—whichever specific school of magic they may be from—it is just energy and it is how this energy is actually manipulated and directed. Stepping beyond the microcosm and on to the macrocosm, there are also no such states as 'black magic' and 'white magic' when it comes to any overriding notions of cultural morality. What is never considered—by moralising, religious individuals when it comes to this topic—is that white magic at one point in history may well have been considered black magic at another point in history, and *vice versa*.

Take, for example, animal sacrifice. The vast majority of people who practice magic today would never consider hurting an animal, let alone sacrifice one during a ritual. Yet, this moral code has only come about because we live in an age whereby people no longer slaughter animals for their own food. The slaughterhouse takes care of this for us. Most people today do not even take a knife to cut individual pieces of raw meat. The local butcher does this for us. How many people reading this book have ever gutted a fish, or removed the entrails from a chicken? So, from a standpoint of modernity and convenience, we can declare sacrificing an animal to be 'immoral', and then we allow the abattoirs and meat processing plants to slaughter and dissect animals for our own busy lifestyles.

The past is always a foreign country when viewed from the present. The moral relativity concerning animal sacrifice today only exists because we have transferred it to someone else. In a different age, a magician sacrificing an animal for a ritual was an act; no more immoral, evil or sadistic than him or her breaking the neck of a goose for their dinner. Personally, I would consider the application of animal sacrifice in rituals to be superfluous and tokenist these days, and therefore a product of needless cruelty. For this reason, I prefer to use the term *modern pathological occultism*, as it is a by-product of trashy pop culture—often coupled with drug abuse by bored and ignorant teens—leading to dreadful and soul-destroying, if not criminal, acts.

The Kingfisher (or Halcyon) represented an animal totem and Heathen symbol of abundance, Spring/rebirth, wealth and romance, who despite their small size are said to be able to ward off thunderbolts. A favourite of the pagan gods, and in Mediterranean regions it was believed that the gods calmed the sea for a period of time in order to allow the Kingfisher to nest and from this came the expression; 'halcyon days'.

(illustration: Thomas Sheridan)

CHAPTER THREE

THINGS FOUND AND OTHERS YET TO BE UNCOVERED

The Druid Code:
Magic, Megaliths and Mythology

The *Bohea Stone* rock art in County Mayo, Ireland was discovered as late as 1987 by a Mr Gerry Bracken, despite being relatively close to a pre-existing standing stone/menhir nearby. How such a spectacular example of rock art had not been found prior to the late 1980s is a mystery in and of itself. It also serves to remind us that there are many more such spectacular megaliths still waiting to be rediscovered. When one stands beside the *Bohea Ston*e each year on April 17 (the start of the growing season), and again on August 24 (the start of the harvesting season), the sun can be seen literally rolling down the northern slope of the Croagh Patrick mountain in the distance.

The mountain itself is deeply symbolic, as it is the site where Saint Patrick is said to have converted all of Ireland to Christianity in 441AD. Saint Patrick knew precisely what he was doing when he picked that particular mountain. A colossal psychic charge is present at the summit of the peak, and this is why it still draws thousands of Christian pilgrims on 'Reek Sunday', which is the last Sunday in July every year. This highlights another issue which we have to contend with: the co-option of Heathen sacred sites and landscapes by Christians. Saint Patrick did not make 'the Reek' a powerful place of magic. The druids had already been there and their presence had to be eradicated from Croagh Patrick, and this 'cleansing' is still going on. No sooner had the *Bohea Stone* been discovered, when the local concerned parties—connected to the Catholic church—jumped on it, proclaiming it to be the 'Chair of Saint Patrick' in order to annihilate (once again), and co-opt (as they always have), the real legacy of the Heathen Irish people who created the impressive artwork, along with the significant solar alignments connected with it.

The mountain had been previously been known as *Cruachán Aigle*, which has been translated as the 'Rock of the Eagle' and was, before Christianity, associated with the mysterious *Crom Cruach*. Portrayed by mediaeval scribes as a dark pagan cult obsessed with human sacrifice and hunting down peaceful Christians, the etymology of their name suggests the *Crom Cruach* were more of a fertility and solar sect. This appears to have been validated with the discovery of the *Bohea Stone* and its seasonal alignments. An interesting inclusion within the fourteenth century manuscript, the *Book of McGovern,* states in poetic verse, that the *Crom Cruach* were still in existence near Kilnavert, in County Cavan almost nine hundred years after Saint Patrick is said to have rid Ireland of the sect.

Interestingly, the small Christian chapel which is now on the summit of the mountain is still referred to by locals as '*An Teampall*' or in English, or 'The Temple'. In the 1980s, it was discovered that the slopes of Croagh Patrick contained significant deposits of a particularly high grade gold ore held within snow quartz veins. As quartz is commonly used in Irish megalithic structures

The Druid Code:
Magic, Megaliths and Mythology

from the Neolithic era, it is reasonable to suspect that the druids were aware of this particular mineral richness of the mountain, and the unique properties of the geology which would have added to the 'charge' of the location. In effect, turning it into a gigantic wand. The same 'wand' which Saint Patrick later used to convert Ireland into a Christian land.

BALLYNAHATNEY OR BALLYNAHATNA IN 1748.
Wright's Louthiana, Book III, Plate III.

Even with the enormous numbers of still standing and remaining megalithic sites around Europe, there have also been some appalling losses and wanton destruction. From growing urban centres swallowing up henges and 'fairy forts', to farmers pulling down dolmens for wall construction, as well as megalithic sites which found themselves in the way of advancing infrastructure and transport routes. Such is the case of 'Ireland's lost Stonehenge' (somewhere just north of Dundalk, Co. Louth) which some have speculated was demolished during the building of the Dublin to Belfast railway line in the 1850s. This is still conjecture, however, as hard information on the structure is difficult to come by apart from confirmation of its existence mentioned within both the antiquarian and public records.

First described in detail by the English astronomer Thomas Wright (1711-1786)—who proclaimed it a "school of astronomy", in 'Louthania'—as being a "ruinous remains of a temple or theatre on the plains...enclosed on one side with a rampart and ditch, and seems to have been a great work, of the same kind with that at Stonehenge in England, being open to the East and composed of like circles of stones within." Wright's 'Louthania' is the present day county of Louth, named after the god Lugh, who also lends his name to Lusitania in Spain and Portugal. Demonstrating that prior to 2500BC, this was a connected culture across the Atlantic regions of Europe.

(image: University of Liverpool archivehub)

There will always be great megalithic discoveries to be made, as the sheer number of sites around Europe is so enormous. The ongoing search for Ireland's "lost Stonehenge", a once large circular complex of huge standing stones and concentric henges in the area north of Dundalk in County Louth—which literally vanished from the archives somewhere between 1748 and 1907—is but one mystery waiting to be solved. It is depressing to think that this complex may well have been a significant *Temple of Lugh* (from which Louth takes its name) and was casually destroyed, or more hopefully, remains buried and is waiting to be rediscovered.

It is worth noting that less than five percent of Tara in Ireland has been properly examined. Not counting the appalling destruction caused by fanatical *British Israelites* who tore up Tara—between 1898 and 1904—in their misguided (to the point of psychotic) attempts to unearth the *Ark of the Covenant*. Unfortunately, *British Israelism* hasn't gone away, and there are still large numbers of Christian fanatics who would eagerly dig up the '*Hill of Torah*' (I kid you not) and many other Neolithic sites given the opportunity.

ANCIENT LESSONS FOR THE MODERN PERSON

In many ways, the same challenges which the druidic and Heathen traditions of Europe were confronted with in the past—from the time of Julius Caesar to the age of the Vikings—with the onslaught of the Roman Empire and then later, by unleashing its most successful weapon of mind control: the *Bible*, that we humans today are now facing similar challenges with the advent of the 'smart' technocratic society. In particular, the rise of the transhumanist and posthuman

The Druid Code:
Magic, Megaliths and Mythology

digital crusades by which a new technological caste system is being imposed upon us all in order to weed out the humans who are no longer compatible with the psycho-digital new order of the future. While at the same time, our technocratic overlords are continually 'improving' all the 'mistakes' that natural selection has created in the humans who will be eventually chosen to be the cybernetic patricians of the future.

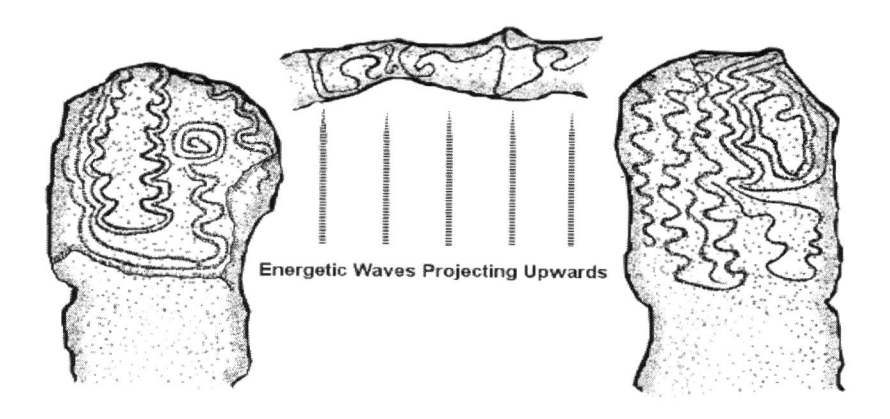

Energetic Waves Projecting Upwards

The remarkable artwork which is contained on a menhir at *Bryn Celli Ddu* ('Mound in the Dark Grove) passage complex in Anglesey, Wales. Its name implies that its function in the past was that of a temple and not simply a place of burial. Above, we see the north face of the menhir (left), the south face (right) and the top edge (centre).

Although it is difficult to decipher the precise meaning of the rock art, what *Bryn Celli Ddu* does provide us with is proof that Neolithic people were aware that energy travels in waves, and from this, they charged the standing stone as a kind of wand. The charge being built up in the top half (at arm's height) and then emitted from the top surface of the stone.

What we are seeing is that Neolithic people were aware of such forces in action and how they could be gathered, stored and transmitted. This awareness of such a concept provides a telling insight into the degree of sophisticated thinking of the time. What we are seeing is the product of a technological and artistic mind. The science and art of the magical force in a single standing stone. Anglesey is also where the British druids made their final stand against the Roman army in AD60.

(illustration: The Triskele and the Dragon website)

The Druid Code:
Magic, Megaliths and Mythology

In terms of our own natural humanity within the oncoming technocratic age of the globalists, the immediate future is looking increasingly bleak for anyone who is perfectly happy just enjoying life as an imperfect human within somewhat passively-vicious limitations of this emerging paradigm. The digital dark magi of the technocratic new order have made no bones about the fact that humans—as we exist now—are an obsolete model to be either selectively upgraded or discontinued. The supreme irony in all this being that they themselves haven't evolved since the time when their own ancestors were throwing people to the lions for sport, while declaring the barbarians around them as being "uncivilised" and in need of Roman rules and culture regardless of if they wanted it or not.

At the same time that this new trauma of transhumanism and posthumanism is being foisted upon us by the new *Caesars* and *pontiffs* of the digital-electro-magnetic spectrum, there is, not surprisingly, a type of awakening also happening in tandem with this. The brighter the light, the deeper the shadow... More and more people are looking towards the world of the pre-Christian consciousness of our European Heathen ancestors. Television shows such as *Vikings*—despite its stereotypical faults—are gaining huge global audiences; ordinary television viewers, who are now aware of the *Eddas* and the *Sagas* in numbers not seen since the so-called 'Dark Ages'. More books than ever are being published dealing with stone circles, barrows, dolmens, henges, cave art, Heathen magic, European mythology and shamanism. People watch the television series *Game of Thrones* and read the books by George R. R. Martin coming away more fascinated by the *Wildlings* beyond The Wall rather than by the imperial dynasties to the south of it. Recognising something of themselves within these fictional, feral characters and 'free' communities. Or, at least, wondering what a world without laws, statutes and government bureaucracy would really be like? This cultural phenomena shows no signs of waning, either.

There probably has never been an opportunity like this in history before, when ordinary people can bring with them all the tools and understanding of the modern world to the 'sacred' megalithic sites, and along with this, partake in one of the few areas of scientific and cultural exploration that puts ordinary people on par with the so-called experts in this field. For if I have discovered one thing from talking to archaeologists and historians regarding the Neolithic megalithic builders of Europe, it is that they know almost nothing about the topic beyond the weight and arrangments of certain stones, along with somewhat subjective dating methodologies. In terms of the cultural and social lives of the people who built these spectacular monoliths and complexes they reduce their humanity to that of primitive animal-skinned automatons in the service of a superstitious death cult. In reality, encounters with the megaliths present shimmering reflection of a hidden world that lies beyond the reductionist world view. Even the hardened skeptic can be caught off guard now and again.

VOTIVE HOARDS AT WOODHENGE AND STONEHENGE

It was a beautiful afternoon in early September, 2015, when something of an epiphany came over me while working at the time on a documentary series dealing with the mysteries and diversity of the world's ancient megalithic sites. A group of us were on location filming in Wiltshire, England, within an area which was once the site of a massive Neolithic timber circular structure known as Woodhenge. The monument at Woodhenge has long since rotted away into the midsts of time, speculation and imagination. Yet, even with only the crude, heavily weathered and worn, concrete modern place markers remaining, the psychic monument of the location itself; remains emotionally, psychologically, if not 'spiritually' very powerful to this very day.

The very perceptively real 'energetic' site of Woodhenge itself, and the purpose for which it was constructed, still remains intact within the negative spaces of the observer's consciousness. Transporting us to a place, located in, and out of, space-time. Between the material world of the here and now, and the 'other worlds' which are only partially hidden within the movements and reflective colours of the shadows which both our sun and moon cast across the landscape. What some of the ancient Irish called the 'fifth province of Mide'; a location unseen by the human eye, but as real and as dynamic as the very literal cosmos of our five senses, but off somewhere else, in the otherworld.

As I looked around at the pastoral vista surrounding Woodhenge, the true nature of the location as being but one specific, individual element within the overall Stonehenge complex in Wiltshire became readily apparent. This was the footprint of a city, a community, and most importantly of all, a statement of cultural presence and not just a collection of isolated ruins and earthworks. The entire landscape itself is a roadmap to human consciousness, our personal and collective destiny, destinations and transient states of existence. The ever-present reminder of constant rebirth and renewal, which echoes the changes in the natural world of both the earth itself and the ethereal vista of the heavens above. An interdependency of not only the earth, sun, moon and stars, but also its timeless fusion within our consciousness and imagination.

One of the prevailing and very plausible growing theories is that this older part of the Stonehenge complex contains, or rather, 'represents' the embodiment of the living world, and that the main monument at Stonehenge itself is a portal to the ancestors who passed into the next reality. This idea makes increasingly vivid sense when you are there on location and move between the actual 'sacred' sites. Woodhenge inexplicably 'feels' like a representation of this world, while Stonehenge takes you to the otherworld beyond.

There is also very good archaeological evidence for this theory, as no bodies have ever been found at Woodhenge. While at Stonehenge itself burials appeared to have been a common practice over the centuries, from the Neolithic age on. The monoliths of the Stonghenge site itself, are not entirely of this world. While their material forms are tangible structures, the negative spaces they wrap themselves around are windblown and star-filled portals to the otherworld beyond the five sense experience of our human mortality. They are supernatural gateways comprised of portals in the form of *Sarsen* and *Bluestone* stone trilithons leading to *somewhere else.*

Although in the material sense, Woodhenge itself does not have the outstanding and awesome colossal monoliths of its close neighbour Stonehenge, the missing spaces where the wooden poles once stood tall, are nevertheless no less emotionally and psychologically capable of something akin to a soft-impact collision within the human psyche of the observer. Woodhenge *still stands*, but not within this reality. It has decayed and long since moved on in its journey to the fifth province which lies somewhere within the 'terminator' of the ever-revolving dance of day and night across the surface of our rotating planet as it spins through the cosmos in constant and never-ending cycles.

As we look at and within the empty spaces of this material world where the wooden uprights of Woodhenge have long since rotted away, we are reminded that one day, we too will leave this material world to begin our own swirling, migratory dance into the otherworld within the ever-rolling flux between sunset and sunrise. Woodhenge reminds us that it is not necessary to see something in order to know it still exists. The long-vanished, organically decayed monument at Woodhenge still has a very real 'power' over the visitor who goes there willing to allow this force to come inside them. It is but a first step into a dynamic and profoundly important landscape which comprises the entire Stonehenge region's visual, psychological, cultural and emotional experience.

This highly theatrical landscape beckons us to embark upon our own personal quest and to explore its secrets and marvel in its never-ending surprises. This same experience is likewise prevalent at other 'sacred' sites such as Carrowkeel in Ireland—where the structures are placed upon a series of extended, finger-like mountains in the shape of a human hand gesturing towards *Queen Meabh's Cairn* atop the summit of Knocknarea. Giant fingers which point further out still, into the mysteries sequestered below the turbulent, sometimes compassionless waters of the Atlantic, and where the visitor can literally touch the clouds as they roll in with the *Gulf Stream* from the lands of the far-off megalithic cultures of the Mayans and the Olmecs.

This same infrastructure of altered states of the natural, supernatural, the conscious and subconscious can be experienced at Neolithic sites all over western Europe from Portugal to Orkney, and from the Aran Islands off Ireland's far west coast, and inland as far as the Harz mountains of Germany. All of these megalithic sites are beautifully adapted within the context of their own geographical potential. They are all complementary petrified brushstrokes upon the canvas of the surrounding environment. Our ancestors considered the landscape in close proximity to themselves to be something that should be harmoniously worked with, and upon it they created a never-ending story of the cosmos and our part within it. They painted experiences of existence and transmigratory states, and their own very personal experience is the legacy which they left to us at places such as Stonehenge, Newgrange, Carnac, Évora and beyond.

The megalith builders were also pragmatic with their stone building. They created astronomical and seasonal observatories, as well as psychological and spiritual portals to the otherworld of the ancestors in order to provide healing and comfort, and they also provided the means of upholding tribal society during traumatic changes, as well as recovery from natural disasters and social upheavals. They provided the fruits and knowledge of experience through application of their magic and their sciences. I used the term 'experience' very much on purpose here, in order to illustrate the unseen, intuitive nature these locations have upon us when we visit them with an open mind, and especially, with an open heart.

The very real perceptible and invaluable power of these megalithic monuments lies beyond their still-remaining stones and earthen mounds, as they are not merely just tombs, temples or tourist destinations. They are living and breathing ancient repositories of necessary experiences for us to engage with. Following this engagement with the stones and their legends, and, if we begin to read and 'feel' their messages, only then do they become our own personal portal gateways to the fifth province of the unseen cosmos. The stones start speaking to us in a language we can finally understand. They speak to the conscious mind by means of simulacra, mysterious energy forces, archeo-astronomy, their geological, magnetic and geographical alignments, and most importantly of all, their *connectivity*. These stone structures communicate deep into our subconscious mind via their mysterious forms, their location within the environment, and are further brought into focus by their connection to mythology, legends and the local folklore associated with them. They open up our senses to what William Wordsworth termed 'other modes of seeing', which take us out of the our present state of consciousness and modern cognitive prejudices.

THE FORM WITHOUT FLESH

The idea of this 'other modes of seeing' being a kind of perpetual transmigration of tribal history and experience can be found in the Irish supernatural entity known as Tuan macCairill, who is a semi-human being, representative of reincarnation, racial collective memories and experiences. His spirit survives a great disaster which destroys early Ireland along with its inhabitants. Eventually his spirit is reborn within the body of a stag, then a boar, followed by a transformation into a bird of prey, and finally as a salmon. He is eventually caught and eaten by the wife of Cairill, a powerful Chieftain. In time, she gives birth to a baby boy who is the human reincarnation of Tuan macCairill. As a man he becomes a Christian, but retains the memory of the ancient history of Ireland which he had lived through when in the form of other animals, and also that of a *Somhlth*; a consciousness, energetic being without form or shape.

Tuan macCairill is also mirrored somewhat in Taliesin—the most significant figure in the Welsh Brytonic Druidism and bardic traditions—and his story also bears many similarities to the Irish druid Amairgin. Taliesin was called the 'shining brow' and had the power of prophecy conveyed through poetic verse. He was the son of the female druid Ceridwen who possessed an enchanted cauldron. After giving birth to Taliesin, she hurled him into the sea, only to be saved by the prince, Elffin. His grave is said to be a cairn called *Bedd Taliesin* on the coast of Wales at Ceredigion. Local folklore states that if you sleep on the stones at night —depending on your personal qualities—you will awake the next morning as either insane, or as a great poet.

The story of Tuan macCairill, both as a human and in *Somhlth* form, tells us much about the pre-Christian attitude towards death and dying. It reminds us of the universality (outside the Abrahamic dogma) of cycles of experiences and sacrifices, and is perhaps best compared to that of the Hindu god *Shiva*. The foreboding process is a stage within a continous journey which all aspects of creation—in the case of Tuan macCairill, both human and beast—are carried constantly into new dimensions on both the microcosm, and greater personal understandings at the microcosm of the individual experience. The dangers being not so much a divine punishment, but rather the risk of not completing all the journeys of life to their end so as to avoid all the risks of each respective experience. The burden of the salmon must be undertaken in its entirety in order for the eventual *Somhlth* transmigration towards the status of human. From this, the consciousness of man can begin to work beyond himself and his corporeal limitations in order to build the framework of the universe going forward by means of developing his own consciousness. The transformation of the *Somhlth* eventually to that of a god.

We see this idea within European mythology time and time again. Cú Chulainn, for example, remains an intriguing archetype simply because he is most certainly not—as is the case with the Arthurian myth—a Christ-like figure. His salvation is completely attained during his mortal existence, and within his own short life, the necessary cycles and stages of mortal existence are embraced with a sense of almost ambitious fury. The *Life-Eager Hero* is also the death-eager hero. Yet Cú Chulainn never loses sight of his own internal cycles of compassion and understanding. He sees these events—such as killing his best friend in battle—as a personal fate, rather than exterior judgements imposed upon him by a single infallable entity. In this sense, the story of Cú Chulainn is more similar in nature to a Greek epic than an *Arthurian* legend. The quest being the fullness of life itself, and the reward is having experienced this fullness for oneself.

If we look at the Anglo-Irish literary revival of the nineteenth century, it was Irish mythology being saved from obscurity by the most unlikely source. Not the Catholic rural peasants who were directly connected to it, but by the Protestant ruling classes whose ancestors came originally from England. Yet their enthusiasm for the native mythology eventually unleashed the flower of Irish nationalism which was to undermine their own powerbase in Irish society. These Anglo-Irish mythology and folklore enthusiasts—Lady Gregory, William Butler Yeats and so on—compiling the legends and popularising them from the comfortable parlours of their manor houses, castles and stately homes, were fulfilling their own archetypal destiny by completing their own cycle. Yeats himself, almost certainly understood this undoing process within the context of his own tribe's *Terrible Beauty*. The cause and effects of unleashing long forgotten archetypes—from the seemingly most benign acts—altering reality for all eternity. The mighty king felled by the bite of a tiny mosquito.

Yet our ancestors previously warned us of our bond to this archetypal completeness time and time again with the mythology they left behind. In the Norse *Eddas*—following a bet—Loki shape-shifts into a fly and bites the dwarven magician named Sindri on is hand, and then he also bites his brother Brokker on the neck and eyelid causing them to bleed. This takes place during the pivotal point during a magic ritual when the dwarven magician brothers are forging Thor's hammer, *Mjölnir*. This interruption by Loki results in the handle of the hammer being much shorter than was intended. It was this defect which would eventually lead to the death of Thor who is poisoned by the bite of *Jörmungandr*, the *Midgard Serpent* after he slays the monster at *Ragnarök*, so the new cycle of creation could begin again. The magic circle is not only made of stone, but also of myth. Completion of the cycle must take place—and *will take place*—regardless of the changes within the material world. Thor's killing of his nemesis *Jörmungandr* was irrelevant. His own cycle was completed.

The intriguing runic inscription located in Södermanland, Sweden carved on an outcropping of granite, features Thor's hammer *Mjölnir*, along with his facial likeness, all enclosed within a magic circle of *younger futhark* runic text. In this case, the power of Thor's archetype is used within the magic circle in order to safeguard the bloodline of a family. A trait also found on Irish Ogham stones. The charging of the rock with the names of certain persons directly connecting these individuals to Heathen gods and goddesses.

(illustration: George Stephens, 1878)

Within the Irish pantheon, in *The Wooing of Étaín*, a jealous druidess turns Étaín —daughter of Ailill—into a fly and then tosses the fly into the air to be carried away by the north wind. After seven years, the fly enters a cup of wine belonging to a concubine of Conchobar the king of Ulster. After she drinks the wine and ingests the fly, she becomes pregnant with a reborn Étaín, who grows up to marry the high king Eochaid. Despite the sorcery of the jealous druidess who transformed her into a fly, Étaín—by means of her *Somhlth*—returns to human form once again to fulfil the destiny that the dark arts prevented her from attaining in her pervious human life.

Another interesting link between the two stories is the eventual death of Conchobar which is almost identical to that of the Norse saga concerning Thor's fight against Hrungnir, which indicates an even more ancient common origin linking both Irish and Norse mythology with the same themes of magic, sorcery, rebirth and completion of cycles of creation expressed within the material world by means of non-material processes.

Victorian illustration which suggests that many of the early Christian crosses of the 'celtic' world may have been recycled from pre-existing menhirs due to their symbolic, social and even electromagnetic attributes. From early basic renderings to the impressive ornate High Crosses of Ireland, the transition was purposely slow, so as to condition the population over a long period of time.

(illustration: The Triskele and the Dragon website)

CHAPTER FOUR

THE SHAMANIC STORY

The Druid Code:
Magic, Megaliths and Mythology

In recent decades, there has been a sizeable body of work presented, concerning complex mathematical alignments and encrypted messages being contained within the design and geographical location of megaliths, as well as within the complexity of their arrangements and overall structural geometry. While there is no doubt that many of these structures do have basic mathematical and geometrical insights contained within them, I personally feel that this field of speculation has been something of a red herring. This typically left brained-only assumption of mathematical decoding of locations such as Stonehenge serves to distract from the entire, and very personal 'holistic' encounters with such places. They are not referred to as 'sacred sites' for nothing, and often, people's initial engagement with megaliths can be very emotionally overwhelming. They inspire us to speculate and wonder in every possible cognitive and emotional manner at their forms and mysteries.

These often impressive ancient stone structures do not exclusively exist as secret engineering codes for locating complex mathematical computations when one approaches them with an open mind and heart. Trying to understand and unlock these codified anomalies cannot be unravelled by merely holding a slide rule and looking for *Pi*. Their stories in stone are as complex as the humans who designed and built them.

Megalithic 'sacred' sites present us with the paradox of solid stone being used to open pathways of perception towards the least tangible and material states. The *Parco dei Petroglifi* in Sardinia contains almost forty 'tombs' hollowed into the solid rock which are known locally as 'Domus de Janas', (Fairy Houses). The site represents a solidified expression of the supernatural world expressed in stone. Adorned with rock art of humanoid-like creatures, the vast site is one of the most energetically surreal I have yet visited anywhere.

(photo: Thomas Sheridan)

This obsession with locating mathematical perfection within megalithic structures has distracted from other aspects of the design pertaining to the detectable electromagnetic effects of the stones themselves. These subtle energy fields contained within the stones of the megaliths are a fundamental aspect of their design, and is generally overlooked by the endless mathematical and extraterrestrial associations made with stone circles and other Neolithic structures. Associations I come to see as being rather cynical, if not sinister distractions designed to mock or disparage plausible phenomenon and anomalies —pertaining to megaliths—that the scientific establishment generally will not touch, as they would fly in the face of their solidified orthodoxy.

A few years back, I made the rather obvious and harmless comment to a historian stating that I believed that the oldest Irish *High Crosses* (the distinctive 'celtic' crosses of Ireland) may well have been rendered from existing menhirs or standing stones due to their symbolic, psychological and perhaps even the electromagnetic qualities present in them. My contention was that in a time long before electromagnetic pollution, humans had a far more sensitive relationship to their environment, and could perhaps sense forces coming from the stones that we modern humans can not. The historian looked as me agape and replied, "you'll be saying the Reptilians made them next!"

Yet, what I had proposed was not in the slightest way an expression of *woo-woo*. I was just implying there possibly were, certain characteristics in the existing Neolithic standing stones that were so important to the community, that rather than destroy them, early Christians converted them into the distinctive Irish *High Crosses* just as they had applied the same incorporation of pre-existing sacred *druids wells* into *holy wells*. The academic had not heard this theory before, so his instinctive response was to revert to ridicule. Yet it was not always like this.

In the early days of radio science, electromagnetic phenomena surrounding megaliths greatly interested scientists of the era, who saw radio as much of a device to make "deep incursions into the spirit realms", as transmitting information across long distances. Leading scientists of the era such as Thomas Edison and even Marconi himself were taken with this idea. Sir Oliver Lodge, a Victorian inventor, physicist, radio pioneer and spiritualist, and who successfully transmitted radio waves at least a year before Marconi in 1894, was one such inventor. The early development of radio led to the development of new ideas based on known energetic frequencies found at megalithic sites in Ireland and Britain where layers of quartz are present in the standing stones and ortostats. The belief was that radio waves—along with other forces found at megalithic sites—were travelling through the *aether*, and that this medium filled all space, including the bodies of all living things. Sir Oliver Lodge wrote a paper for *Encyclopaedia Britannica*, which was ignored soon after publication, and has all but been forgotten in spite of his ground-breaking discoveries into radio transmission.

Electromagnetic-, and even plasm-based phenomena surrounding megalithic sites has been long observed and documented, but remians strangely sidelined to make room for *Pi* and landing sites for alien spacecraft. Eliphas Levi, the brilliant French occultist, outlined the phenomena known as 'astral light', an effect which has been observed countless times over the centuries being emitted from the stones at West Kennet Long Barrow near Avebury in England during certain lunar cycles. Yet so much of the recent history of megalithic study has been reduced to the coldness of the slide rule and the log tables, when there is so much more to be investigated.

MADE FROM THE SAME STUFF

Regardless of their place in far-off antiquity or up to the very present, we humans continue to remain very complex creatures, and these megalithic structures reflect our human complexity in every way imaginable. I myself, believe in many things which are unseen, as I have observed their shadows move constantly across the face of this world. We all have had these magical, fleeting insights and experiences. Rarely do they grab our attention and force us to look more deeply. The truth always waits for you to be ready for it to reveal itself to you, and not the other way around.

The emotional energy and aesthetic of the ancient megaliths, even when they have been ravaged by everything from religious intolerance, agriculture, urbanisation, bureaucracy and ignorance, still manage to communicate with us on some powerful subconscious level. Even some archaeologists have admitted to me that there were moments when they put down their equipment and rationality, only to find themselves emotionally, if not (whisper it quietly) spiritually, overwhelmed when working at some megalithic dig site when the sunset or sunrise was just right and they found themselves caught up in the magic of these mysterious stones and earthworks.

Their ability to call us has personally led me to walk for miles, in the wind and rain, across the often soaking and boggy, mountainious landscapes of rural Sligo where I live in the northwest of Ireland, only to find myself—for no explicable reason—drawn to a cluster of remote trees and not being satisfied until I was in their centre. Then, to discover much later on (via an old Irish *Ordinance Survey* map) that the precise location where I stood was the centre of an ancient Rath, or 'fairy fort', where the semi-mystical race, the Tuatha Dé Danann, are reputed to be laying in wait for the day when they are called to return to this reality and save Ireland.

The ring of trees are allowed by farmers—even in this day and age—to grow unhindered around these 'fairy forts' so that livestock and even children, do not accidentally wander into the domain of the *Sidhe* (*Aos Sí;* pronounced "Shee", the people of the mounds), lest they be carried into the fifth province of the otherworld. This is the origin of the phrase 'away with the fairies', and believe me, as prosaic as I like to think I generally am, I agree with the old farmers in this respect.

In the early 1980s, a future Irish billionaire, Sean Quinn, knowingly ordered his quarrying company to demolish the four thousand year old Aughrim Wedge Tomb, at Ballyconnell in County Cavan, to further expand his growing quarrying and concrete empire. By 2012, the billions he had accumulated were gone, along with his once mighty construction and insurance empire. Quinn himself was left with less money in his bank account than when he ordered the demolition of Aughrim Wedge Tomb twenty five years previously.

Several older people in rural County Cavan issued dire warnings back in the early 1980s, claiming that Sean Quinn's attack upon the *Sidhe* would lead to the ruin of both himself and his family. This is precisely what happened. In fact, no sooner had Quinn removed the megalith than there was a sudden increase in his fleet of trucks mysteriously breaking down, losing control, and going off the road. Quinn then attempted to replace the megalith stones in their original arrangement, but this proved an impossible task. To this day, people tell me that he is regretting his violation of the *Sidhe*. Not only has his business empire collapsed, but the knock-on effects of his empire collapsing has led to massive unemployment levels in the border region.

The present otherworld, according to Irish mythology, came about as the result of a diplomatic arrangement to divide Ireland between two conflicting factions: the Milesian Gaels, who were to take the world above (consciousness/materialism), and the Tuatha Dé Danann who departed to the world below (subconsciousness/psyche). This could also be an allegory pertaining to the fracturing of the human mind into the speaking brain, and the part of our cognition which listens and obeys (in a sense, ego creation) which is echoed in several other mythologies, and became an idea popularised by Princeton psychologist Julian Jaynes in his 1976 book *The Origins of Consciousness in the Breakdown of the Bicameral Mind*.

This is not to imply that there is no historical evidence that groups such as Tuatha Dé Danann did not actually exist as a real tribe in ancient Ireland. They may well have been very real in some historical sense, and indeed, there is plenty of evidence which collates actual locations in Ireland and Scotland with Irish mythology. However, over time, history merges with myth, and from this a form of psycho-history emerges. Nevertheless, there may be some powerful cognitive reason for this, as mythology is often the repository of human survivial through the traumas of the past. The mythology thus serves as a warning from the ancestors. The Tuatha Dé Danann were defeated, but they were not destroyed.

VITAL SIGNS

The veil being lifted between the material world and the otherworld is something many of us have experienced at least once in our lives. So it was at the precise moment within this contemporary version of space and time (early 2016), that members of a documentary crew and I were discussing the mystery and possibilities of Woodhenge, and in particular, its relationship to the nearby Stonehenge complex itself which includes the adjacent Durrington Walls superhenge, that the world's media—unbeknownst to any of us at that moment—

was in a great state of excitement, reporting that a 'Stonehenge Two' had been discovered. Its location determined to be under the very same circular embankment which we had been contemplating, just as the press releases on the discovery were being reported around the world. A message from the fifth province was delivered via the couriers of the collective unconscious. Another votive hoard of the psyche uncovered.

However, the previous morning's visit to the great stones at Stonehenge had already given up a taster for the main event that was to come at Woodhenge the following day. Not being the type given to being constantly overcome by such metascientific epiphany, and finding myself one of the very fortunate and increasingly limited number of people who will have been privileged enough to have been allowed inside the centre of the Stonehenge monument itself—as the sun rose on a perfectly still and cloudless morning—I was overcome by a sense of enticing welcome and powerful revealing.

I truly never expected that the actual Stonehenge stones themselves would display such a mass of migrating colours and pulsating hues, as the long shadows of the rising sun moved across their surface, revealing dancing simulacra and meandering, weaving tonal changes. I was also pleasantly surprised to discover that not only are sounds perceived very differently when inside Stonehenge, but also how the perception of one's own inner voice—inside one's head—is also strangely experienced. It was as if I was hearing my actual authentic thoughts for the first time; very similar to when one hears their own voice played back for the first time on a recording device. It was that surprising to me. However, it should not have been, as I was within the ultimate man-made magic circle.

The Druid Code:
Magic, Megaliths and Mythology

However, more than anything else, it was while inside this assemblage of great stones that I finally realised what Geoffrey of Monmouth meant when he wrote that Merlin had taken the stones of Stonehenge from Ireland to Salisbury Plain using 'scientific knowledge'. It was a metaphor for the secret knowledge and workings of the druids to pass on carefully guarded secrets, often by using mythology connected with megaliths created by a previous—although not unconnected—culture, to deliver important messages and information to the tribal population and especially, to future generations. Suddenly, everything fell into place for me. The photons of the morning sun being absorbed and bouncing among the surfaces of the great stones had revealed to me a narrative for a mysterious and missing order of ancient holy men and women, linking them not only to the European stone monuments of the Neolithic Age, but also to the aftermath of a great traumatic cataclysm which swallowed up the lands of our ancestors and changed their lives, and the destiny of Europe, forever.

Although the link between the missing continent of *Atlantis* and Stonehenge may on the surface appear to be a highly tenuous association, it is one that many have speculated upon over the centuries. To begin with, we must discard the name "Atlantis" itself, along with the *Classical* depictions of toga-wearing figures being washed away by the sea. A more fitting imagery from which to apply this association would be the metaphors and allegories contained with the Norse story of *Ragnarök*.

Anyone who has ever stood under the central triathlons at Stonehenge is instantly struck by the sensation that the structure itself comes from somewhere else. You are standing within what feels like an alien landscape. It is a completely different sensation than stranding inside the ruins of, say a Norman castle, or a Roman amphitheatre. We know what these structures are and who built them, and more importantly, why they were built. With Stonehenge, we simply haven't a clue. Add to this that we cannot even comprehend who, how or why these immense stones were brought to this site. The entire experience feels 'alien' in the truest sense of the word. Not alien, as in from another planet, but rather, alien in terms of the consciousness of the people who built them compared to that of our own. Is the loss of *Atlantis* also referring to the the loss of the consciousness which built Stonehenge and the other great structures of the European Atlantic regions? Perhaps the entire trajectory of the European magical tradition, from the druids to the *Chaos Magic* of the 1980s, has been a continuous subconscious desire to return to *Atlantis*?

THE PETRIFIED TRANSMISSION

The following day at Woodhenge—while I was still pondering the concept that our mysterious lexicon of the ancient sites of Europe could be more comprehensively uncovered using an overall holistic approach based on applying everything from archaeology and astronomy to deciphering mythological archetypes, all applied in tandem by observing developing cultural manifestation —that perhaps the most incredible group synchronicity of my entire life was unleashed with the 'Stonehenge Two' announcement. This 'spiritual' experience, for that is what it felt like in the most clearest descriptive sense to me, fused the material world of experience with the fifth province of knowing.

Finally, I understood why Odin's information-gathering ravens, *Huginn* and *Muninn*, represented 'thought' and 'memory' as they flew over the human-percieved world of *Midgard*. They allow us to connect our rational cognition

The Druid Code:
Magic, Megaliths and Mythology

with that of the supernatural. For this is what had taken place at Woodhenge as we were considering the nearby Durrington Walls at the same moment that academics and ordinary people around the world were in state of great excitement at the discovery of the literal remains of approximately one hundred or so huge stones discovered using ground-penetrating radar technology a few metres below the Durrington embankment. Along with these large stones, other structures in close proximity to the Woodhenge site were also discovered, including a large timbered hall. A genuine *Valhalla* of the Neolithic!

Part of the *Sarsen Circle* at Stonehenge. The famous site, which to this day continues to create wonder and reveal mysteries, and which still surprises and captivates even the minds of even the most casual observer. Every manner of possible mathematical formulae and geometric theory has been presented in an attempt to explain the stones and their relative position to the cosmos. Yet, one aspect that is often overlooked, is that these are doorways, or portals, to link different states of existence together. The negative spaces in between are as relevant as the massive stones themselves. Something of a 'light and shadow' of the material meets the immaterial, thereby fusing the conscious and subconscious minds as one.

(photo: Thomas Sheridan)

This incredible synchronicity finally and very personally validated for me the long-held assumption that the Stonehenge complex was one of the largest human settlements in Europe during the Neolithic era. A great settlement that was more than just merely people and great structures, but also a powerful expression of art, culture, human destiny and magic. The Stonehenge complex is a trans-Neolithic particle collider of sorts, which is still colliding into the consciousness of people like myself in the most remarkable and surprising of ways.

THE DRUIDIC GHOSTS IN THE EARLY CHRISTIAN MACHINE?

Prior to this remarkable synchronicity, I had been researching the idea that the druids of pre-Roman/Christian Europe, rather than having been wiped out with the advent of Christianity, had instead gone 'underground' within the emerging power structures of the new order of Roman laws, taxation and culture. Acting as something akin to *Fifth Columnists* within the Roman power networks so as to ensure that their knowledge and especially their mythology was not completely consumed and obliterated by the new Abrahamic religion from the Middle East. So that, rather than allowing themselves to be annihilated as pagan martyrs sacrificed to the traumatic changes of the era's rapidly changing politics, religion and culture, these druids—as living repositories of history, genealogies, poetry, satire, medicine, magic and science—had instead become the 'Merlins' of the *Arthurian* legends.

Merlin was based on a very real Welsh warrior-hermit-seer named Myrddin Wyllt, and was described as being both 'the son of the devil (druid) and the servant of God (Christianity)' within the *Grail* stories of the Middle Ages.

The Druid Code:
Magic, Megaliths and Mythology

Playing the Roman game, so to speak, but not fully in the game, as such. Merlin's reality and mythology is a useful example of how we can understand the workings of this *Druid Code* and what it reveals to us. The actual historical data relating to Myrddin (Merlin) is recorded following a 6th century battle which took place at Arderydd in 573AD.

The records tell us that he 'went mad' when the fighting was over. Myrddin appears to have been afflicted with something akin to *Post Traumatic Stress* from witnessing the violent deaths of his relatives and friends. As a result of this breakdown, he fled deep into the dense forest along the Scottish Borders. It was there that Myrddin underwent a profound shamanic experience of sorts, and from then on, would only emerge from the woods to give counsel and deliver prophecy.

Therefore, we can extract from this historical evidence that the character we have come to know as *Merlin the Wizard* was ostensibly, Myrddin the semi-hidden druid operating within the power structures of the post-Roman imperial paradigm whose own magical transformation came about as a result of trauma. A trauma, generating a narrative of powerful truths and realisations, and whose power is capable of inspiring both illiterate serfs and great intellectuals alike. The transformation of Myrddin's trauma was reassembled into a magical system of communication and memory which reached deep into the psyche of those exposed to its power.

This may also explain why Saint Patrick insisted that priests ordained at the Eamhain Mhacha (Navan Fort) complex—near present day city of Armagh in Ulster—were to be the only ones trusted to deliver the *Gospels* to the native Irish. Did Saint Patrick want the druids in the early Irish church as part of a

The Druid Code:
Magic, Megaliths and Mythology

public relations coup, or did he want to keep an eye on them?

Through his own network of spies and informers, Saint Patrick had likely become aware that several druids ('snakes', if you will) had infiltrated the early Irish church—perhaps following the fall of Tara as a Heathen power site—and who were secretly attempting to keep the 'old faith' alive at the highest administrative levels of the church. But why? What was the reason why the druids retained and wrote down the ancient Irish mythologies in order to ensure they were preserved for future generations?

This nineteenth century Irish drawing illustrates how many early (and even much later) Christian sites built their churches and cemeteries upon previously Heathen 'sacred sites'. The tombs of the Christian faithful in something of a 'higher heaven' above that of the assumed pagan 'tombs'.

We can see clearly the motivation here; to both capitalise upon the enormous spiritual and energetic footprint these Neolithic and later pagan sites had among the local community, while at the same time, to literally 'bury' the old faith with the new. The same process was also applied to Heathen festivals and calendar dates which became holy feast days of Christendom. In time, the ancestors' spirits became 'demons' and 'ghosts', while their powerful archetypes within the Irish and other native European tribes were reduced to simple fairy tales and meaningless old country customs believed to have borne out of superstition and ignorance.

(image: The British Library Collection)

As mentioned in *Chapter One*, the famous Irish epic, *The Children of Lir* is essentially a moving lamentation for the loss of the old faith among the people of Ireland with the coming of Christianity. The druids created—or more likely, utilised already existing methods of recovery from social trauma—as a healing device in the guise of folklore to deal with the cultural/spiritual upheavals with the transition to the Christian era. The druids had performed their task of cultural crisis management and social healing for which they had been be created to do. Their elixir, was mythology, folklore and the power of the bard.

SECRET WHISPERS IN THE SCRIPTORIUM

The is also evidence within the Christian power structures in Ireland of something of a hysterical paranoia—concerning the power and influence of the druids. Almost 600 years after the arrival of Saint Patrick. The *Book of Ballymote* contained within its pages complex instructions on deciphering druidic coded messages transmitted using the Ogham (pronounced 'om') system of writing, and how to translate it into Latin. Long after the Anglo-Norman invasion of Ireland, Christianity was still in a precarious state in Ireland, as the vast majority of the population steadfastly adhered to pagan customs and ritual celebration dates and festivals, just as their ancestors had done so, going right back to the Neolithic and perhaps even to the Mesolithic era. This single page of decoded encryption almost certainly demonstrates the concern within the Irish church fathers—regarding the possible operational existence of druids—many hundreds of years after the arrival of Saint Patrick. Such was their paranoia that they even refer to the runes as 'the Viking Ogham'.

In recent decades, much has been made of the 'authenticity' of the methodology of the early so-called *Celtic Church* and their defiance against the Pope, by incorporating pagan worship into Christian religious services. In reality, any theological disputes between both were purely academic, and there is little hard evidence to suggest that the *Celtic Church* was self-consciously developed as a structural hybrid between paganism and the Christian church in terms of their rites and sacraments. It was more akin to a pre-conditioning of the population in anticipation of the arrival of political Christianity from Europe. Rome was coming anyway, and so the Irish druids became 'Christians' as a matter of political and social expediency. This not only ensured their own personal survival, but also the historical and cultural legacy of the pre-Christianised Irish.

Most of the actual writing down and retention of the Irish mythology record was undertaken long after the *Synod of Whitby* (664AD) had merged the Celtic church into the Roman church. The Irish druids appeared to have waited until Rome was in charge and then they 'jumped ship' so to speak, as they possibly saw no threats from the early isolated Celtic Christian outposts (obscure cult compounds at the time, which could be easily infiltrated and influenced) clinging to wave battered, rocky shorelines and remote islands. It was Rome, afterall, who slaughtered the British druids, and if there were any scores to be settled, it was with Rome.

THE SERPENTS RETURN

This highlights another neurosis within the so-called early 'celtic' and the later Roman version which came intensely to the fore with the Norse raids on

The Druid Code:
Magic, Megaliths and Mythology

European monasteries during the Viking era; that being that the arrival of the pagan Norse might return the Britons, Picts, Irish and others back to the 'old faith'. Indeed, this does seem to have happened to a degree, (at least culturally) as Anglo-Saxon scribes in the court of Charlemagne expressed dismay that not only did the Christian peasants living in close proximity to the monasteries fail to come to the aid of the 'defenceless' monks during the Viking raids, but soon afterwards began wearing their hair in the fashion of the Heathen Norsemen.

The reality is that the monks in these monastic outposts often tended to be heavily armed and well-trained former knights who were generally despised by the neighbouring secular population whom the 'humble men of God' treated hardly any better than the cattle or livestock on their monastic lands. We can clearly see in the *Book of Ballymote* that even as late as the 1400s, the Christian church in Ireland was still struggling to maintain their hold over the consciousness of the Irish people, and any possibility of secret druids posing as monks, priests, and even bishops would have been of great concern to Rome.

The pagan emerging from under the Christian veneer was an ever-constant worry for the early church fathers. This era of the Middle Ages was a time when intolerance towards heresy was taken to an industrial level by the Roman church with the genocide of the Cathars by the *Inquisition* in southern France during the horrific—and 'hellish' in every possible sense of the word—*Albigensian Crusade* initiated by Pope Innocent III in 1209. Almost a thousand years after its arrival in western Europe, Christianity was still only managing to hold onto its power over the population through oppression, cutting deals with royalty (along with other powerful nobles), and sheer militaristic brutality. Paranoia was rampant, and heretics, in the form of 'sons of devils, and servants of God.' returning the masses back to worshiping nature, pagan gods and especially goddesses, along with venerating the ancient mysterious stone structures, was not taken lightly.

Antiquarian woodcut from 1700 of the sequential Heathen ritual mounds in Uppsala, Sweden which are punctuated by the church of *Gamla Uppsala*. The mounds are dated to approximately 500AD and represent Sweden's oldest known historical structures. Folklore decrees that three of the *Haugr* (mound or barrow) venerate the Nordic gods Thor, Odin and Freyr. The location is considered to be one of the most important sites in Europe for the study of psycho-geography, ley lines and geomancy (landscape magic).

The landscape and the church of *Gamla Uppsala* dominate the surrounding countryside as each mound progresses towards the largest mound, which was once adjacent to a major pagan temple and which is now occupied by the church. The replacement of important Heathen sacred sites is a common occurrence all over Europe, often as a symbol of co-option and suppression of the previous tradition. The church at *Gamla Uppsala* makes a definitive statement in this regard.

(illustration: Suecia Antiqua et Hodierna)

The Irish church, having been essentially created by the druids before the arrival of Roman Christianity with its secret codes of Ogham writing and tolerance towards pagan feast days, must have produced a rather unique society in Ireland during and after the Middle Ages. The legacy of this pagan influence within Irish Christianity (and Irish society at large), the Catholic church in Ireland has still not managed to come to terms with. As late as 2015, a Rev Dr Chris Hayden—a priest from the notorious paedophile-infested Ferns diocese in the southeast of Ireland—embarked on a remarkable diatribe in the Saint Patrick's Day edition of

The Druid Code:
Magic, Megaliths and Mythology

the *Irish Times* against pre-Christian Ireland, which, if it was applied to any other religion or race would have been considered hate speech. He stated that our Irish ancestors were 'dark, terrible and savage' and that 'Druidism was based largely on human sacrifice' within an article condemning the rise of NeoPaganism in Ireland today. In actuality, there is far more evidence to suggest that Catholicism is based on raping children more than there is evidence to prove that human sacrifice was central to the druids' practices. This coming from an individual whose former fellow cleric—Fr Seán Fortune—made pornographic films of himself raping young boys, while being protected by the same diocese. A 2002 BBC documentary entitled *Suing the Pope* discovered that several of Fr Seán Fortune's victims had committed suicide as a direct result of the Ferns diocese ignoring their complaints of sexual abuse. In other words, using them as human sacrifices to the infallibility of the Catholic church.

Highly engineered and beautifully ornate Neolithic rock art on display at the *National Museum of Archaeology* in Valletta, Malta. The spiral motif, so common to Irish Neolithic rock art tradition, is also found on this Mediterranean island in great abundance. According to Maltese legends, these Neolithic monuments were created by a race of giants who were the first inhabitants of the island.

(photo: Thomas Sheridan)

With a mentality such as this in 2015, is it any wonder that the Irish druids—following the arrival of Saint Patrick and the country converting to the new faith—communicated secretly to one another by means of Ogham within the growing power of the Roman church in Ireland over a thousand years ago?

COUNTER PROPAGANDA

A Christian monk would have found himself rather uncomfortable deciphering this 'blasphemous' script, and this might explain why many Ogham stones ended up on their sides rather than in their original vertical position. A rather famous example are the Ogham stones uprooted and inserted as lintels in order to face directly into 'Ireland's gateway to Hell' is at Oweynagat Cave, among the vast—but today, depressingly ravaged and bleak—Rathcroghan-Cruachán megalithic complex in County Roscommon. One of the Ogham stones, rather fantastically, contains within the translated text a line clearly identifying this location to 'mythological' Queen Meabh of Connacht in the heart of what is reputed to be the capital of her ancient kingdom. Here we have tanigible evidence of oral mythology connected with the stone monuments of the past. A genuine smoking gun of the *Druid Code* in effect.

Perhaps a druid in the Middle Ages, or even much earlier, placed the Ogham stone in that position inside the cave as a message to future generations at a time when Christianity was involved in replacing—as well as creatively editing—Irish legends with ones from the Middle East? During this same period, the Christians were converting Irish gods and goddesses into saints (these were not pagan-hybrids as such, as they were deemed fully Christian), as well as renaming megalithic and mythological locations using terms such as 'hell's this', 'devil's that' and 'pagan sacrificial murder altars', in order to culturally obliterate their origins as well as the cultures and individuals connected to them. Even so, it was almost as if the early Christians knew something of the history of these European 'Walls of Jericho' that told of an ancient disaster for the people who built them with their pagan craft and witchery.

At the same time this Ogham stone was being preserved inside Ireland's hellmouth, Irish druids were making the choice of becoming *Fifth Columnists* operating within the Christian church, or taking up a career with the emerging bardic tradition, known as the *filid*. The *filid* survived for centuries as a central aspect of Irish society and remained highly influential as an elite class of pseudo-secular druids—in all but their original title—within Irish life and society for many hundreds of years after the arrival of Saint Patrick. The *filid* performed the function of workers of magic and healing, interepreters of *Brehon* law, personal counsellors to the chieftains, and most important of all—at a time when a brilliant satire could destroy an entire kingdom—poets. How the *filid* were even tolerated in the Christian world of Ireland is remarkable in and of itself, and serves to demonstrate just how many concessions the Roman church had to make to 'sons of devils and servants of God' in order to survive as a social force in Ireland.

The universal tenacity of such ideas was summed up perfectly by Carl Jung when he wrote in *On the Relation of Analytical Psychology to Poetry,* "Just as the individual's conscious mind needs to be brought into greater harmony and balance with the countervailing tendencies of the unconscious, so a particular culture needs to readjust its collective perspectives through the agency of myth and symbol. It is the mythmaking artist who discovers the compensatory archetypal image that the age and culture require for greater balance."

ALL GOBLINS ARE PAGANS

When I tell people that the Irish peasantry still believe in fairies, I am often doubted. They think that I am merely trying to weave a forlorn piece of gilt thread into the dull grey worsted of this century. They do not imagine it possible that our highly thought of philosophies so soon grow silent outside the walls of the lecture room, or that any kind of ghost or goblin can live within the range of our daily papers. If the papers and the lectures have not done it, they think, surely at any rate the steam-whistle has scared the whole tribe out of the world. They are quite wrong. The ghosts and goblins do still live and rule in the imaginations of the innumerable Irish men and women, and not merely in remote places, but close even to big cities.

At Howth, for instance, ten miles from Dublin, there is a 'fairies path', whereon a great colony of otherworld creatures travel nightly from the hill to the sea and home again. There is also a field that ever since a cholera shed stood there for a few months, has broken out in fairies and evil spirits.

Sligo is, indeed, a great place for fairy pillaging of this kind. In the side of Ben Bulben is a white square in the limestone. It is said to be the door of fairyland. There is no more inaccessible place in existence than this white square door; no human foot has ever gone near it, not even the mountain goats can browse the saxifrage beside its mysterious whiteness. Tradition says that it swings open at nightfall and lets pour through an unearthly troop of hurrying spirits. To those gifted to hear their voices the air will be full at such a moment with a sound like whistling. Many have been carried away out of the neighbouring villages by this troop of riders. I have quite a number of records beside me, picked up at odd times from the faithful memories of old peasants. Brides and new-born children are especially in danger. Peasant mothers, too, are sometimes carried off to nurse the children of the fairies. At the end of seven years they have a chance of returning, and if they do not escape then are always prisoners. A woman, said still to be living, was taken from near a village called Ballisodare, and when she came home after seven years she had no toes-she had danced them off. It is not possible to find out whether the stolen people are happy among 'the gentry', as the fairies are called for politeness. Accounts differ. Some say they are happy enough, but lose their souls, because, perhaps, the soul cannot live without sorrow. Others will have it that they are always wretched, longing for their friends, and that the splendour of the fairy kingdom is merely a magical delusion, woven to deceive the minds of men by poor little withered apparitions who live in caves and barn laces. But this is, I suspect, a theological opinion, invented because all goblins are pagans. Many things about fairies, indeed, are most uncertain. We do not even know whether they die. An old Gaelic poem says, 'Death is even among the fairies', but then many stories represent them as hundreds of years old.

The Druid Code:
Magic, Megaliths and Mythology

An image of a typical pre-Christian Irish 'savage', along with an example of the remarkable and intricately designed gold jewellery from the same era on display in the the *National Museum of Ireland*. Within the *Ancient Ireland* wing of the museum, is this large, colourful painting of an Irishman wearing examples of the same jewellery on display, and looking like one of the *Morlocks* as described in H. G. Wells for his 1895 novel, *The Time Machine*. Half naked and tanned, while we all wait for a suitable grunt-like noise to be emitted from his lips...

The logic being presented here by the so-called Irish experts, being that the ancient Irish people could develop all the technical and creative skills to build stunningly exquisite metalwork, complex engineering and masonry, while gaining sophisticated knowledge about astronomy, as well as developing agricultural sciences, and all this held together with a rich culture. However, they were somehow then incapable of developing textiles for clothing and remained more than half naked.

Apart from the obvious climatic issues with dressing like a Polynesian islander in the middle of an Irish winter, the utter nonsense behind these 'caveman'-like portrayals of our Irish, British and other pre-Roman European ancestors shows no signs of waning among academia, as well as with general population at large. For all we know, the people of the ancient past age may have sported elaborately-decorated clothing to complement their beautiful metalwork, while living in attractive and ornate houses engineered in wood, and which today, we only have postholes in the ground to know where they stood and how large they were. The decay of organic materials from the Neolithic and later eras has created a void which has been filled in with Roman-originated propaganda and stereotypes which are widely accepted to this day.

(photo: Thomas Sheridan)

The Druid Code:
Magic, Megaliths and Mythology

The world is, I believe, more full of significance to the Irish peasant than to the English. The fairy populace of hill and lake and woodland have helped to keep it so. It gives a fanciful life to the dead hillsides, and surrounds the peasant, as he ploughs and digs, with tender shadows of poetry. No wonder that he is gay, and can take man and his destiny without gloom and make up proverbs like this from the old Gaelic- 'The lake is not burdened by its swan, the steed by its bridle, or a man by the sold that is in him.'

-WB Yeats (1890)

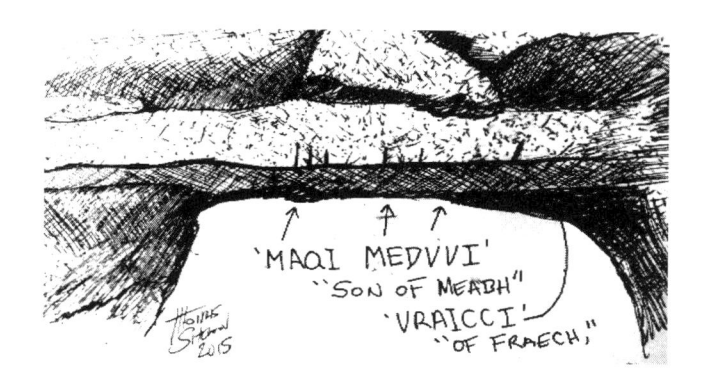

The remarkable Ogham Stone lintel installed inside *Oweynagat Cave* in the heart of the vast Rathcroghan-Cruachán complex in the west of Ireland. One of two Ogham Stones inside the cave known as Ireland's 'Gateway to Hell'. The above example contains an Ogham script (just visible on its lower edge) which translates as 'of Fraech, son of Meabh'. A direct association between the location itself and the legendary Queen Meabh who was said to have ruled Connacht from Rathcroghan-Cruachán.

It cannot be overstated how important this artefact is, as it verifies the actual existence of Queen Meabh, who was previously believed to have been a mythological figure with no basis in historical fact. This Ogham Stone is on par with the *Rosetta Stone* of Egypt, or the discovery of Troy by Heinrich Schliemann in terms of its importance in bringing a genuine historical flesh, to the bones of what was once considered mere mythology.

(illustration: Thomas Sheridan Field Notebook)

What makes the transition between Heathenism and Christianity in Ireland of the period—within the context of the druids' infiltration of the early Irish church—so unique, would have been attitudes towards non-material entities. To the Christians, these would have been all considered to be "demons" and emissaries of the Devil, yet we can probably assume that druids were involved in the summoning up and invocation of these entities as part of their magic. The Irish mythological and folklore tradition makes many references to 'monsters' from the otherworld entering into our own.

The cave at Oweynagat is particularly associated with these inter-dimensional beings, and it is fair to assume that the 'monsters' which the Christians claim to have emerged from the cave were connected to dogmatic neuroses concerning entities which may have been unleashed or summoned by druids inside the cave itself. To this day, rituals are still performed within the inner chamber of the cave, if the magical paraphernalia left around is anything to go by. There is also a powerful sense within the lower chamber at Oweynagat as being something of a portal to the real show hidden behind the stone rock face on the right hand side as one enters. Legends speak of Oweynagat being connected to the equally mysterious *Caves of Kesh,* dozens of kilometres away in County Sligo. Indeed, one does get a sense that the entire Rathcroghan-Cruachán region may well be a vast subterranean world, and the numerous mounds and other structures on the surface are but a hint of what may lie below the topsoil interconnecting the vast limestone caverns which this part of Ireland is filled with. Perhaps a real life version of the *Hollow Earth* theory waiting to be discovered?

Without going too deeply into my own experiences with such entities, I can assure the reader that they do indeed exist, as when they appear in and around megalithic sights they are usually in the form of unusual animals. In my case, they tend to appear as enormous hares which have no fear of humans. In fact, the opposite scenario applies, I can assure you. I have also, on occasion, witnessed what has become known in recent times as *Shadow Beings*, almost-human forms made of a dark mist.

At the *Parco dei Petroglifi* in Sardinia, among the so-called Janas 'fairy' houses, are carved into the solid rock some of the strangest and most unsettling of Neolithic rock art forms including images of frankly disturbing humanoid-like beings which stare back at the viewer from across the centuries. Inside one of the chambers, I caught sight of a moving, humanoid-shaped, darkened mist, identical to what I have have also seen in the remote highlands of the Ox Mountains in Sligo. A figment of my imagination brought about by the heightened sense of drama such locations can generate? Perhaps, and perhaps not. However, these experiences were very 'real' indeed, regardless of their origins being deep within my neurology, or perhaps arrivals from the otherworld. Either way, both are equally valid in terms tearing apart the stoic illusions of our modern lives. I believe it was the Irish novelist and playwright Brendan Behan who remarked that we are all subject to 'daylight atheism' until darkness falls...

The demarcation line between fairies and demons is almost indistinguishable from a pagan context, and it was probably the druids themselves within the early Irish church who made this distinction on purpose, lest the Irish lose their unique cultural relationship to elemental entities at a time in which they were all subjected to being declared 'demons', which had also taken place in most of Europe during this period of history (Scandinavia excluded). A good example of this would be the *Šetek*, a Slavic and Bohemian ancestral spirit, considered to be an omen of good luck to have one living on your property. This image of a tiny, Pan-like being with cloven hooves and goat-like horns allowed the Christians to turn this somewhat endearing spirit into a miniature demon in the service of the Devil himself.

The respectful fear of the *Sidhe* in Ireland had practical considerations, too. As the nineteenth century French occultist Eliphas Levi stated, "The love of such beings by a Magus is insensate and may destroy him." One of the reasons for this is that the magician develops a more close relationship with his or her elementals and familiars than with the human race. This might well explain the hermit-like nature often applied to the druids. While Merlin was in the woods as a hermit on the Scottish Borders, he was devoid of human company, but may have found himself surrounded by non-human companions.

THE SLEEPING SEER

Druids were often called upon to use deep sleeping to solve a problem within the community, or even to select a new leader of the clan. Almost certainly this consultation within the dream state involved communications with elemental spirits. In the 1870s, a term was coined by the Victorian neurologist William Carpenter concerning the unconscious creativity of working with a familiar or elemental spirit which he called the *Unconscious Celebration*. These nocturnal guides will sometmes wake us from a deep sleep with the answer to some problem we are seeking the solution to at the time. As Carpenter stated, "Our personal *Familiar* is a great deal more than a walking dictionary, a housemaid, valet de place or a barrel-organ man... He is a novelist who can spin more romances than Dumas."

Carl Jung referred to such dealings with elementals and familiars as states of

Autonomous Complexes contained within the psyche, and these complexes behave much like independent beings. These demons, elementals and spirits are, according to Jung, "naïve awareness of the powerful inner effect of autonomous partial systems". That is to say these internal beings can not be brought into a *Tupla*-like manifestation of an actual being which can be observed in waking states. In fact, this desire for manifestation of a non-earthly being is one of the primary goals of most occultists in numerous cultures and schools of magic. In this respect, Jung was probably wrong. However, as Jung himself was sailing so close to the rocky shores of academic vitriol, his feelings on the matter can be almost certainly be seen as something of a professional compromise in this regard.

In 1955, the brilliant English artist and practicing magician Austin Osman Spare painted a pastel work entitled *Druidesque*. Influenced by the *Symbolism* and *Art Nouveau* styles of artistic expression, the body of his artwork work is generally noted for depictions of demonic and sexual imagery but yet, in *Druidesque,* Spare presents us with a haunting vista of beauty and longing among the shadows of a bucolic landscape dominated by a single standing stone. After developing his own ideas of proto-psychology, Spare became interested in Theosophy and magic, and underwent a brief association with Aleister Crowley. From this, Spare began to develop his own magic practice and philosophy which resulted in grimoires, entitled *Earth Inferno* (1905), and *The Focus of Life* (1921), amongst others.

Spare was captivated by the creation of familiars and elementals and, like Merlin, chose to live in isolation, in Spare's case; in the East End of London with a company of spirits, rather than being in the company of other humans. *Druidesque* is a breathtakingly beautiful work which shows a group of druids around a standing stone as a golden sun sets in a blazing purple sky. Off into the distance, a winding stream vanishes into the far horizon. The druids pictured in the work appear tired, forlorn and melancholy, as if their work was done. Yet the meandering waterway leading into the distance suggests that their magic will go on forever. The large standing stone in the foreground of the painting is to remind us that Austin Osman Spare's own magic was a continuation of what the druids had begun. As Spare would be dead not long after painting *Druidesque*, the irony of his own now highly influential magical legacy was not lost on him, as he joined the stream of continuous magic which had initially poured forth from the primal well of the druids.

CHAPTER FIVE

THE MYTHOLOGICAL TALES ARE WRITTEN DOWN

The Druid Code:
Magic, Megaliths and Mythology

During the period when the famous Ogham stone lintels were being placed inside 'Ireland's entrance to Hell', (Roman) Christian monks were also coming to the realisation and understanding of the power of Irish mythology being very much alive within the consciousness of the population, and thus, they attempted to create their own 'Christianised' versions of the Irish mythological record. Although, once again, it is highly plausible that there may have been secret druids, or clergy with Druidic sympathies (if not fears), making sure that as much Irish mythology and pre-Christian history was retained under the guise of Christian editorialisation.

A clear indication of this altering of Irish mythology—following the direct control from Rome—to make the old gods and goddesess fit more appropriately within the biblical creationist timeline, is the legend of Cessair, who was reputed to have been a grand-daughter of Noah, and who came to Ireland because "She thought it probable that a place where people had never come before, and where no evil or sin had been committed, and which was free from the world's reptiles and monsters, that place would be free from the Flood."

This fabrication by the Christian scribes in Ireland later became a central aspect of the absurd *British Israelism* movement of the Victorian era, which sought to solidify ancient European history with biblical timelines, often with pernicious political and imperial agendas in mind. Even so, there was indeed a very real cultural memory of the seas rising and swallowing up not just Ireland, but much of the European Atlantic seaboard, and which, unlike the flood of Noah, there is tangible and emerging scientific evidence to validate these Irish and other mythological stories of a great flood swallowing up a vast landmass of western Europe. The early Christian monks knew this, and attempted to co-opt the story for their own dogmatic ends with the biblical overlay.

The migration of early Christian monks to even more remote parts of the country and eventually to islands off the coast—after Christianity had achieved a growing early foothold in Ireland—also betrays the 'cult'-like aspect of the early Irish monks who were eager to relocate to more and more isolated locations that were free from "reptiles and monsters", producing an almost neurotic urge which sent them to the cliff tops of Skellig Michael, an island off the coast of County Kerry, although even early English Christian sources claim that the island was home to the sons of Breogán, who are specifically mentioned as being Celtiberians. One has to wonder if these monks isolated on the remote islands began to experience visions of their own *Shadow People*? Eventually, the Christian monks apparently found Skellig Michael to be also filled with "reptiles and monsters", and like any cult, moved their compound to Iceland, long before even the Vikings repeated these voyages in their magnificent longships. Which ironically enough, displayed carved "reptiles and monsters" on their 'Dragon Ship' prows.

The Christianising of the Irish mythological stories was a cultural, if not psychological version of what later religious Puritans in Scotland undertook when they attempted to destroy the many megalithic sites in Aberdeenshire. As the rock star and megalithic researcher Julian Cope points out in *The Modern Antiquarian*, there were simply too many megalithic sites to destroy, and they were too deeply connected to the natural topography of the landscape that the Puritan 'stone killers' just gave up in the end. The same result took place with Irish mythology, as the archetypes and subconscious narratives within the Irish mythological record were just too rich, and likewise, too deeply connected to the topography of the landscape they were set within. Try as they might, the Christians, and later on in history, the completely absurd *British Israelites*, could not find a place in the British Isles for Jesus to change water into wine.

THE RAVEN AND OTHER HARVESTERS OF THE SLAIN

Comparative mythologies reveal tremendous insights when we discover archetypal interconnectedness between them. Following the Christianisation of the Irish mythological record, and later on in history, the same Biblical overlay was attempted with the Norse *Eddas* and Viking *Sagas* under the Icelandic editorial department of Christendom; Snorri Sturluson (who shows all the signs of being a secret Viking version of a bard or *walwōn* himself) and who wrote down the legends of Thor, Odin, Freya and Siv, as well as the wonderful tales of the *Yggdrasil Tree* and *Asgard*. It just goes to show, that you can't keep a good archetype down if the mythology from which they sprang is so powerful that it reaches deep into our collective subconscious minds. It shall endure and resonate with humans as long as we are still humans. Which is not surprising, as many of

The Druid Code:
Magic, Megaliths and Mythology

these mythological archetypes are very similar across different, and not so different cultures.

Laurence Dermott (1720-1791) is another interesting figure strongly associated with Irish Freemasony, who moved from Ireland to London, becoming very influential within the freemasonic circles of the city at the time the British Empire was approaching its zenith. Considered by many to be a controversial figure who generated as much suspicion as praise, he is generally considered by the historians of the main Irish and British lodges as having the secrets of the 'ancients'.

Among these, was his alleged ability to teach people how to become 'invisible'. This power was also a well-documented skill of the druids during the early years of Christianity in Ireland. In one legend, Saint Patrick himself has to learn the magic of invisibility in order to locate the druids. What is suggested by 'invisiblity' may well be a metaphor for disguise and being hidden in plain sight.

The illustrations above are from Laurence Dermott's *Minute Book of the Ancient's Grand Lodge* (right) and text from the Book of Dun Cow (left), an example of some of the oldest written Irish. The similarity between the *Old Irish* alphabet and Hebrew is readily striking. It has even been suggested by some that the *Old Irish* script was derived from Ogham and then purposely stylised on either Hebrew or Greek in order to bypass any Roman influence. Old Irish script remained in common use in Ireland until the 1950s.

(illustration: The Triskele and the Dragon website)

By using comparative mythology, we can detect cross-cultural similarities which allow us to develop a holistic interpretation of how the minds of ancient western Europeans viewed their own existence, and by osmosis, then takes us one major step closer to developing a more humanistic understanding of the megalith builders of the Neolithic age and what messages they left for future generations. How this legacy may have impacted culturally upon later civilisations and what they can tell us about the psycho-history of a particular group or subculture, or indeed, the collective unconscious of humanity as a whole.

One example of this from within northern European mythological traditions is the idea of the 'Goddess of War' being a powerful archetype, acting somewhat as the supernatural counter-version of the earthly natural mother. The idea held sway that just as a mother was present at the time of birth, an archetypal, supernatural 'death mother' or non-earthly soul-harvesting female entity would ease the passing of men—who had generally fallen in battle—into the next world. Men dying on battlefields have long been known to scream out 'mother!' while in the final death throes, and perhaps this is how the mythology came to be. So it is not at all surprising that both Irish and Norse mythology share a very similar connection to female deities as either goddesses of death, and/or 'collectors of the slain': the *Badb* (pronounced 'baeiv') of the Irish mythological pantheon and the *Valkyries* of Nordic tradition. In all cases where this supernatural archetype is present, prophecy generally plays an important, if not pivotal, role in the events as they unfold.

In the Irish tradition, the *Badb,* literally meaning "crow" or "raven", is a zoomorphic war goddess who assumes the earthly form of the "battle crow", and her presence forms part of the *Morrígna* along with her sisters, *Macha* and the *Morrígan*. Similar to the *Valkyries* of the Norse pantheon of war goddesses, the *Morrígna* can appear alone or in groups of usually three women on the eve of, during, or following a great battle, and are often the travelling fateful companions of 'familiars' of heroic warriors. Within the Anglo Saxon narrative, a raven, hovering—in anticipation of an easy meal above an army—is described as the *Wcelceasiga*, literally translating as "the slain-choosing one", and is almost identical to the Germanic/Norse *Valkyrie*, demonstrating just how deeply-rooted this idea was within northern European cultures. An archetype also rooted in a very ancient past.

One can easily imagine how ravens and other corvids would have congregated around, and assembled among megalithic structures as soon as they were erected. In fact, visiting Stonehenge myself, I soon noticed a rather entertaining and very approachable *unkindness* of ravens congregating among the stones. Having been absent for nearly three centuries, these remarkable birds have returned to Stonehenge in recent years. We can only speculate as to why the ravens have returned, but we can be equally sure that it is symbolic of something profound.

ANCIENT ORIGIN OF THE RAVEN-GODDESS-HARVESTER

We know that in the Neolithic period of western Europe, the defleshing process of excarnation was commonly practised. Generally speaking, the body of the deceased was placed upon a platform of some elevated design—to keep it safe from rodents and other feral mammals—and then ravens and other flying carrion would eat the flesh of the deceased until all that remained was the large bones and the skull. This explains why finger and toe bones are rarely found inside burial plots, as the ravens and crows would have carried them off. The larger bones would be then placed inside burial urns to be interred within mounds and chambers and, as some have speculated, pregnant women would later give birth within these mounds, next to jars containing the bones of their deceased loved ones so that the soul belonging to the ancestor's bones would be reincarnated at the moment of birth into the new infant.

Unfortunately, this speculation has inspired and led to *Modern Pathological Magic* activities at megalithic sites and other historic locations in recent years, particularly in England, locations such as West Kennet Long Barrow, the Rollright Stone Circle, and other locations in Devon and Cornwall. These ceremonies generally take place around the *Summer Solstice* and represent a disturbing trend. I myself have seen the aftermath of suspicious animal sacrifice magic activities at Neolithic sites in both Ireland as well as in Sardinia. These are not NeoPagan, modern Druidism or Wicca rituals. They are most certainly connected to modern *Modern Pathological Magic* cults, or perhaps just disturbed individuals. They are modern misinterpretations of pagan cults which come from a time when animal killing was an everyday event, and not a by-product of immaturity and drug abuse.

TRANSMIGRATION CHAMBERS

Some of my own field work has led me to believe that the passage mounds themselves—with their cruciform floor plans—may represent the female reproductive system. With the entrance being the vagina, the long passageway being the uterus, the left and right chambers being the fallopian tubes and the back chamber being the umbilical cord. From this, it is not difficult to imagine that over time this Neolithic inter-relationship of the female, the transmigration of souls and the raven's role in all this evolving into the idea of these remarkably intelligent birds being seen as 'collectors of souls'.

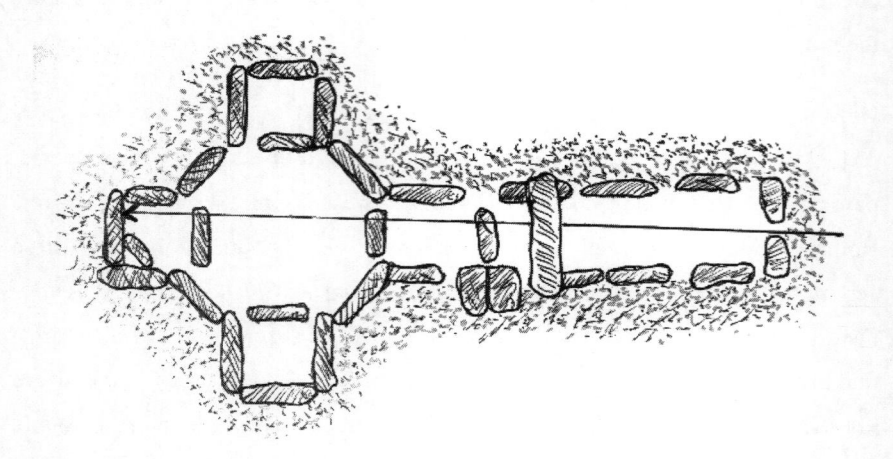

Looking intriguingly similar to a classic Irish *High Cross* design laying down, the floor plan of *Cairn T* at the Loughcrew Neolithic complex in County Meath, Ireland, is one of the thirty or so cairns at this location. The site contains some of the most remarkable examples of Irish Neolithic rock art. It was here, in 1982, that American artist Martin Brennan and co-researcher Jack Roberts observed that both the passage itself and chamber of *Cairn T* are oriented towards the equinox sunrises. The discovery made the front page of national newspapers in Ireland at the time. The straight line in the image above shows the approximate path of the sun as it hits the highly decorated back stone (number 14), one of the more than two dozen ortostats inside the cairn.

(illustration: Thomas Sheridan)

Returning to the Irish and Nordic concept of the war goddess, they are almost always associated with ravens at pivotal moments in the mythological narrative. The female 'war-witches/demons' are sometimes literally portrayed as goddesses, other times as human female witches with terrifying superpowers of magic and prophecy. In all cases, these females—be they supernatural beings or earthly witches—were the choosers of the slain, and very often were connected with the notion of prophetic fatalities and doom. This archetype was so powerful among the Irish and the Vikings in particular that one can only imagine the intensity of the psychic and supernatural mind storm which took place on the eve of the *Battle of Clontarf* near Dublin on 23 April 1014, when a complex set of alliances comprised of Irish and Norse warriors on both sides brought their archetypes of both the *Badb* and the *Valkyries*—into their combined and collective consciousness—as one enormous battle which took place not only on the battlefield itself, but also within the battlefield of each and every psyche present that day. According to Viking accounts of the *Battle of Clontarf*, a group of *Valkyries* were sighted, weaving the destiny of the leaders as both harbingers of fate and prophecy, charging many on the battlefield with a terrifying weakness that eventually overcomes the warriors on both sides.

Such psychic attacks upon the warriors would have had real after-life consequences, as cowardice could prevent them from being elevated towards becoming post-mortal, supernatural beings themselves. Such as the *Berserkers*—who would have also been present on the day at Clontarf—being carried up by the *Valkyrie* to Odin's long hall at *Valhalla* in order to transmigrate into the state of *Einherjar* so they could prepare to fight alongside Odin and Thor during the cataclysmic end-time of *Ragnarök*.

Being shape-shifters similar to the Irish *Badb*, the Norse *Valkyrie* were also feared when arriving in the guise of attractive rural maidens who bring wine or mead to the heroes, causing them to under-perform in battle, having been led astray by these sexual, witch-tricksters. 'Softening them up', so to speak. The intended purpose of these shape-shifting war goddesses being such, was to make the warriors psychologically weak, so their 'ravenesque' form might dine more easily upon their flesh following the battle. All undertaken as a symbolic 'toll' for transporting the dead warrior's soul into the next world. Therefore, the shape-shifting war goddesses' powers of prophecy were looked upon with dread and loathing by warriors on the eve of battle by some, and an opportunity for afterlife greatness by others.

Central to the Norse, Irish and Anglo-Saxon mythology is that of the raven arriving at the moment of a heroic death in order to transport the warrior's soul to the otherworld. The origin of this folklore comes directly from the Neolithic age, when deceased persons were hoisted high upon excarnation tables so that their flesh could be eaten by ravens and other flying carrion. The bones would then be taken down at some later stage and processed for burial, usually inside an urn.

The raven, in several mythological traditions, is also a trickster and shape-shifter, often in the guise of a beautiful seductive maiden, or an old hag. In heroic tales, the raven in the form of a female will be seen as symbolically connected to the warrior about to meet his fate. However, the arrival of the raven proper, ultimately validates the valour of the hero by transforming and transporting his deeds and life story into earthly legends, while taking his soul to the otherworld to be among the gods.

(illustration: British Library Collection)

Along with battlefields, try to imagine when, following a major natural event such as tsunami, there remains a landscape filled with vast amounts of dead humans and animals who had not been washed out to sea. The only creatures who would survive such devastation in large numbers would be the ravens, crows and other corvids who would swoop down from their mountain refuge as the 'harvesters of the slain'. Any surviving humans—from that point on—would take careful note of the behaviour of ravens, as it has always been known that animals can sense the coming of disasters before they strike. Odin's two ravens, then, quite literally, become, 'memory' and 'thought' in the truest sense of the words.

THE ALCHEMICAL DEATH OF CÚ CHULAINN

The Irish mythological hero Cú Chulainn represents what the great American mythologist Joseph Campbell termed the '*Life-Eager Hero*'; an archetype who forever walks in the shadow of his or her own imminent death. Therefore, the hero's path is to indulge in heroic deeds in order to 'live' beyond the confines of his or her mortal existence, transcending death towards cultural immortality through great achievements and valour. Cú Chulainn is also heavily associated in the Irish mythological record with the magical concept of glamour. That is, a spell or enchantment making a person see what the magician wants them to see. Forever taunted and tricked by female satirists who are the human personification of the *Badb* battle, or death premonition crow, Cú Chulainn's destiny is not so much at the hands of the *Badb*, but rather, the supernatural entity is a reminder of his duty as a *Life-Eager Hero* to partake in deeds which are both heroic and memorable enough so as to 'live' beyond his early death through myth and folklore. This idea of post-mortal existence magic may present us with an insight into what the megalithic builders were driven by: the need to create impressive 'immortal' monuments of their great culture so they would survive every possible future natural and social change which may obliterate their own mortal existence.

In the Irish mythological epic the *Táin Bó Cúailnge* or "*the driving-off of cows of*

Cooley", it tells of the war against Ulster by the forces of Connacht under Queen Meabh (pronounced 'maeve') and her husband Ailill against the teenage Ulster warrior Cú Chulainn. Again, we can see how the corvids (in this case, crows) represent a powerful archetype on the Irish battlefield, as they did later in history upon the Viking battlefield. The awesome potential of the *Morrígna* within the Irish ancient psyche being equally as powerful as that of the *Valkyries* within the minds of the Viking warriors.

Within the *Táin*, the *Morrígna* foretells of many deaths while demonstrating shape-shifting powers by transforming into various human forms, birds of prey and other creatures. At one point—the *Morrígna*, in the form of a cow—may offer a drink of milk from one of her teats so as to offer refreshment to a tired warrior, such as is told about Cú Chulainn which then transforms the young warrior into a kind of demon. This suggests the possibility of a psychedelic (DMT-Dimethyltryptamine) substance in the milk which transformed Cú Chulainn into a terrifying and hideous super-being of incredible bravery and fighting ability;

> *"The first warp-spasm seized Cú Chulainn, and made him into a monstrous thing, hideous and shapeless, unheard of. His shanks and his joints, every knuckle and angle and organ from head to foot, shook like a tree in the flood or a reed in the stream. His body made a furious twist inside his skin, so that his feet and shins switched to the rear and his heels and calves switched to the front... On his head the temple-sinews stretched to the nape of his neck, each mighty, immense, measureless knob as big as the head of a month-old child... he sucked one eye so deep into his head that a wild crane couldn't probe it onto his cheek out of the depths of his skull; the other eye fell out along his cheek. His*

mouth weirdly distorted: his cheek peeled back from his jaws until the gullet appeared, his lungs and his liver flapped in his mouth and throat, his lower jaw struck the upper a lion-killing blow, and fiery flakes large as a ram's fleece reached his mouth from his throat... The hair of his head twisted like the tangle of a red thornbush stuck in a gap; if a royal apple tree with all its kingly fruit were shaken above him, scarce an apple would reach the ground but each would be spiked on a bristle of his hair as it stood up on his scalp with rage."

The similarity to the Viking *Berserkers,* who were also sometimes known to ingest hallucinogenic plants before a battle, is apparent here, and both these examples may provide a significant insight into the role which entheogenic plants and herbs may have also played in the lives and development of shamanic cultures right back to the earlier Neolithic age. Significantly, ravens and crows are also mentioned in the text, as the *Badb*—this time in the context of the ravens —being an actual combatant during the fighting of the battles themselves. In the *Ulster Cycle* version of the *Táin Bó Cúailnge*, Cú Chulainn, on the way to battle, encounters the *Morrígan*, who has shape-shifted into an old hag. To his dismay, Cú Chulainn realises she is polishing his own armour while removing the blood by dousing it into a river.

THE WATERS OF LIFE AND DEATH

The symbology of the river (along with waterways and coastlines in general)— as we shall see, plays an enormous part in both the mythology and, location of several important megalithic structures—representing the 'crossing over' and consequently, in this case, an omen of Cú Chulainn's own death in the upcoming battle. Later on, as Cú Chulainn is dying—having been mortally wounded by Lugaid's magical spear—he straps himself upright to a standing stone, using his own entrails as ropes so he can die on his feet. At the moment of his passing, a lone crow lands upon his right shoulder, signifying the arrival of the *Badb* and the fulfilling of the *Morrígna's* prophecy.

The location of this event is purported to be the three metre high standing stone at Clochafarmore near Knockbridge in County Louth (named after the god Lugh). This serves to illustrate that although these standing stones were erected by Neolithic cultures—sometimes thousands of years before the time associated with Cú Chulainn—it also demonstrates how succeeding cultures overlaid their own supernatural and cultural identities upon these stones and other megalithic structures. Keeping them 'alive', so to speak. However, the similarities and archetypal interconnectedness reveals to us a continuing social narrative which brings us one step closer to understanding the culture and values of the megalithic builders of the Neolithic age. Only by application of this holistic approach can we breach the chasm left in the wake by archaeological and academic history.

WIDENING THE EVIDENCE, EXPANDING THE HORIZONS

I make no apology for the fact that I have been a life-long polymath and I owe much to the influence of authors and great minds such as Colin Wilson, Graham Hancock, Joseph Campbell, Carl Jung and Rupert Sheldrake. I consider my work within the bounds of acceptable rationality, where I am as both equally as comfortable with Charles Darwin as I am with Immanuel Velikovsky. I consider all these sources valuable resources, and my exploration into this topic is towards a greater understanding of the human story—in all its complexities and faculties—rather than that of an exclusively spiritual or mystical journey. However, I also can't deny that my encounters with the stones have not left me unaffected in this regard. Take what you wish from this; it is my very personal journey of discovery, and you, the reader, should drink from this well and then, if you so wish, add your own personal piece to the story. The example presented above with the prevelance of ravens within western European mythology is indicative of this approach. When we widen the sphere of evidence, we expand the possibilities for answers, and thus open up new previously shunned paradigms. For example, a typical 'scientific-only' mind—who also happens to be a hardcore atheist—will instantly discount any stories pertaining to art, mythology or folk history concerning cataclysmic floods which may have torn apart entire civilisations in the past, due almost entirely to their negative reaction to the Hebrew story of *Noah's Ark*. This also serves to highlight how damaging biblical stories have been in skewing and also tearing asunder the history of ancient Europe, as even today, otherwise excellent researchers remain obsessed with proving that, somehow that Jesus Christ was in England, or that Tara is connected to the court of King David and the *Lost Tribes of Israel*.

It is also a mentality that is incredibly degrading to people of ancient Europe and seeks to mock and belittle their technical and cultural achievements. The same can be said for the tragically enormously popular comtemporary subculture which proclaims that only by means of visiting alien spacecraft and intergalaltic technology could momuments such as Stonehenge have been constructed in the first place. We were not created as the slaves of an alien god. Such thinking is reconstructed fundamentalist Christianity, with concepts such as *Original Sin* likewise being repackaged.

The *Midgard Serpent* is a mythology common to Norse, Saxon, Old English and the Gothic legends, and shares many commonalities with similar folklore around the world, including the mysterious Mata of Irish folklore. In the Norse tradition, the world of men known as Midgard, is encircled by the world serpent *Jörmungandr*. The *Midgard Serpent* plays a central destructive role within Norse mythology, often involving encounters with Thor. This includes the pivotal battle between *Jörmungandr* and Thor during *Ragnarök*, when the serpent emerges from the ocean to poison the skies with its venom before both *Jörmungandr* and Thor mutually slay one another.

Remarkably, there really is a world serpent which wraps itself around the globe and lives beneath the sea—known in the more literal and prosaic sense—as the active region of volcanic mountains and earthquake where the earth's tectonic plates meet. Even more incredible is the fact that the serpent's head is located in the north Atlantic west of Scandinavia, and to the north west of Ireland and Britain, and shapes the *Porcupine Bank*, with the serpent's eye being the island of Iceland. A perfect geological simulacra of an ancient myth.

Is it possible that the legend of the *Midgard Serpent* is rooted in some distant ancestral or archetypal knowledge of this geologically unstable region which encircles the planet, and is responsible for the majority of the world's most volcanic-, earthquake- and tsunami-prone regions? Was it *Jörmungandr* who destroyed the lost continent and civilisation we have come to know as *Atlantis*? Was this also the cause of the mysterious events of 2500BC which depopulated Ireland and Orkney for hundreds of years? On a synchronistic level, such an idea is remarkable. However on an archetypal level, it makes a valid case that we are dealing with profound human experiences carried through the ages within folklore.

(illustration: The Triskele and the Dragon website)

Chapter Six

Chains of Discovery

The Druid Code:
Magic, Megaliths and Mythology

As David Lewis-Williams points out in his groundbreaking *The Mind in the Cave*, there are two types of scientific argument used for approaching the research of ancient cultures. The first is the *Cable-like* method, which will intertwine several strands of evidence into a cohesive, holistic examination leading towards an open-ended speculation. Even if the cable comes apart, the individual strands can still provide valuable conduits of discovery and valuable data. The second method is the *Chain-like* method where one piece of evidence is chain-linked to the next, moving towards a 'sustainable' but completely interdependent trajectory. However, if one of the chain links is later determined to be false, then the entire argument falls apart and everything is discarded, along with the false chain link.

This almost fascistic application towards scientific discovery has only resulted in a stagnation of imagination and creativity—especially in the fields of ancient history and cultures—which are incredibly complex and varied due to their very underlying human nature. Any mainstream speculation is then to be overseen by 'scientific' gatekeepers who are often self-appointed. Gatekeepers, who place the broken chain link, along with the entire chain of speculation (no matter how valuable or insightful) into the same rubbish bin as the single false argument or discredited chain link's overall integrity.

This has been a most unfortunate aspect relating to how mainstream historians and archaeologists approach the megalithic sites of Europe. What works when developing a code of software most certainly does not work at an archaeological dig site. There is little or no credence given to what exterior data can be determined to tell us more about the people who built these structures and what led them to doing so. More importantly, why did the megalith builders suddenly stop using stone, and instead, began building almost exclusively in wood and other materials and thereby, losing all the stone working technology which they had developed up until that point? While it is likely that the Neolithic builders of Stonehenge and Newgrange were almost certainly as skilled in the use of wood for construction purposes as they were in stone, due to the organic nature of wood, the material simply rots away. In Ireland, there appears to be a colossal time frame, whereby stone was discarded as a building material in favour of wood, only for stone to come into use again with the construction of the famous Irish Round Towers. These are significant mysteries which are generally overlooked.

Yet there is one strange anomaly inside the chamber of *Bryn Celli Ddh* at Anglesey in Wales, where a large standing stone in the centre of the cairn was discovered in recent years to actually be a petrified tree trunk. The television actor Michael Bolt discovered what generations of archaeologists had missed. I myself also have strong suspicions that there are at least two examples of petrified wood being mistaken for stones at two of the cairns at Carrowkeel in County Sligo. What could cause wood—which is structurally integral to the construction of some of these apparently Neolithic structures—to petrify in thousands, rather than millions of years? There are several possible answers. Firstly, that the wood—due to the unique, electromagnetic forces contained within the surrounding stones—can petrify inside a cairn or other megalith at a far faster rate than in, say, a bog or mud flat. Secondly, that these cairns are far, far older than the official three- to five-thousand years date, and finally, that the people who built these megaliths in the Neolithic age possessed some technology which allowed them to turn wood to stone in a relatively short time frame.

All three possibilities are, quite frankly, amazing. But so is a major and important artefact such as a fossilised tree trunk inside a very well known and excavated megalith which hundreds, if not thousands of professional academic archaeologists somehow missed. The *Bryn Celli Ddhu* anomaly proves that on the official level, almost nothing is known by academics on how and who built these structures, as non-professional researchers and artists continue to make the most amazing discoveries that the archaeologists constantly miss while wearing their death cult goggles at these sites. Their failure in identifying the petrified tree at B*ryn Celli Ddhu* clearly demonstrates the limitations and flaws within the Chain-like method. What may work in the science or technical development lab, cannot be applied out in the field to megalithic structures.

THE PSYCHOLOGY OF SURVIVAL AND EXPERIENCE

Carl Jung's rediscovery of the Western alchemical tradition in the early 20th century unearthed a previously lost canon of psychic personal self-realisation which was practically identical to his theories concerning the process of *Individuation* as specific stages of psychic development leading to the 'rounding out' of one's personal life story. Jung put forth the idea that on one hand, there is the natural process of growth which takes place in every living thing, and which occurs unconsciously. This can be further augmented with consciously processed stages of inner development according to precise doctrines and practices. That being, the conscious mind monitors what is happening, and strives to manipulate the lifestream into a kind of heroic self-adventure and exploration of the universal journey of the hero, which resonates in all cultures through various myth and legend.

Rituals, storytelling and symbolism help to reinforce this lifestream into the psychic memory of the unconscious mind. Contained within every member of the tribe, it then becomes the unconscious *memory well* of all who are exposed to it. This would have been the primary purpose of the druid's storytelling and their passing on of ancient mythology: to keep the stories 'alive' in the psyche of the tribe when all else had been decayed or destroyed, and the 'magic' of the storytelling and bardic performance would have been the primary conduit to get there.

As previously mentioned, what happened to me at Woodhenge on that glorious afternoon of synchronicity, magic, memory and experience finally proved to me that Carl Jung's theory of the *Collective Unconscious* was an undisputed fact. Within this twilight shadow world, there are networks of unseen threads woven throughout the fabric of the material and corporeal universe—in much the same way the *Norns* of the Norse *Eddas* weave the destiny and fate of all living things next to the well of *Urðarbrunnr* and the foot of *Yggdrasil*, the world tree, while two beautiful swans swim and feed in the waters below, and that such synchronicities allow us to read the ongoing transmissions of the Druidic and other compatible/earlier proto-shamanic traditions of western Europe as a kind

The Druid Code:
Magic, Megaliths and Mythology

of transneural network of the archetypal and the elemental.

The very real technology of these megalithic structures, along with the landscapes they inhabit, when 'charged' with the mythology connected to them, perform as something akin to relay stations of the subconscious mind, transmitting their codes outside of linear time and space. That is precisely what happened to me during those sunny two days we spent filming in Wiltshire, when by default, both myself, and my colleagues had all logged into this network, and in my own case, this experience also answered my question concerning the survival of a Druidic and European shamanic 'default' underground existing right to the very present.

The *Kernanstown Cromlech* (or Brownhills Dolmen) in County Carlow, Ireland, with its enormous capstone, of perhaps one hundred and twenty tons, making it the largest in Europe. Located on top of a hill, the monument may extend deeper underground to a possible large chamber below. Having never been excavated, its official age (3-4000BC) is basically a guess as to its actual antiquity. *Kernanstown Cromlech* is representative of what are known in Ireland as 'Portal Dolmens', as the entrance is flanked by two othostats (upright stones). Some Portal Dolmens also contain a 'gate stone' at the entrance.

(illustration: Thomas Sheridan)

The discovery of 'Stonehenge Two' beneath Durrington Walls created as much excitement worldwide as the hype for the latest smart devices within the news pages and sound bites of the world's media. Visitor numbers to places such as Newgrange and Tara in Ireland and other ancient 'sacred sites' continue to rise. People now regularly wander off the tourist trails to locate and touch remote dolmens in muddy farmers' fields, or to enter passage mounds on barren hilltops just so they can interact with the stones and wonder about their own ancestors, driven by an often inexplicable need to encounter and imagine who constructed such stones, and then marvel at how they selected these specific places so as to erect megaliths upon them in such precise geographical and astronomical alignments.

THE HEALING STONES

Very often, people are brought into this territory through a life trauma or a personal reflection upon their own life course and decisions made in the past. I have lost count of the numbers of people I have met at these 'sacred sites' who were very open about having undergone everything from the recent death of a loved one to a messy divorce, or just a major personal shift within their own lives. Just ordinary people, from all walks of life, who were just trying to find some meaning to their own lives, and the wider, overall human experience. What was it about their personal 'real world' experiences which brought them to a stone circle or a dolmen? The primary reason for the sense of wonder that standing stones personally evoke within us—and which they continually provide to generation after generation—is due, I believe, to their profound sense of mystery. They generally have no obvious narrative, syntax or 'hard' design/artistic features, yet they are filled with all the meanings and realisations we are willing to pour into them and take from them when needed. This is due, I personally feel, to the people connected with them, having been through an experience which so deeply affected them that they literally had to rebuild their own consciousness in order to survive. Hence, why people who have been through the slings and arrows of their own personal misfortune arrive at such places.

The *Mên-an-Tol* megalithic site in Cornwall, England is an unusual clustering of stones containing a famous hole stone reputed to have healing properties, and is safeguarded by a 'Piskie' (fairy) which is the Cornish equivalent of the Irish '(*Aos Sí*) *Sidhe*'.

It is possible that the hole at *Mên-an-Tol* was created by natural forces, and this would have still infused the rock with as much of a magical charge as if the hole had have been carved by humans, being brought and erected on site as something of an offering from the otherworld to this world. A kind of a reversed votive horde of the Neolithic. Now one of England's most famous and beloved megalithic structures, it has even been celebrated in song by the rock band The Levellers.

(illustration: Thomas Sheridan)

In a sense, sacred stone circles and other megalithic sacred sites become recovery clinics of the psyche. The stones themselves can also become a mirror of purity and realisation into a world of control and corruption, war and hatred, as they have remained the same throughout history, as all else we are forced to experience constantly changes. Yet the stones of the sacred sites have remained. These stones and their mythologies representing a 'stripped to the bone' truth that is both raw and honest. We have no hard proof of the names of the people who built the stone structures of western Europe, how old they actually are, or what was their absolute purpose. Even the methods and manpower to move and erect these structures remind us that life is indeed a great mystery. When we enter the *fifth province*, we enter into a blank canvas, an empty journal, and a dream which has yet to be dreamt. Among the stones and within our mythology we find the pigments, so we can begin to paint our own picture. In some ways, the ancient ancestors knew more about you than you ever knew about yourself.

THE WATERY WORLD OF LOUGH GUR

One of the strangest menhirs in Ireland is located at Grange in County Limerick, is known as *The Stone of the Tree* and is called such due to it being linked—at some metaphysical level—to a tree which is said to be still growing at the bottom of nearby Lough Gur. The folklore states that the still-living tree is surrounded by the ruins of a sunken city. According to the visiting French engineer Charles Vallancey—who was taken out on a boat in 1812 after the lake water level had receeded—"When the surface of the lake is smooth, one may see from a boat the drowned city, its walls and castles…It astonished me to see such immense irregular blocks and rocks under water, when nothing similar is to be found in the vicinity." Later it was suggested that Vallancey had seen sunken crannogs (moated houses). However, these are always built of wood and earth and never stone. Assuming he was telling the truth—coupled with local folklore—then something remarkable may well be waiting to be rediscovered at the bottom of the lough.

The legend of the supernatural tree at the bottom of Lough Gur being represented by a standing stone near the lake is, itself, most interesting. Comparisons have been made with the Norse *Yggdrasil* 'World Tree', which contains three roots that extend to the well *Urðarbrunnr* (where the three Norns spin the destiny of all living things) by the spring *Hvergelmir* (which is the primary water source for the tree and is filled with snakes and dragons), and another to the well *Mímisbrunnr* (where Odin sacrificed one of his eyes to attain wisdom). It is difficult to speculate how the menhir on the lake shore relates directly to the magical tree at the bottom of Lough Gur. However, a mythology of this uniqueness does not come without some deeply vital meaning connected with it.

Is *The Stone of the Tree* a double of a similar stone beneath the surface? Why would a story concerning a sunken city develop within the region, and then be directly represented by a standing stone on the land? As we know from Cormac O'Neill's testimony at Newgrange in 1699, these folk memories are very ancient indeed, and, as with the folklore memory of a very real solar event at Newgrange, the sinking of a city beneath Lough Gur has to be rooted in something factual as well as mythological. Along with this, we also have another archetypal connection between Irish and Norse mythology originating from a possible single, ancient source.

THE TIMELORDS BEYOND SUMER

In 1913, Carl Jung had a dream in which he was walking through a Neolithic landscape of mounds and barrows in northern France when the dead, ancient ones contained within them started to come to life. However, in his dream entry Jung stated that the Neolithic corpses would only resurrect from the dead when he looked directly at them. The famous psychoanalyst's subconscious mind was making it clear to him—through his dreams—that while to his conscious mind he considers such structures as megalithic mounds and passageways as purely repositories for the dead generations of the past who built them, within his own subconscious mind, the people of the Neolithic were very much alive.

This, then, started a period in Jung's life from which he began to study native cultures and mythology from all over the world in order to get to the core of not only the archetypal native within himself, but within humanity as a whole. Jung was unable to explore his own European indigenous culture, as it was basically non-existent within his native Switzerland, so instead, he sought out the remote tribes of Africa and the Americas for this purpose.

His ignorance of Irish mythology is a great shame, for he no doubt would have uncovered a deep repository of archetypal and magical fuel that would have sat well within his own work. In particular, his theories concerning the arrangement of triple deities as an archetype in the history of human spirituality being echoed all over Irish mythology with the triple goddesses of *Brigid*, *Morrígan* and the earth mother goddesses of the ancient Irish named *Ériu*, *Fódla* and the *Banba*. Irish mythology represents a vast archive of cultural, historical and spiritual insights on par with the *Vedas* and the *Puranas* of the Indian subcontinent in terms of reinforcing national and cultural identity, and is no less potent and ancient in both its scope and appeal. During the struggle for Irish independence, the legends of Cú Chulainn, Ferdiad, Queen Meabh and other mythologial warriors from epics such as *Táin Bó Cúailnge* were invoked by nationalists to foster a sense of hereditary and racial self-awareness in defiance of British colonial rule. Likewise, a few decades later, Hindu nationalists sought independence from the *British Raj* by summoning up the racial memory of their own mythologcal heroes from the verses of equally ancient epics such as the *Mahabharata*.

Perhaps unique in a northern European context (along with the more recent Icelandic/Nordic *Sagas*), the near miraculous survival of the Irish mythological record contains within their volumes an enormous archive of events—being a mixture of both the literal and the allegorical—and which ultimately seeks to enrich human understanding, while reinforcing ideas of social cohesion, survival from trauma, loyalty and destiny.

These tales are also an archive of secrets. Secrets contained within stories of the most fantastical, and also more mundane details. Epic battles of both the external and internal states of experience which encapsulate the full expression of the human story. All taking place within a timeframe spanning hundreds, if not thousands of years across an epic landscape comprising of humans—both ordinary and extraordinary—while also featuring a supporting cast of supernatural beings who, while being divine in nature, are also very often possessed with human-like attributes and shortcomings.

As we have seen, long before the antiquarians, archaeologists and tourists arrived, locations such the spectacular *Brú na Bóinne* megalithic complex—located along that curious bend of the river Boyne in County Meath—was saturated in tales of the Tuatha Dé Danann (who brought the practice of ritual magic to Ireland) and this legacy was not always one of an appreciation for great mythology such as we enjoy today. Until the early 20th century, *Brú na Bóinne* was considered by the most superstitious country folk living under its shadow to be among the most ominous domains of the *Sidhe (Aos Sí)*.

This fear of their own historical past was imposed upon the rural dwellers by Christians in order to change their ancient customs, and from this, their culture too. This paranoia was common among both Catholic and Protestant rural Irish alike. By filling the subconscious mind with fear of devils and demons which lurk inside the earth and strange ancient places, it creates an association which in due course projects the fears of the psyche onto these elements upon the landscape. However, this fear of megalithic sites being connected to the Devil was far less hysterical in Ireland when compared to other parts of Europe.

The Scottish philosopher David Hume, in his *Treatise of Human Nature* (1789), stated that 'custom, then, is a great guide to human life.' The customs of the Irish rural folk had been re-engineered from reverence for the *Sidhe (Aos Sí)* to outright terror in many cases. But what was the root of this fear? The actual *Sidhe* themselves, or a posible traumatic racial memory which their 'awareness' subconsciously might unleash within ordinary people? Irish rural folk of the Christian era lived not only in extreme fear of encountering a fairy, but also their 'fairy mounds' and 'forts' were off-limits, too. There was also a belief in 'fairy roads' or 'passes'—invisible corridors of supernatural transportation and energy forces connecting the ancient *Sidhe* sites to one another—which were considered ruinous to build one's home upon.

THE PARALLEL WORLD OF THE FAIRIES

The most interesting aspect of the fairy faith in Ireland is that the *Sidhe* themselves were considered more akin to another type of reality, or a kind of parallel universe—somewhat culturally similar to our own—rather than a type of psychedelic mystical dream experience. As with the rural Irish, the *Sidhe* also maintained farms and kept livestock, and this brings up a very interesting Irish folk tradition which states that if a human somehow entered the world of the *Sidhe*, they came back with reports that not only were the fairies unskilled farmers with badly maintained and poor yeilding farms, but that the *Sidhe* themselves also had a deep resentment for the proficiency and skills of human farmers.

Young rural boys were known to be sought out for abduction by the *Sidhe* in order to bring human farming skills to the otherworld. As a result, young boys in some remote parts of rural Ireland—as late as the early twentieth century—were dressed as little girls and given names such as 'Mary'. It is also been suggested that Oscar Wilde's own mother dressed her son in girls' clothing when he was a young boy for this same reason, and some others have speculated that this is also the origin of the slang term 'fairy' being used to denote a homosexual male. The propaganda runs very deep indeed...

The *Sidhe,* on the other hand, are said to be brilliant musicians who had their own school of Irish music and which humans often heard being played by the fairy pipers and fiddlers among hawthorn bushes and lonely sand dunes during moonlit beach walks. Much of the traditonal folk music of County Sligo is still referred to as being from 'fairy tunes' in origin. The *Sidhe* (*Aos Sí),* and the otherworld in which they existed were also believed to be moving at a much faster speed—within their own reality—than the one which humans occupy. Hence, why a sudden swirl of dust, or a sudden rustle in the hedgerows on a calm day was known as a 'shee goaithes', and considered to be a sign that the *Sidhe* were in the immediate area. The concept of the *Sidhe* being still present within the Irish landscape—albeit, within a different reality—ties in well with the legend of the Tuatha Dé Danann being banished into the otherworld following their defeat at the hands of the Milesian Gaels.

This also might suggest a part of the idea of the *Sidhe* representing an aspect of human consciousness that has been placed to one side, as it has fulfilled its purpose for the time being. We are told that the Tuatha Dé Danann will return again when Ireland faces its greatest danger. What is the danger that awaits Ireland? The same traumatic event which the Irish *Mythological Cycle* tells us that first brought the Tuatha Dé Danann from the lands to the north of Ireland when they were surrounded by 'dark clouds' and where they 'brought a darkness over the sun lasting three days...'?

If there is one attribute we can point to in order to demonstrate that the Irish mythological record is more than just simple folk stories having no basis in fact, then it is the numerous correlations between the 'sacred sites' and actual real locations spoken of within the folklore itself. More importantly, many of the individuals and locations contained within the mythology can be verified as having been real people and actual locations with tangible proof. The mention of Queen Meabh on an Ogham script inside Oweynagat cave—right in the heart of her 'mythological' kingdom at Rathcroghan-Cruachán, County Roscommon—clearly links the reality of this location with the mythology. This is surprisingly common at 'sacred sites' all over Ireland, and remains, what makes Irish mythology so unique in that we can actually 'verify', or at least, substantiate, its social, if not historical ligitmacy.

For example, Tara was an active social, political and cultural centre from the Neolithic era right up to the Middle Ages. If we compare this to Stonehenge, which was abandoned and unused for thousands of years, it is clear that Irish Neolithic, and perhaps even Mesolithic sites, carry valuable information and cultural manifestations well into the era of written documented and recorded histories. Unlike, say, the *Arthurian* mythology, which was applied to Glastonbury in England by enterprising monks seeking to capitalise upon pilgrms, we can (liberally) take much of the written history of Ireland up until the early sixteenth century as something of a continuum—albeit, within a highly dramatic backstory—of the early ages of Irish life and culture, when we apply the latest research into the remarkable tenacity of folklore and mythology to survive intact across thousands of years.

TO THE WATERS AND THE WILD

Come away, O human child!

To the waters and the wild

With a faery, hand in hand,

For the world's more full of weeping than you can understand.

The Druid Code:
Magic, Megaliths and Mythology

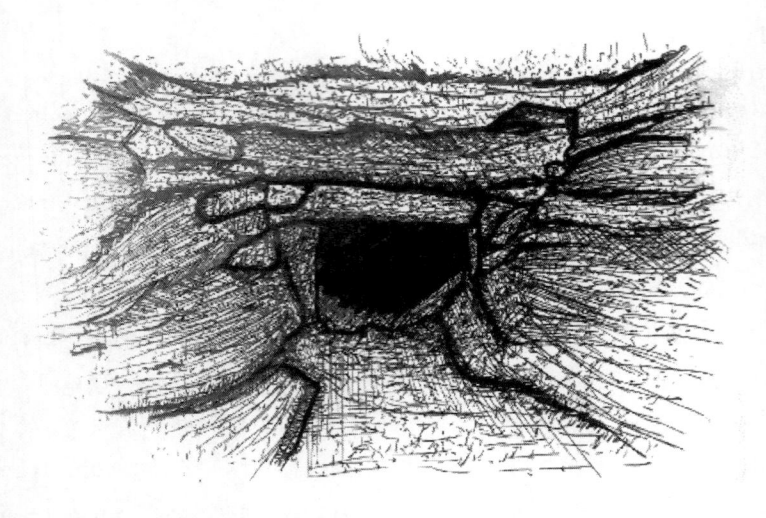

The 'Hellmouth' inside Oweynagat (the Cave of the Cats) below the megalith-filled landscape of Rathcroghan-Cruachán in County Roscommon, Ireland, which was considered by early Christians to be Ireland's entrance to hell. Still used in Heathen rituals to this day, the cave leads to a naturally vaulted underground chamber possessed with remarkable acoustic properties.

Strongly associated with being the domain of the *Morrigan* goddess of warfare and death —especially at *Samhain* (Halloween)—Oweynagat plays an important part in several Irish mythological tales and more importantly, contains an Ogham stone inscription clearly identifying the location with Queen Meabh in the heart of her kingdom. Here we have hard evidence of a megalithic complex going right back to the Neolithic era directly connected with mythology, and the evidence to link them all together.

(illustration: Thomas Sheridan)

The above quotation is from the first stanza of the William Butler Yeats' poem *The Stolen Child,* which was a product of the poet's intimate and personal exploration of the folklore of County Sligo. Yeats, also being a member of the magical order of the *Golden Dawn,* was well aware of the power of mythology and folklore as a method of cultural exploration of social and personal 'magical' experiences. Magical in the sense of moving ideas and desires from the cognitve *will* into material reality. This process works in both directions; in that a particular piece of art or artistic performance can move the individual experiences of the material manifestion through the artform or perfomance into a 'magical' state. Yeats himself, wrote a rather lengthy essay on magic in which he stated:

> "...for all men, certainly all imaginative men, must be for ever casting forth enchantments, glamours, illusions; and all men, especially tranquil men who have no powerful egotistic life, must be continually passing under their power. Our most elaborate thoughts, elaborate purposes, precise emotions, are often, as I think, not really ours, but have on a sudden come up, as it were, out of hell or down out of heaven. The historian should remember, should he not? angels and devils not less than kings and soldiers, and plotters and thinkers. What matter if the angel or devil, as indeed certain old writers believed, first wrapped itself with an organized shape in some man's imagination? what matter 'if God himself only acts or is in existing beings or men,' as Blake believed? we must none the less admit that invisible beings, far wandering influences, shapes that may have floated from a hermit of the wilderness, brood over council-chambers and studies and battle-fields.

Yeats, who spent many hours wandering the landscape of Sligo, and no doubt, pondered its many mysterious ancient ruins (five thousand ancient sites in the county alone), is telling us here in this passage that a kind of transcendental awareness is a prerequisite for understanding the hidden landscape(s) behind the visual one. One of the founders of the *Golden Dawn,* and a close associate of Yeats, was occultist MacGregor Mathers who, inspired by *Enochian Magic,* suggested that the most effective manner whereby a person might pass into another reality and communicate with non-human beings was to concentrate upon a magical symbol and then look towards a blank wall until the sheer focus of the act produced a vision of the same shape upon the wall large enough for a person to pass through.

Incidentally, the flamboyant Elizabethan occultist Edward Kelley—who collaborated with John Dee to bring forth the *Enochian* language from the spirit world—came from the powerful Uí Maine dynasty, who also claimed to be direct descendants of the Tuatha Dé Danann, and part of the kingdom included Rathcroghan-Cruachán. How Kelley acquired his frankly astounding magical abilities, and from this, came to enjoy the patronage of the most powerful people in Europe during the *Renaissance*, remains a total mystery. Was Edward Kelley a living repository of some Druidical tradition within his own family bloodline, and because of this was employed to open up portals into other planes of existence and into the parallel worlds? His spectacular successes, along with his understanding of magic, was far beyond anyone else in Europe at the time. The likes of MacGregor Mathers and Edward Kelley were essentially continuing a magical tradition going right back to the shamanic tradition of the megalith builders. Portals and doorways, questions and answers.

When the Anglo-Norman historian Henry of Huntingdon wrote in 1130, "Stonehenge, where stones of wonderful size have been erected after the manner of doorways", his remarks were far more astute than he realised. Is this not precisely what we do when we walk through the portals of the trilithons of Stonehenge and the openings of the many megalithic structures all over the world? The original English name for dolmens in Ireland was, afterall, 'portal' dolmens. There was no doubt that by passing through negative spaces between these petrified portals—sometimes carved into the solid rock of a megalithic structure—that one is crossing a threshold into another reality. Hence, what

Yeats was doing with his poetry and other works. He was creating literary and magical portals which came directly from his own personal intimacy with the folklore and megaliths of Sligo.

This sense of consciousness flux became personally apparent to me when, in 2015, I took part in the *Blue Raincoat Theatre*'s production of the Yeats play *The Land of Heart's Desire,* in which I played the role of Fr Hart; a priest, whose own Christian faith is ultimately subordinated by the arrival of a fairy into a rural Sligo homestead. The play was an outdoor production which took place literally under the summit of Ben Bulben—a table mountain saturated in mythology and folklore—and it was during the performace of this play that I found myself experiencing a profound shift in consciounsness. It was essentially akin to what some might call a shamanic experience of sorts, and the trigger was simply being immersed inside a work of art dealing wth the folklore of the location in which the story was set. I also realised the full power of what the Druidic experience must have been in times past, and why their stories and bardic traditions retain a profound ability to carry the narrative of a society and its experiences across vast periods of time.

The area in and around Ben Bulben has long been associated with a supernatural race known as the *Gentry* who had abandoned the countryside for a more comfortable life in the cities of Europe. It isn't hard to extrapolate from this as being symbolic of the millions of rural Irish who fled the countryside from the time of the *Great Famine* onwards. Creating something of a modern compensatory mythology to deal with the loss of their neighbours, family members and social circle.

Yet this is not what people who live in the shadow of the mountain where I also happen to have my art studio state when recounting the stories told by their grandparents. Well into the 20th century, people who lived in the shadow of Ben Bulben believed in, and reported encounters with the *Gentry*. Who are we to say they were delusional or making these stories up? Walter Evans-Wentz, the highly-regarded American anthropologist who published the first English translation of *The Tibetan Book of the Dead,* reported in his 1911 book, *Fairy Faith in Celtic Countries*:

> "The Ben Bulbin country in County Sligo is one of those rare places in Ireland where fairies are thought to be visible, and our first witness from there claims to be able to see the fairies or 'gentry' and to talk with them. This mortal so favoured lives in the same townland where his fathers have lived during four hundred years, directly beneath the shadows of Ben Bulbin, on whose sides Dermot is said to have been killed while hunting the wild-boar. And this famous old mountain, honeycombed with curious grottoes ages ago when the sea beat against its perpendicular flanks, is the very place where the 'gentry' have their chief abode.
>
> Even on its broad level summit, for it is a high square table-land like a mighty cube of rock set down upon the earth by some antediluvian god, there are treacherous holes, wherein more than one hunter may have been lost for ever, penetrating to unknown depths; and by listening one can bear the tides from the ocean three or four miles away surging in and out through ancient subterranean channels, connected with these holes. In the neighbouring mountains there are long caverns which no man has dared to penetrate to the end, and even dogs, it is said, have been put in them never to emerge, or else to come out miles away."

CHAPTER SEVEN

LAND OF THE GENTRY

The Druid Code:
Magic, Megaliths and Mythology

In 1996, a team of archaeologists led by the Swedish professor Göran Bürenhult working on a dig site at *Carrowmore Megalithic Cemetery* (as it is commonly but misleadingly titled) in County Sligo published a report which was to challenge everything previously assumed about the timeline of ancient Irish history, and, in particular, the accepted notions of Neolithic Ireland in terms of an agriculturally-based culture having arrived—from Britain and Europe—some time after 4500BC. Which is also the accepted starting date for when all megalithic structures in Ireland were being errected.

The population of Ireland continued to grow during this phase until evidence suggests a sudden and catastrophic collapse in the population some time around 2500BC. At the same time, the Neolithic community at Skara Brae in Scotland, likewise, suddenly vanished, and the site remained unoccupied for the next six hundred years. Interestingly, this is also the same period which the major structures at Stonehenge are believed to have been erected. As most of the Neolithic communities of Ireland were living in coastal settlements—due to the heavily forested and wild interior—this population loss therefore mostly occurred in coastal regions at locations such as Carrowmore.

When the 1996 site investigations into the Carrowmore complex were completed and the findings published, it was revealed that the Carrowmore complex was at least five thousand years old. Radiocarbon dates by Professor Göran Bürenhult and his team indicated that one of the monuments dated to at least 5400BC. This is a full millennia before the Neolithic age was supposed to have even arrived in Ireland, and placed the construction of Carrowmore well inside the Mesolithic era (8000–4000 BC). Making it—at the time—one of the oldest surviving man-made structures on earth.

It was a sensational discovery, and one which should have generated as much excitement as the fantastic discoveries being made at Göbekli Tepe in Turkey, which were also revealing their own very ancient origins during the mid 1990s. One would think that Irish academics would have greeted this fantastic discovery with enthusiasm and even pride. That here—on the far northwest Atlantic coast of Ireland—was one more ancient site which would place the country at the forefront of ancient European civilisation and culture.

In actuality, the Irish academic establishment were deeply sceptical of the dating methods from the moment of the announcement, if not, almost disparaging to the point of hysterical condescension in some quarters. Almost immediately, the mainstream Irish academics set about to discredit Professor Göran Bürenhult's dating methods, even if none of the sceptical archaeologists and historians were present on the actual site at Carrowmore during the complex excavations.

The Druid Code:
Magic, Megaliths and Mythology

The central chamber of the *Listoghil* (or tomb 51) passage mound which is the largest of the megalithic structures at Carrowmore in County Sligo, Ireland. First explored by the antiquarian George Petrie in 1837, the excavated site today provides an excellent insight to the design and engineering techniques used by the Neolithic builders. All the other structures at Carrowmore appear to be focused upon *Listoghil* as if it is a central point of collection for the other megaliths nearby.

Although Carrowmore is at the centre of a part of Ireland rich in mythology, there are no known tales directly pertaining to this location that, as yet, anyone has successfully identified. It is almost as if the Carrowmore complex represents a forgotten or lost culture. More cryptically, the megalithic structures adorning the hills all around Carrowmore are directly connected to mythology. What happened at Carrowmore—near sea level—which left no memory?

(photo: Thomas Sheridan)

The high priests of Irish academia from their plush, tenured offices in far away Dublin were not going to allow their sacred timelines to be pushed back by several thousand years. Timelines which, for the most part are completely arbitrary—representing a legacy of Victorian validation of fanciful biblical migration assumptions—and which to this day remain still entrenched into the academic consciousness with an almost inflexible adhesive of agreed-upon consensus. It literally takes one generation of academics to die off before any challenging data is taken seriously enough to be even considered, let alone examined. In the meantime, every effort is undertaken to then, 'correct' the challenging data as it arrives.

Their reaction tells us so much about the fallacy of the Western timeline of discovery. Carrowmore was probably older than the civilisations of Sumer/Babylon, and flew in the face of the very literal 'biblical' timeline mentality of mainstream archaeology and their long-cherished *East to West* migration theory.

The Irish academics asked themselves, 'How could people on the fringes of Europe, in remote Country Sligo, be creating large scale megalithic infrastructure, along with all the human resources and social stability required to undertake this, when they were obstenibly scavaging, proto-humanoid 'savages' out in the back of beyond, far from the real heart of civilisation located in the Middle East?' If we lived in a world where mythology was used a tool to help unravel such mysteries, then the *Atlantis* idea would come running to the fore of speculation. In time, the carbon dating was declared 'flawed', and was soon 'corrected'.

Carrowmore is lucky to have survived at all. Sligo County Council wanted to build a landfill dump on the site (which had already been established as an important Neolithic ritual location by that time), and one gets the impression that some mainstream archaeologists in Ireland would have been content to have seen this happen, especially in light of Professor Göran Bürenhult's discoveries. Following a legal challenge in the early 1980s, the site was saved from the ravages of bureaucracy, and today, Carrowmore has become a popular site for tourists visiting the nearby city of Sligo. Carrowmore now resembles a golf course with manicured grass embankments, along with the small and rather typical visitors' centres. However, it still survives.

ENERGETIC FOOTPRINTS

Like so many 'protected' Irish megalithic sites, Carrowmore feels energetically 'dead' and sterile when compared to, say, Avebury in England, or the remarkable *Parco dei Petroglifi* near Cheremule in Sardinia with its *Janas* (fairy) chambers. It somehow suggests that Neolithic sites respond in kind with the attention and respect which people bring to them. It is as if they are charged or 'switched on' at some deep primal energetic level by our feelings and inclinations towards them, coupled with our respect for the people who created them. In the past, Irish folk customs and traditions charged these sites with overlays of indigenous mythology and festivals of celebration. Today, we are told that the great megalithic structures of Europe were created by animal skin-wearing proto-humanoids. This problem is not just an Irish one; in places such as Malta, the dehumanisation of their own megalithic builders is practically state-sanctioned, if the illustration in museums and visitors centres' are anything to go by.

Meanwhile, locations such as Avebury in England—still open to the public without admission charge—are filled with New Age and NeoPagan *Hippies*. While on the surface it may seem twee and corny, are these people the reason why Avebury sings and Carrowmore sleeps? I challenge anyone to walk the embankment at Avebury and then proceed along the standing stone-lined avenue, over Windmill Hill, then observe the man-made Silbury Hill appearing as one reaches the crest, and finally, follow the path up towards West Kennet Long Barrow without being emotionally, if not spiritually affected. These sacred sites belong to all humanity, and by our engagement with them, we create the 'sacred landscape' and the sites react to whatever emotional and intellectual inclinations we ourselves possess while encountering them. After all, we are made of the same stuff.

The academics, on the other hand, have reduced many of the Irish megalithic sites to cold, dead laboratories. Almost becoming default 'stone killers' by their lack of insight into the human complexities of their meaning, and belittling the importance of their mysteries. These sites are always considered to be either primitive death cult compounds, or exclusively, places of human and animal slaughter, and all the other possibilities for the most part, are discarded by mainstream archaeologists and historians. In many ways, Carrowmore has ironically become a dumping ground of sorts: for all the cushy, cold consensus which allows mainstream Irish archaeologists to copperfasten their accepted guesstimates and prejudices onto experiences they will never fully understand and do not want to understand.

Presently, there are thirty 'tombs' at Carrowmore, with dozens more lost to land reclamation and quarrying activities during the Victorian era. Conservative estimates put the number of structures presently on the site at being between sixty and eighty. The largest monument is the still impressive and semi-restored *Listoghil* (the only cairn at Carrowkeel), which is surrounded by several satellite mounds. Today, something of a dissected structures designed for easy tourist access, *Listoghil* is notable for both its strange, carved symbols, and also how the centre of the cairn performs the function of something of a 'collector' for all the other structures surrounding it.

THE CLOVERHILL ROCK ART ANOMALY

There are precious few examples of rock art known to exist among the Sligo megalithic landscape, and the most important ones can be found among the remains of a most interesting and puzzling cairn about five hundred metres from the main Carrowmore complex at Cloverhill. Discovered about two hundred years ago by a farmer ploughing the field, this truly unique site had already lost its kerbstones by the time of its 'discovery'. Although the rock art at Cloverhill has been badly weathered, it nonetheless presents a true mystery, in that representations of different eras of rock art designs appear to be present on four decorated stones.

On one stone, which faces the entrance, there is the petroglyphic style typical of megalithic stone art of Britain and Ireland, including the common circle and dot design. The other three decorated stones which face into the chamber have rather elegant, curvilinear chevrons looking very much like stylised ram's or bull's heads locked into combat, as well as other graceful forms. The subtle execution of the motifs on the three inward facing stones is truly remarkable, suggesting the possibility that perhaps two separate artists undertook the carving of each stone, or that some of the stones were brought to this location from somewhere else in order to form something of a Neolithic, or earlier, art gallery.

Some have suggested that the Cloverhill cairn is of a later, 300BC 'celtic'-era construction. However, apart from the curvilinear designs bearing something of a likeness to the European celtic *La Tène* period from about two thousand years later, there is little else to suggest that the cairn is of a more recent construction. If anything, to my eyes, the artwork is strikingly similar to rock art I have seen in Malta and Sardinia, which is far older in origin. This brings up another issue; in

The Druid Code:
Magic, Megaliths and Mythology

that the older the European megaliths are, the more likely we are to find they contain art and artefacts of a more elegant and refined level of craftsmanship and skill. We seen this from Orkney to Sardinia and at other locations. It is almost as if the stone builders reached a period of refinement and decorative skills, and then this was lost, and a later Neolithic culture had to begin again from scratch. Perhaps the more stylised artwork on the Cloverhill stones are from an earlier period, while the petroglyphs are from a more recent time?

A sample of some of the rock art from the Cloverhill cairn in Sligo, Ireland—as could best be determined by the author on a recent trip to the site—which is now heavily overgrown and vanishing at an alarming rate. Rock art at Sligo megalithic locations is exceptionally rare among the five thousand known sites in the county. Which adds further to the tragedy of their deteriorating condition. A far cry from how they looked in 1888 when beautiful rubbings were made by the antiquarian, W. G. Wood-Martin and which are now held in the *Sligo County Library*.

The designs contained on the Cloverhill orthostats are very different from what can be found in the Boyne Valley or elsewhere else in Ireland. Located near a complex where some sites have been determined to be as old as nine thousand years, the assumption was made in the late Victorian era that the Cloverhill artwork is more recent than the Neolithic. However, this is merely guesswork based on the curvilinear 'ram's or bull's' head type chevrons on some of the stones bearing a passing resemblance to 'celtic' *La Tène* style of central Europe from around the third century BC. Could Cloverhill be the oldest of all Irish rock art designs? The distinctively stylised 'ram' or 'bull' head designs also bear an uncanny, if not striking similarity to very ancient rock art at places such as the Ħaġar Qim temples in Malta.

(Illustration: Thomas Sheridan Field Notes)

Regardless, these people placed art and design at the centre of their communities and social life as a reflection of the natural art forms of the landscape and environment around them. In every sense, they were a truly 'cultured' people and not the animal skin-wearing neo-primates we see illustrated on the walls of countless archaeological visitors' centres.

Carrowmore is somewhat unique when compared to other sites in Ireland—such as Loughcrew and Newgrange—as there are no lintel-covered passage tunnels (portals). The more one looks at Carrowmore, the more unique it becomes when compared to similar sites around Ireland and Europe. Lying on the western edge of Europe and being so very ancient in its location, and with something of an almost psychological orientation towards the west and the Atlantic Ocean, its place on the Coolera Peninsula is also very significant. More than anything else, Carrowmore—when we look beyond the manicured lawns in and around the tourist-friendly structures—evokes the same sense of profound antiquity that we can also see at places such as *Ġgantija* on the Maltese island of Gozo, in that they would appear to belong to a far older period than the Neolithic timeframe which they have been slotted into by accepted convention.

TIME LINES ON THE LANDSCAPE

From my own investigation of megalithic sites in both Ireland and elsewhere, is that there appears to be two very distinct phases of culture and design. *Phase 1*: prior to 2500BC and *Phase 2* which recommences the secondary phase of Neolithic structures following the 2500BC 'events'. The date of 2500BC being significant as it indicates the possibility of a major disaster(s) which befell western Europe that may have included a tsunami(s). An environmental convulsion which decimated the populations of the Atlantic coastline regions and may also be related to environmental shifts within the Mediterranean regions which we can quantify by the desiccation of the Sahara, with evidence of the Nile water level significantly lowering in Egypt during the same timeframe.

Determined by academics to be an 'early Christian fort', the *Grianan of Aileach* is a tiered amphitheatre-type circular structure. Contrary to the official dating of the site, it is strongly connected with the mythology of Nemedians. First surveyed in the 1830's, the site affords spectacular views of Donegal, Derry and Tyrone. Its suggested use as a fort has to be called into question, as the walls are impractical for defence. They can be easily scaled, and missiles can also be hurled into the centre from outside the boundary walls with ease.

The interior of the structure has remarkable background noise removal properties due to its unique shape, which suggests that it was some form of ancient meeting place where discussions could take place from one side to the other without a need to raise one's voice beyond normal speaking level. In 2016, a drone camera operator proved that the *Spring Equinox* sunrise shone a long shaft of light through the small portal entrance. Ostensibly proving that the site was of pre-Christian origin and not from the sixth century fort as is officially stated.

(photo: Thomas Sheridan)

The Druid Code:
Magic, Megaliths and Mythology

The megalithic complexes in Sligo offer us a unique window into the two phases as both eras are present within a small and limited geographic area. The comparative mythology also offers tantalising allegories and similarities—echoed all across the mythology of the megalithic builders—concerning a previous age of 'giants', in which water plays a significant aspect. Humans have a remarkable capacity for incorporating social trauma within the shallow shorelines and deepest abysses of our collective psyches. Look, for example, at the mythology of the Titanic sinking, or the September 11, 2001 attacks upon New York City. The lingering trauma of these disasters impacted profoundly upon the consciousness and the subconscious of millons, if not billions of people.

When the initial personal and cultural shock of the experience wears off, a kind of compensatory mythology begins to heal the very real emotional trauma of the experiences. The visceral horrors of war are always replaced with tales of heroes and gallantry. In terms of the 9-11 events, the experience for millions was replaced with the conspiracy theories surrounding what happened on the day. Likewise, the 'unsinkable' Titanic has been the womb of endless conspiracy theories concerning 'what really happened?' This is our modern mythology gestating before us. It does not matter that most people find it annoying, offensive or shocking. It is a phenomena rooted deeply within the human psyche.

Does the manifesting of this trauma-induced mythology in the form of conspiracy theories indicate that the sinking of the Titanic and 9-11 never took place? Quite the contrary; they make the events more real and more deeply entrenched within the collective human condition, because myth is the most authentic repository of human experience. We retain the emotional and psychological impact of the events as trauma within the mind, and then, in time, this emotional record is replaced with a mythological compensation. A mythology which then begins to slowly submerge deep into the human subconscious in the form of folklore and legend.

The further back in human history the event—which sparked the mythological compensation that occurred—the deeper it sinks into the subconscious. However, it never completely vanishes into some forgotten abyss to decay among the entropy of its own antiquity and obscurity. The experience always remains fully intact, and given the right social and psychological/psychosocial triggers (which are not always necessarily traumatic) it can erupt with seismic convulsions back up to the surface again. However, they can also gently float back up to the surface as recollections of ancestral experiences. The stones of the sacred sites give us this experience and much more.

It is impossible to experience these stones of the great megaliths by viewing them as being apart from the ancient artists and engineers who designed and created them. They are petrified echoes of their consciousness sent forward in time. Their design, complexity, location and chronologies only tell us so much, and on the surface at least, very little about the sentient awareness of the people who created them. For this, we need to look at the mythology of the regions associated with them.

When I embark upon a field trip to explore megalithic sites, I take with me the local and tribal folklore and myths connected to them. This approach is perhaps the only reliable method which allows us to understand the people behind their creation, and more importantly, what became of them.

THE FIRST PHILOSOPHER'S STONE

Let's get to the heart of the matter as to what these ancient megalithic sites are at their very basic state. They are expressions of imagination and creativity. In other words, they represent a kind of philosophy in the form of their art, along wth their geographic/environmental locations and orientations towards astronomical alignments and so on. The approach is not a scientific one in the way that we, in the post-*Enlightenment* era, understand what science is, for as remarkable scientists and engineers as the megaliths builders were in their own way, they were not gestated exclusively in the womb of technical details. It is far closer to what we would call 'magic'. They were also products of the earliest form of *Natural Philosophy*, and an ability to bring the fire within their minds into tangible material form. The trajectory of their *will* and desires growing like a flower from within their subconscious as imagination and dreams, expressed with a very real artistic flair. An artistic flair that just happened to result in impressive engineering and logistical achievements. There is no realisation without the dreamer, and there is no dream without the imagination.

Next to art, I cannot imagine anything more vital to the development of the human story than its twin sister, philosophy. It is the *will* to dream out loud and create possibilities. When we gaze up at the often inconceivable engineering feats of the megalith builders, what we are seeing is their philosophy in stone. Dreams and visions made manifest and hurled into the future as mysteries which allow us fleeting glimpses of a humanity that was once very different to what we presently experience. Yes there is complex engineering. Yes, there are very real social, administrative and scientific applications required to have constructed these monuments in the first place. This, however, was simply the technical necessities which were rooted in a subliminal awareness that came from a place of underlying consciousness so very, very different to the one we humans possess today.

The largest stone quarried, transported and then erected upright by Neolithic people, is the so-called *Broken Menhir of Er Grah,* located at Locmariaquer, Brittany. Illustrated here during the early 1800s, no one can explain how such a colossal monolith was stood upright for so long, nor how it was knocked over and broken with such force. This region surrounding the Gulf of Morbihan was almost certainly flooded in the past, which also resulted in the highly decorated cairn at Gavrinis now being situated on a small island off the present shoreline.

(illustration: The British Library Collection)

These people did not quarry and erect monoliths such as the colossal *Broken Menhir of Er Grah* in Brittany, France for merely religious reasons alone. It is indeed incredible to us today to consider that these people quarried and then moved a seventy-foot stone weighing nearly three hundred and fifty tons, and then stood this huge megalith upright at least four thousand years ago. They undertook this incredible task because they were very different human beings than we as a species later became. Another form of consciousness resided inside them with a very different economy of reason that we today can't easily grasp.

The Druid Code:
Magic, Megaliths and Mythology

The ego had yet to be fully formed, as there was possibly little need for it at the time. It was a permanently induced magical state which placed them in a constant *mind-over-matter* state of existence. What made them like this is anyone's guess. Colin Wilson speculated that the same forces that allow a mother to lift a two-ton car off her child after an accident were somehow accessible on-demand to the megalith builders. Perhaps some shaman or holy men or women —by means of chanting, or perhaps following days of induced states of altered consciousness—created a situation whereby average humans could move these large stones and stand them upright with remarkable ease. We will probably never know if this is the case. One thing is for certain: rolling logs, simple ropes and earthen ramps can't place a sixty-ton stone on top of a plinth several metres off the ground using basic engineering techniques. And it never will.

How the currently Broken Menhir of Er Grah would have looked when it stood upright. The largest piece of stone quarried and moved across the landscape, and then placed upright by Neolithic people. An engineering feat impossible even in the twenty first century.

(illustration: Thomas Sheridan)

The Druid Code:
Magic, Megaliths and Mythology

The Coolera or *Cuíl Irra* Peninsula in County Sligo, Ireland sits at the heart of one of the most megalithic-rich landscapes in Europe with some of the structures having been dated as far back as six thousand years. Despite being on the very edge of Europe, this part of Ireland demonstrates that prior to the rise of Sumer, complex and advanced civilisations had developed on the fringes of the Atlantic Ocean during the Neolithic age.

(photo: Thomas Sheridan)

CHAPTER EIGHT

WITHIN AND WITHOUT THE MAGIC CIRCLE

The Druid Code:
Magic, Megaliths and Mythology

I n order to understand how, and more importantly, why, the megalith builders created these remarkable structures, we have to somehow attempt to get inside their heads and try to understand how their consciousness expressed itself cognitively. Trying to do this with a post-*Enlightenment* scientific mind is akin to putting a square peg in a round hole. It is not going to happen. They solidified their own existence in stone, and later, their descendants did the same, in story. Between both, we have a bilateral conduit back into the complexity of their world from the vantage point of the complexity of our own. Yeats expressed this beautifully in his poem *Fergus and the Druid*:

This whole day have I followed in the rocks,

And you have changed and flowed from shape to shape,

First as a raven on whose ancient wings

Scarcely a feather lingered,[...]

THE HILL OF THE MOON AMONG THE LANDLOCKED ISLANDS

Behind Carrowmore and dominating the coastal skyline of north county Sligo is the impressive mountain of Knocknarea (Hill of the Moon), with the so-called *Queen Maebh's Tomb* (*Miosgán Méadhbha*) sitting upon its visually striking limestone summit. Described as a large cairn being approximately sixty metres (200 ft) in diameter with a height reaching about ten metres (33 ft) high, the structure is one of the largest buildings of its kind in Ireland, and remarkably, has never been excavated. Perhaps the largest megalithic monument of its kind in Europe which still remains unexplored.

Dated at around three thousand years old (but this is just a guess using 'accepted timelines' with no hard evidence to disprove it isn't much older), the cairn is visited by thousands of hill walkers every year who can make their way up the mountain from two well-maintained hiking trails. The view from the summit presents a spectacular vista of the Sligo ritual landscape. Yet there is also something of a natural orientation towards the ocean, which is just below Knocknarea at the popular surfing village of Strandhill.

The biggest mystery of all is why no attempts to explore the site have been undertaken and with no plans for the foreseeable future to open up the cairn and discover what may lay inside. Speculation ranges from mainstream academics either wanting their own names personally connected with any potential great discoveries unearthed inside, to suggestions by some quarters that looking inside might result in discoveries which would undermine the archaeological orthodoxy regarding accepted 'facts' concerning Neolithic Ireland. In more prosaic terms, it would be a financially expensive project, but not an insurmountable strain upon public funds.

When one climbs to the summit of Knocknarea and then observes the landscape below, he or she are looking down on one of the most archaeologically wealthy landscapes found anywhere in Europe, in which all types of Irish megalithic monuments are to be found within a single location. However, one overriding factor also comes to light. Apart from the Carrowmore complex (and the nearby site at Cloverhill), the remainder of the cairns and other ancient monuments are predominantly atop hills and mountains: Knocknashee (Hill of the Fairies), Mulkatly Hill, Keshcorran, Carrowkeel, Slieve Daeane and Doomore atop the mysterious Ox Mountains. Forming something of a ritualistic landscape among the sky, it is as if these were originally constructed as isolated islands above the equally mytholocially wealthy *Plain of Reckoning* below. Created at a time when the sea levels were either higher than they are now, or somehow rose unexpectedly at one point, and with this, the ancient megalithic builders made contingency for this happening again in future by elevating their sacred sites atop these landlocked islands in the sky. Indeed, if one utilises a mapping simulator to increase the sea level in the region, the 'island' nature of these hills becomes readily apparent. There are other clues too, suggesting the possible aftermath of a tsunami, such as the large quantities of shells on high ground in the region, as well as large boulders which appear to have been subjected to coastal erosion scattered all across the Ox Mountains.

The name "Sligo" is derived from the Irish '*Sligeach*', and means "abounding in shells" and indeed, enormous mounds of mainly oyster shells are found in large middens—not all of which appear to be man-made—along the county's coastal areas. Sligo is a place where the ocean and land—including the inhabitants—are interchangeable within the folkore of the region as much as in its geography.

THE MYTHOLOGICAL OVERLAY

In the northern half of the island of Ireland there is no figure more greatly connected to the landscape than Queen Meabh. In Ulster—where she was considered the leader of an adversarial tribe from Connacht—the vast waterways of Lough Erne are named after the high priestess/druidess in the service of Meabh, and from which an ancient tribe of the region, the Érainn, took their name. Even more interesting is that Meabh and her court—which included the priestess/handmaiden Erne—all retreated towards Lough Erne when a giant emerged from from the cave of Oweynagat in the heart of Meabh's kingdom at Rathcroghan-Cruachán. Fleeing from the giant, Meabh and her court departed this reality by dissolving into the waters of the lough. Ulster folklore states that below the waters of the lough there is also a submerged city which is home to the Fir Bolg ('men of the bag'), one of the early races of Irish pre-history.

THE MYSTERY AT TANREGO BAY

Irish mythology is lavishly resplendent with previous races, tribes, kings, queens and heroes who meet their end, or face their ultimate fate upon or beneath water. These stories were told for generations by druids representing an oral tradition going back in far-off antiquity until Christian (or allegedly Christian) monks began writing them down in the format of the Irish *Annals* and other great mythological cycles of ancient Ireland. Within sight of Queen Maebh's cairn and below the waters of the picturesque and tranquil Tanrego Bay lies a stone circle known in the past as *Cú Chulainn's Tomb* (although locals are oblivious to its existence today), which is below the water level most of the time. There are also some badly weathered cairns on the shoreline nearby forming something of a neglected and delapidated megalithic cluster.

Tanrego Bay in County Sligo where the author has located a previously lost (officially 'destroyed') megalithic stone circle which is below the water line most of the time except during very low tides as is shown here. Some stones from the circle are indicated with white lines, while the remainder of the circle is semi-visible just protruding above the waterline behind it. The single line points to *Queen Meabh's Cairn* atop the summit of Knocknarea mountain in the distance. This part of Sligo is typical of the 'ritualistic landscape' of the Atlantic Neolithic societies.

(photo: Thomas Sheridan)

It appears to have been built by the same people who constructed nearby Carrowmore, and this would suggest it being of very ancient antiquity, as well as having been constructed at a time when the shoreline was much further out to sea than it is now. Once again, local tradition deemed it appropriate to name the stone circle after another Irish hero who met his moment of destiny during a mythological battle among the waters. What is particularly frustrating with this stone circle, due to its submergence in the bay, is that it is officially deemed to be 'destroyed' by archaeological surveys and therefore is no longer recognised as a legitimate megalithic site.

In 1779, the Dutch artist Gabriel Beranger, visited Sligo, and took a keen interest in the local megaliths and especially those found at Carrowmore and Tanrego Bay. The results of which are some beautiful watercolours and illustrations of their condition at the time of Beranger's investigation, along with well-detailed ground maps and other important illustrations. Although Tanrego Bay and its surroundings are treated with as much diligence and importance as Carrowmore by Beranger, he noted other structures which today are still not positively identified including some cairns on the nearby *Hill of Skreen*.

These lost megaliths included something named the "Green Stones", and he also drew a plan and view of a ring of stones on the beach at Tanrego Bay. This is the aforementioned *Cú Chulainn's Tomb* I have managed to identify through my own visits to the location, along with a possible avenue of stones leading towards it. This serves to further illustrate how we are still in an ongoing battle to preserve the megalithic structures of Sligo and the stories they tell, as well as the still-important role the ordinary researcher can play in supplementing the work of archaeologists and historians. The most important question for me regarding the stone circle at Tanrego Bay is why there is a megalithic structure under the sea most of the time? This is not uncommon by any means in the west of Ireland, or at places such as Orkney, where more and more complex and impressive megalithic structures are being found off the coast all the time.

THE BLACK PIG TSUNAMI?

One of the most cryptic of all the Irish folklore tales is that of the 'Black Pig', which features in several legends mostly set in the northern half of the island of

Ireland. The general plot line essentially follows the same narrative: a giant black pig (or black boar in some versions) ravages and destroys huge sections of the Irish landscape, wiping out all in its path. Its fury is such that its colossal strength forms new valleys through mountainous landscapes with its sheer unstoppable mass, and gouges out long trenches with its snout and tusks as it moves across the lowlands to eventually meet its demise in the ocean.

The *Black Pig's Dyke* (*Claí na Muice Duibhe*) is a series of earthen trenches, which runs form the borders of Leitrim/Sligo right across to the other side of Ireland to the Irish Sea at County Louth. Although parts of the trench had been turned into basic fortifications around 350BC, the common assumption is that these fortified sections were once part of a great defensive wall protecting Ulster from the kingdoms of Connacht and Meath to the west and south. This 'Great Wall of Ulster' theory, loses it traction when we consider that the defensive sections are all disconnected from one another. More likely an existing natural trench was altered by local tribes for holding and protecting livestock. Cattle being the main form of currency and accumulated wealth in Bronze and Iron Age Ireland.

The so-called *Grave of the Black Pig* is a rather cryptic mound near the beach at Enniscrone in Sligo. In the legend itself, some fascinating and rather revealing metaphors jump out from the overall narrative. After being chased into the sea by a band of survivors, the pig—and this is extremely important to take note of—then returns from the ocean and causes devastation upon the landscape once more. Finally, a band of warriors chased the Black Pig back into the ocean at nearby Easkey. Although sometimes the two locations—Enniscrone and Easkey—are interchangable depending on the telling of the story. Even so, the story does not end with the watery demise of the Black Pig. The legend of the destruction in its aftermath reveals even more tantalizing clues. Along with the devastation to the landscape, farms and human life, a further horror is unleashed when it is discovered that the Black Pig had covered the landscape in poisonous bristles which caused the death of any human or animal who came near to them.

Along with bull/bovine cults, the pig or boar represents one of the 'power animal' totems of ancient Irish society, as well as being a constant within mythology. The pig/boar archetype is considered something of a sacred animal, as both a means of survival and a destructive force. The tale of the destructive Black Pig which devastated large parts of the Irish countryside during a rampage, hints at something more profoundly allegorical in terms of an environmental catastrophe upon the landscape. While in the *Fenian Cycle of Irish Mythology*, the tale of the eloping lovers Diarmuid and Gráinne ends tragically when Diarmuid is killed by a giant demonic boar among the slopes of Ben Bulben in County Sligo.

(illustration: The British Library Collection)

Now let us use an allegorical method of deduction to unravel the legend of the Black Pig as an environmental catastrophe told within mythology; in this case, a tsumani, along with the destruction to the landscape, lives, property and livestock, tsunamis leave a toxic landscape in their wake. Once-fertile lands are essentially sterilised for decades afterwards. The entire biological cycle of the arable and natural landscape is destroyed from earthworms up to the tops of still-standing trees. Water wells are poisoned and riverbanks are turned into vast stagnant marshes. The basic requirement for any human society and infrastructure is stripped clean from the landscape and along with this, the means for survival. All that is left of human habitation in the case of a Neolithic society are two things: the stones of the man-made megaliths, and the ravens harvesting the slain...

Now just imagine the surviving members of communities in 2500BC at coastal regions such as County Sligo (or around the Gulf of Morbihan in Brittany), running to high ground as the tsunami makes its way inland. When the waters receded back into the ocean from whence it came, and they gaze upon the landscape to behold the loss of topsoil, trees and wood buildings. Nothing but blackened mud and the once-mighty trees uprooted and laying on their sides like the hairs on the skin of a black pig. The only thing left on the landscape to have escaped the disaster and remained standing were the great stone megaliths built by their ancestors. Everything else had been taken by the sea god Manannán mac Lir, a god who incidentally is also the owner of a magical pig whom he eats partially each evening, only for the pig's flesh to regenerate in the morning.

This allegory of the magical swine of regeneration is also possessed by the Norse god Odin, and remarkably, both are the primary pre-Christian deities of the Isle of Man (Manx) which is now waterlocked (having been once connected to Britain) in the middle of the Irish Sea. Is this legend of the *Black Pig* a traumatic mythological repository concerning the same tsunami which caused the mysterious depopulation of Ireland and Skara Brae in 2500BC? Is this same massive tsunami from the Atlantic which may have also toppled the *Grand Menhir of Er Gra*h in Locmariaquer, Brittany?

When the tsunami receeded, the coastlines of the Atlantic Neolithic regions changed forever. Valleys and low-lying regions were now under water. Entire communities were lost. As the megalithic builders of ancient coastal Europe looked around, the search for 'answers' began in earnest. What had become of the many humans taken by the sea gods? They were in the otherworld, of course. Now a whole new compensatory mythology was required to explain their absence, and how both this world and the otherworld had shifted their demarcation line away from the land and the skies and beyond to under the sea.

STORIES, STONES AND SIGILS

Following a lecture I gave in 2016 to a group of overseas visitors—who were on the Irish 'megalithic trail', so to speak—concerning the subject of the megaliths of Sligo, which also included the respective folklore and mythology connected with them, I accompanied this group of mainly Americans and Canadians to view the horned cairn (as I prefer the older 'official' terms) at Creevykeel not far from my art studio. While we were inside the 'court' area of this magnificent structure, and as we were considering its mystery and location within the landscape—one of the few Irish megalithic sites which most certainly remains energetically highly 'charged'—that one of the group asked me if it was true that the druids practiced human sacrifice.

When I replied that there is some hard evidence beyond the Roman propaganda (which is occasionally hyperbolic and overblown) that some druids did indeed indulge in acts of human sacrifice during periods of extreme hardship, that I could clearly observe several members of the group wince upon hearing this.

They did not want to hear that the druids—in some instances—took the life of another person (often a captured prisoner) as part of some desperate life sacrificial ritual. By "life sacrificial ritual", this term is used to denote the last desperate measure when all other magic has failed. However, we must also bear in mind that these ritual killings—as far as we can tell—were a rarity and nothing like the industrial scale of mass blood sacrifices that the Incas and Mayans of the Americas got up to when their own magic failed and their own gods completely abandoned them, viscerally demonstrating that when magic goes wrong, it goes very badly wrong, indeed.

When the science and art of magic is submerged under the miasma of spirituality and religion, elemental demonic forces begin to prey upon the priest class and aristocrats of the tribe by infecting the weakest psychic links among them. From Nero to Caligula, to Chairman Mao and Pol Pot (secular magi, but magi nonetheless), the results are horrifically self-evident for all to see. When the single chain that links the dynamics of a tribe or an entrenched concept breaks, the lower half of the chain crashes downwards as it is sacrificed to save the dogmatic top links of the chain. When a cable breaks a single strand, the cable remains fully intact along the length of its course.

Monotheism and dictatorships are chains from the top to the bottom, while polytheism and more anarchist-inclined social orders are cables made up of individual strands, and therefore, one broken strand will do far less damage than one broken chain link. Hence, why ancient Irish society lasted so long, and remained intact for thousands of years. It was a European indigenous social cable model made up of many strands around a central, accessible core. Even so, now and again, one strand or more will break as a result of all manner of social factors. At times, this leads to human sacrifice, but always on a limited and localised scale. Druids were still human men and women, and subject to the same light and shadow of the complex human condition.

To be honest, upon telling the tourists that some druids did perform human sacrifice, I found that I did not want to admit it to myself. There is something about the image of druids that wants us to see them as living embodiments of Tolkien's *Gandalf,* or even as a benign Odin in his simple robes walking the shoreline of the fjords in search of wisdom. The reason for this misty-eyed image of the druid in popular culture—from the late 1700s onwards—is a result of a 'romanticization' of their image, which has, in effect, created a very unrealistic portrayal of who the druids actually were, and what their role within their respective communities really was.

Another reason for the enduring appeal of the druid within popular culture can be found in what Carl Jung referred to as a "wise old man" archetype, which he termed the *Senex*. This aspect of the psyche emerges towards the latter stages of life as a person begins to achieve *Individuation* or a rounding out of one's life. It is a comforting archetype borne out of experience of life and the wisdom attained from such. Within younger people, there is an instinctual desire towards one's own self-actualisation, and we all developed a sense of fondness of the elder sage we see in others.

In 1978, Marie-Louise von Franz—the Swiss psychologist who specialised in the interpretations of fairy tales and of alchemical manuscripts—wrote in her essay, *The Process of Individuation*, "If an individual has wrestled seriously enough and long enough…the unconscious again changes its dominant character and appears in a new symbolic form…as a masculine initiator and guardian (an Indian guru), a wise old man, a spirit of nature, and so forth." We see this not only in Merlin of the Arthurian legends, but also, all throughout Western culture from Obi-Wan Kenobi in *Star Wars* to Leopold Bloom in James Joyce's *Ulysses*.

LUGH's ARRIVAL AT TARA

One of my personal favourite episodes in the Irish mythological record is that of the arrival of Lugh *Lámhfhada* ("long trailing arm") at the gates of Tara. Lugh is a powerful solar deity not only in Ireland, but all over Europe, lending his name to both Lusitania in Iberia, Louth in Ireland, Lyon in France and perhaps even lent his name to the city of London. He was also one of the first Heathen Irish deities to be re-engineered—in a negative sense—by Christian missionaries from Rome, who reduced his status to that of a lame, goblin-like creature disparagingly known as 'little stooping Lugh', and from this where the term 'Leprechaun' was derived. Even during the Victorian age, Irish rural peasants had been made so fearful of Lugh's Christianised negative image, that on his feast day of *Lughnasadh* (1 August), in memory of his foster-mother, Tailtiu—now Teltown, County Meath—they would avoid any location connected to him entirely.

The reason for this degradation of Lugh *Lámhfhada* was that he enjoyed the archetype of the wizard-god in the guise of a necessary catalyst for destruction and change rather than salvation and sainthood. This makes his image extremely powerful, as his Heathen magic demonstrates tangible human qualities and skills that any of us can attain if we choose to work towards their development, and thereby giving us more improved odds against the challenges of life and the natural world. Such gods and goddesses are not invisible power archetypes who bestow us with their mercy. Rather, they are gods and goddesses who create and inspire us to apply our own intuitive abilities and talents. Lugh was also the father of Cú Chulainn, the great hero of the *Ulster Cycle*. This father and son relationship is very significant, in that the father represents the intention of the subconscious mind (art), while the son represents the engagement with the material world (science). For there can be no earthly hero without a subconscious cause and effect to unleash the full potential of the *Life-Eager Hero* (change).

Within the collective archetypal concept, this can be viewed in terms of Cú Chulainn representing all humans as being the earthly sons, daughters and apprentices of the god Lugh (or other similar culturally-specific deities and their inter-relationships, such as Arjuna and Lord Krishna in the *Bhagavad Gita* for example). A terrifying prospect for the first Christians in Ireland to come face to face with, as it was wherever the *Gospels* were first exported. Which is why the second wave of (Roman) Christians arriving in Ireland instantly sought to destroy the image and power of Lugh among the Heathen Irish. Ultimately, their strategy failed, due to the Irish druids having already co-opted Christianity in Ireland before the arrival of Saint Patrick.

Upon his arrival at Tara, Nuada was the *High King*, and his guards refused Lugh entrance into the site. Now let us consider the significance of this act of refusal. We have what is ostensibly a god being refused access to the court of a king by a lowly guard until Lugh the godhead, proves his worth. We are now very much in the world of magic here. Tara being the magic circle, Nuada being the magician and the guard representing the circumference of the circle to protect against any hostile entity or forces from entering, and therefore violating and endangering the integrity of the magical enclosure. There are an estimated thirty to forty thousand raths, or ring-like enclosures with raised circular, sometimes conjoined surrounding mound(s) officially listed in Ireland. Most are estimated to have been built prior to the arrival of Christianity. Are these simply earthen forms of magic circles rather than defensive fortifications? One thing we do know for certain is that the Christian Irish termed these enclosures 'fairy forts'. Perhaps indicating the nature of the Heathen occupants who continued to live inside them (away with the fairies) after the arrival of Christianity? The main 'royal' sites of Ireland are all known for their circular mounds, including the conjoined examples on the *Hill of Tara*, which Lugh attempted to enter.

When the guard at Tara asked Lugh to present his credentials, Lugh then listed an array of skills and talents from smith, bard, historian, harpist, to warrior, magician and craftsman. Agreeing that Lugh was all he claimed he was, only then was he allowed access into the magic circle of the location. Lugh then goes on to become a great champion, who eventually slays Balor of the Formorians at the *Second Battle of Moytura* in County Sligo. Nuada himself is killed in this battle by Balor, who in return is then slain by Lugh. As in the Cú Chulainn story, there is a tremendous sense of magical destiny that transcends beyond that of the individual deeds of heroes, druids and kings. It is a charged continuum. Lugh possesses all the qualities of druids in terms of skills, talents, sorcery and valour, and is not a romantic figure by any means. He is pragmatic and necessary. Like a force of nature. He is not the only possible redeemer, and his archetype reminds us that we all have a duty to work and strive towards our own earthly salvation.

This would have been a daunting social and cultural hurdle for the first Christians who set foot on Ireland's shores to have to deal with. Not only was there no *original sin*, but that 'sinning' was actively encouraged at times in order to generate new and alternative dynamic forces. A social order operating in the same manner as any good scientist, constantly testing and retesting the hypotheses of their own existence as a means of developing new paradigms within the individual and the society, that would allow a better chance of survival of challenges arising in the future.

Each man and woman were aware and accepting of their flaws, because the gods themselves were flawed. This idea presents a rawness of humanity that is then left to the individual to personally work on, rather to atone for their sins which are absolved from above through middle men with the only approved 'magic' on offer: religion. This is also the *Shadow* of *Jungian* psychology. The traumas of the subconscious mind within the depths of the psyche need to be raised to the surface and dealt with, rather than forced deeper into the abyss of one's self, only to come exploding back up to the surface with an even more convulsive destruction of the personality, or, in a collective sense, the tribe. Jung knew well the importance of mythology as a safety valve of the *Shadow*. When taken in this way, the concepts of good and evil, right and wrong evaporate into a miasma of valuable insights and personal learning processes.

We can also see how this idea was reflected in the Norse deity of Loki. A tiresome and disruptive trickster god, when viewed with Christian eyes, he is simply a menace and a disaster waiting to happen. A liar, deceiver, troublemaker and ultimately the destroyer of all the *Æsir* gods. To the Heathen mind, Loki's apparent perdition is merely a representation of one specifically of the natural forces of destruction and rebirth that is self-evident from the wider cosmos to the smallest hungry microbes, and on to the awesome gravitational pull of a galaxy. **Loki exists because he needs to exist**. He is there to remind us all that, like Lugh's interrogation at the gates of Tara, we must always look for the light which casts the shadow, rather than just the shadow itself. This is firstly an individual process allowing us to see 'negative' spaces as being the part of the whole.

When viewed in these terms, Loki is not a devil; he is an asset. Like Lugh's entrance to Tara, he reminds us all that our own magic circle is not an act of fate. We created it ourselves, and we are personally responsible for the forces we bring to it and take from it. Monotheism, on the other hand, places us in the top to bottom chain link of a precisely demarcated world of good and bad, right and wrong and so forth. New Age doctrines follow the same tangent. There is no shadow work, only shadow boxing, and we strike out at the phantoms on the wall while missing the main target. Lugh's association with light is significant here, as the light cast by his shadow is the light which allowed all to see the full intent of Balor *of the Evil Eye*.

Lugh, in recent times, has also been associated by some as possibly being a comet, with his long arm trailing behind him. So there may well be some very real cosmic implications to his nature. Perhaps Lugh's archetype was rooted in some far off astronomical event which the earlier builders of the megaliths were aware of? In time, this cosmic cycle is then transformed into the subconscious forces of the human condition as mythology and allegory. However, the impetus remains the same; that only we can save ourselves. This realisation goes a long way to demonstrate just how very different the European indigenous Heathen consciousness is when compared to the later Christian consciousness.

It also explains why, much later on in history, the romantic version of the druids was cultivated. They were made Christ-like, yet this also became the catalyst for the resurgence in the popular interest in the Lughs, Odins, Gandalfs, Veles (Volos) and Merlins and so on. As with the discovery of the *Broighter Hoard* in 1896, it ultimately closed a magical spell cast in the far off distant past, and then, in true magical form, revealed itself in the most poetic and very surprising of ways.

CLONEHENGE

The modern image of the druids is one which grew out of the same period of British artistic expression that produced geniuses of the calibre of William Blake (himself the son of Irish immigrants), and William Turner during the height of what we now refer to as the *Romanticism* movement. The *Romantic* era cultivated an artistic and philosophical Europe-wide movement which took place during the first fifty years of the nineteenth century. This movement was basically a result of poets, artists and other bohemian types undergoing something of a 'spiritual' experience within the natural world, and from this, attempting to create an aesthetic language in order to convey (or capture) the 'super reality' of these events. Many of the *Romantic* poets and philosophers ended up committing suicide in one manner or another, as they lacked the psychological understanding in order to fully comprehend their own profound experiences.

By the time the movement had run its course, the *Romantics* were epitomised by the philosopher Nietzsche climbing mountains in search of his dead god only to find salvation with a horse held tightly in his own arms as it was being flogged on the streets of Turin. The *Romantic* movement still produced the initial spark of insight that would lead to the modern idea of what we consider Druidism to have been. In terms of the underlying aspect of the *Druid Code*, Nietzsche's *Eternal Recurrence* probably represented the first popularisation of the idea within western Europe since the druids of the Classical period. *Eternal Recurrence* is the concept that, with enough time, coupled with a finite number of circumstances, events will recur over and over again into infinity, and that all existence and forces has been recurring, and will continue to do so, in a self-similar manner for an infinite number of times across infinite space and time. This was both the most important and most misunderstood legacy of the *Romanticism* movement.

In essence, the *Romantics* failed to acknowledge that the light cannot exist without shadow. Rather than try to live with the dark side of the human condition, many *Romantics* strove to deny it out of existence. The result of this, of course, is that it destroyed many of them. Yet, perhaps it was this lack of their own 'shadow work' during the *Romantic* era which created a wider, and highly idealised, interest into the spiritual lives of the 'ancients'. *Romanticism* was also a cultural reaction towards the rapid industrialisation of the period—along with the resulting enormous social upheavals—as millions of rural dwellers departed the land forever in order to work within the urban shadows of Blake's 'dark, satanic mills'.

At its heart was a philosophy that man is a kind of god, and his artwork and philosophy is a means to move one step closer towards his divine state. Much of it was brought about by the same kind of escapism which the Gnostics—although using a purely spiritual trajectory—also sought to escape from their own earthly prison. A prison which was created by the same *Demiurge* super-demon whom they believed was the god of the *Old Testament*. The *Romantic* movement, on the other hand, believed that man's destiny was to move towards a higher state of development through connectivity with the natural world. So it is hardly surprising that the revival of an interest in Druidism took place around the same period. The changes brought about by industrialisation were particularly convulsive in the central and northern regions of England, where what had remained of English folk traditions and cultures—which had not been ethnically cleansed by William the Conqueror with his *Harrying of the North* (1069–70)— were finally diluted into the wheels of urbanised industry as the last of the English and *Brytonic* mythological cycles dissolved into the soot-filled streets of Manchester, Bradford, Sheffield and many other emerging industrial cities.

It was this final loss of English rural cultural heritage (although similar folk movements took place in Germany at the same time) which led the *Romantic* movement to embark upon their own desires to keep the old ways alive. Albeit in a rather unrealistic manner. Interestingly, some combined a form of early NeoPaganism with Christianity in order to paint a picture of a rustic and more idealised England which, at the time, was being submerged into the black fog of anthracite and charcoal infernos of (black) pig iron.

This period was epitomised by the outstandingly gifted Samuel Palmer (1805-1881), who was to become one of the greatest English visionary *Romantic* painters, printmakers and writers. The son of a Baptist minister, Palmer, like Blake and Turner, was also a Londoner, and who was first exhibited at the *Royal Academy* at the age of fourteen, despite him having no formal training. His work remains deeply moving and hauntingly melancholic—with nocturnal landscapes of rural Kent—outstanding for their dream-like qualities. These artistic expressions were derived within a NeoPagan-esque group known as *The Ancients*. Members of the group—including Palmer—would wander the English countryside under full moons attempting to recapture the ancient spiritual energies of the landscape. It was certainly a naïve approach, but it was also groundbreaking at the time, and resulted in some remarkable paintings and illustrations. It was during this same period that Druidism—or rather, something of an unconscious Druidic revival—became fashionable among the British artistic and upper class sets. So naturally, those with the financial means, coupled with appropriate levels of eccentricity, embarked upon building megalithic follies, or 'Clonehenges', as they are disparagingly known today.

These follies in stone were equally complemented by spiritual follies surrounding supposed recreations of a particular (if not peculiar) version of Druidic rites and rituals which remain with us today. However, even this faux notion of Druidism which was cultivated during this period, nevertheless has a very real value in and of itself. It represents something akin to the discovery of a votive horde of an idea which was later more fully understood when systems of complementary mythology and analytical psychology came along. This trajectory of developmental awareness over the course of time is no different than Cormac O'Neill telling a visting Welsh antiquarian about the Dagda at Newgrange in 1699. A sychronistic unearthing of a seam of racial memory and archetypal resonance was taking place.

STUKELEY'S RITUAL LANDSCAPES

The *Romantics*—that being the ones who turned their attenion to the megaliths—could not have adhered their own artistic philosophy onto the ancient landscape of Britain without an underlying 'spiritual' identity connecting both stone and spirit. This had already been provided by pioneering freemason, biographer of Issac Newton, and Anglican minister William Stukeley (1687-1765). Even today, Stukeley's investigations and theories concerning the two most famous English megalithic locations—Avebury and Stonehenge—have left an enormous cultural legacy that continues to impress upon the collective cultural consciousness. Contemporary ideas such as the Celtic Church being a Heathen-Christian hybrid came directly out of Stukeley's own theories.

Being a clergyman (and an ardent freemason), William Stukeley was in no doubt that the stone circles of Britain and Ireland were built for one specific purpose: they were temples of the druids. He created the popular idea of the ritual, ancient landscape, and by all accounts, he may well have been correct. Except that his 'celtic' druid priests did not create the megalithic complexes at Avebury, Stonehenge and elsewhere. However, it is reasonable to suspect that they may have used them for their own rituals during much later periods. He was also the first to speculate that the megalithic sites were possibly connected to the *Atlantis* civilisation of Plato. This is not to say that some proto-shamanic culture did not build the great megaliths of western Europe. On that count, Stukeley was probably correct, as were later researchers who came along and discovered specific alignments to certain celestial events. It was William Stukeley's timelines which were wrong. His basic ideas of megalithic stones relating to astronomical cycles have since proven to be sound.

Considering the period when William Stukeley undertook his monumental investigations of Stonehenge and Avebury, his work remains remarkable in terms of his conclusions. Conclusions which were almost certainly derived from his own interest in Freemasonry. For example, he worked in tandem with the legendary astronomer Edmund Halley (of the comet fame) to determine that Stonehenge was aligned to magnetic north in order to generate magnetic forces within the stones themselves, and from this, they dated Stonehenge to 460BC.

As the long-term aftershocks of the Puritanical era of British society had begun to wane, educated people started to take a serious interest in the megalithic stone monuments left by the ancients. Although antiquarians in general still looked upon the people who built these stones as uncultured barbarians, something of a sweeping romanticism of "ancient magicians and giants" gradually became applied to the monuments by freemasons, artists and poets.

In this early Victorian illustration of Carnac in Brittany, we can see the stones portrayed almost akin to an alien landscape. However, within a sweeping epic scale, so as to inspire awe and wonder. Such images of the British and other European megalitic sites played a major part in the creation of the modern Druidism Revival movement.

(illustration: British Library Collection)

Stukeley's vast miscalculation concerning the age of the monuments was due in part to the fact that, at the time, it was not known that magnetic north wanders and does not remain in a fixed position. Another factor was the age-old—an unfortunately ever present—desire to fit all human history within the timelines of the *King James Bible*. Nevertheless, Stukeley's work was groundbreaking on numerous levels, and despite its flaws, it continues to inspire to this day. Within his own lifetime, he had turned the mysterious—and often 'satanic'—ancient stone circles and mounds of Britain and Ireland into something of a fashionable phenomena that not only put a human connectedness upon the megalithic sites, but also inspired the later *Romantics* to build 'druids temples' of their own. On the other hand, while creating a greater public interest into ancient monuments, the speculation presented in Stukeley's work also created stereotypes which remain stronger today than ever.

EVEN BETTER THAN THE REAL THING?

The most infamous of these fashionably recreated 'druids temples' constructed at the height of the *Romanticism* movement is located at Ilton in Yorkshire, and was built by the English writer and philosopher of some note: William Danby (1752 – 1833). The 'temple' is complete with a 'druid's altar stone', a 'heel stone' in order to simulate the one at Stonehenge, and numerous other typical, and not so typical, homages to the megaliths of ancient Britain. These follies were nothing more than products of vanity and exclusivity, on private lands designed to keep out the same rural peasants whose ancient folk culture, that the likes of William Danby were purporting to be saving from the same industrial onslaught which ironically, their own business interests had foisted upon the English poor.

Even more ironic, there was no shortage of actual genuine ancient megaliths in Yorkshire, including the impressive and tellingly named *Devil's Arrows* at Boroughbridge, which are some of the most impressive standing stones (menhirs) found anywhere in Britain, Ireland or elsewhere. These stones form part of the expanded Neolithic landscape of the *Ure-Swale* region, which includes the spectacular and highly-significant Thornborough Henges.

Surrounded by genuine 'Temples of the Druids', the likes of Danby and many others sought to build their own fantasy versions instead. Within his *Druids Temple* folly at Ilton, the pageants and performances undertaken and improvised by Danby and his fellow 'druids' became the basis of what many people today consider the druids of the pre-Christain era rituals to have been. Nothing could be further from the truth. This softened image of stage-Druidism would be akin to some future generations restoring a lost Catholicism based upon Bing Crosby movies, while ignoring everything from flagellants whipping themselves, to fully re-enacted crucifixions taking place in the Phillipines at *Easter*. Druidism, like any effective spiritual tradition which lasts for significant periods of time, has to incorporate the darker aspects of the human condition and personal/collective suffering. Something that the modern druid revialists still go to great lengths to deny and ignore.

ANIMAL GEO-MAGNETISM

Something of a misunderstanding has developed in recent times—mainly within *NeoPagan* circles—that the ancient European druids were some kind of a shamanic tradition. While there are indeed tantalising images of the god Cernunnos—most famously portrayed upon the *Gundestrup Cauldron*—resplendent with deer antler head attire similar to that of Siberian and Slavic shamans, in reality, there is little proof that druids embarked on special and specific ritual journeys to otherworldly domains. Either by psychedelic substances or drumming—while taking the guise of spirit animals or otherwise

—and then returning back with prophecy and healing information.

Great excitement was generated with the discovery of an ancient red deer antler headdress at Hook's Cross in Herefordshire, England a few years ago. However, apart from this being uncovered during a dig at a Roman BC site, it would be just as prosaic to speculate that it may well have been a party or theatrical headdress belonging to some entertaining Roman as much as it being proof of druids partaking in shamanic rituals. Nevertheless, the zoomorphic archetype would have been a profound element within the idea of supernatual entities connected to the wild landscapes.

The symbolism of the deer-headed god or man represents a universal archetype being evident in deities such as *Pan* (Indo-European), *Brân the Blessed* (Wales), *Wayland the Smith* (Norse/Anglo Saxon), *Conall Cernach* (Ireland) *Karnayna* (Alexandria) and of course, the Christian Devil himself. None of these 'horned gods' are associated with shamanism. Druids, as portrayed in the Irish record, were more likely to use dreaming during normal sleep in order to make important decisions, such as the selection of a new king and so forth. Even so, it is probably very likely that the European druids had their origins in some basic proto-shamanic culture during the earlier Mesolithic period which later 'refined' the concept towards the druids of the pre-Roman era.

THE OAK MEN OF THE NORTH AND WEST

The term 'druid' was long taken to have been been derived from the proto-European term for 'oak' which is 'dru' and is also found in adjectives describing something or someone who is 'strong' or 'firm'. However, in recent times, the

Croatian linguist, Ranko Matasovic, has interepreted the term as possibly meaning 'strong knowledge'. In any case, the association of the druids and the oak is so intertwined that both terms are perfectly compatible when used in tandem.

We are always going to be talking in terms of metaphors and allegory, and so the druid, being the oak of the community, had the deepest roots into the earth of the human psyche and experience, with the strongest trunk and branches to withstand the greatest tempest, and was also capable of living and producing acorn seeds for hundreds of years. The oak wood itself is highly resistant to insects and disease due to its high tannin content, and when incorporated within buildings, oak beams are known to grow stronger as they age. The term 'tannin' itself, is derived from from '*tanna*', the *Old High German* word for oak tree, (as in '*Tannenbaum*'). So the universality of the oak metaphor is clearly apparent.

In Ireland, the oak tree is the symbol of County Derry derived from the Irish '*Doire*', meaning oak, while another Irish county, Kildare, in Irish '*Cill Dara*' or the 'Oak Church'. The huge supporting columns of the great Gothic cathedrals are long believed to be a representation of the sacred oak groves of the European druids. Again, the Christians took what worked in the Heathen world and engineered it for their own purposes. They were acutely aware of the powerful energies which Heathens celebrated in both forests and among stones, and the Gothic cathedrals were an attempt to solidify both into a single, and controllable experience.

The sacredness of the oak in European folk magic is recalled in J.G. Frazer's epic work on magical ritual, *The Golden Bough*, in which he outlines the serious consequences within Saxon society of someone stripping the bark from an oak tree. The culprit's navel would be nailed to the area of the oak where the bark had been stripped, and then they would be forced to walk around the tree trunk until their intestines had become completely unravelled as a sort of bandage, around the area of stripped oak bark. Then the guilty person would die from this ritual, and his own blood would then nourish the roots of the oak. The life of a man for the life of an oak. The implication being that an oak tree was more than a part of nature disconnected from human society, but that the oak tree **was** also a part of human society as much as any person. The protection of the oaks was given to the 'Oak Men'. Their service was to that of Nordic/Saxon diety Donar or Thunar: these being alternate names for the Norse god of thunder, Thor. Donar was connected with fertility, spring rains and the end of the darkness of winter. The Teutonic traditions of the Yule Log and the Easter Oak all derive from the Donar/Oak Men cult, the survival of Winter and the oncoming revival and restoration of Spring.

CRANNÓGS, NEOLITHIC AND LATER WOOD STRUCTURES

During the Neolithic period in Ireland, artificial islands known as crannógs were constructed by driving oak pilings into the soft beds of lakes and marshes. Along with protecting people and livestock, the crannógs were also symbolic in that they were connected to the idea of crossing water, boundaries and transformation. It may even be the case that the crannógs were first developed as a result of widespread flooding. The need to create dwellings which would be able to withstand sudden rises in water levels without being washed away?

This brings up one more factor concerning the vast gulf of archaeological and artistic evidence which was lost between the Neolithic and the Dark Ages due to the organic nature of wood. What kind of buildings did people design and create in ancient times? If they had the ability to create the stone complexes of the scale and impressiveness of Stonehenge and Carnac, then we can only imagine what they were also capable of building using wood. This lack of architectural evidence based entirely on unearthed foundations and stump posts left in the ground has been the only basis for why reconstructions of Neolithic and later buildings look more like they belong in central Africa than in northern and western Europe. The archaeologists have no idea what the structures looked like above foundation levels. So they apply a 'primitive' model in every case as the baseline of pre-Roman dwellings.

Back in my school days, we were shown a history film which portrayed the Roman arrival in Britain in 55 BC under Julius Caesar. The Romans were shown in the film as cultured, manicured and technology-possessing sophisticates, while the native Britons were shown to be near ape-like, grunting proto-humanoids, wearing animal skins and living in mud huts. The fact that this was a British-made documentary, and showed how British historians viewed their own ancestors, made me wonder about how they must have viewed the Irish from the same period! In fact, even today, the *British Museum* in London remains a monument to the greatness of *Roman Britain*, while 'celtic' Britain is treated as something of a family embarrassment and given a token exhibition space.

Things are better in Ireland, and there is ongoing research and discovery into possible building types that were used outside the Roman empire. High-quality wood was readily available from the Alps to the Arctic Circle and yet, wood still decays with time and weather. Hence, why there are little or no great pre-Roman cities and large public buildings remaining in northern Europe, apart from their foundations which can still be uncovered. However, these structures did exist and only now—starting on a small scale—are archaeologists beginning to understand just how potentially magnificent northern European Heathen architecture may have been. Rather than just circular mud and straw huts, a picture of elegance and stylish buildings is finally emerging. There is much evidence of large halls and other structures at major pre-Christian sites such as Tara in Ireland, and Uppsala in Sweden. Rediscovered Iron Age and later wood-built urban landscapes are being unearthed all the time. Thanks to the work of reconstruction archaeologists at locations such as The *Irish National Heritage Park* in County Wexford, an image of elegant and impressive wood and thatch buildings are beginning to finally emerge, and which is slowly recreating the almost 'enchanted' urban landscapes of northern Europe from the Neolithic period to the Dark Ages.

Try to imagine these communities of impressive wooden structures, halls, temples and homes clustered together in clearings between the immense old growth forests of Europe, and some being linked together by a complex network of wood roadways built wide enough for two chariots to pass one another at speed. Imagine the occupants of these communities dressed in lavishly-coloured fabrics of natural pigments and adorned with jewellery of the most intricate and complex patterns and designs. Then, imagine families retreating to their homes at the end of the day to gather around a central hearth fire and create magic, poems and legends which danced among the embers and sparks. Suddenly, our ancient ancestors do not seem so alien and foreign to us, after all.

This lack of above-ground building design from the time between the Neolithic and the Roman era is somewhat tantalizingly revealed by the remarkable early Christian *Stave* churches of Norway with their architectural design and ancient wood. Generally attributed to the Middle Ages (when Norway became Christian), these structures may have even been eariler Heathen buildings converted into churches in the Middle Ages rather than purpose-built during this period. Is this any less plausible than the known fact that many early Christian churches all over Europe were constructed upon pre-existing pagan sacred sites, or that just about every Christian *Holy Well* in Ireland and Britain were once *Druids' Wells*?

OLD CHURCH OF HITTERDAL.

The ancient 'stave' churches of Norway provide a possible insight into the kind of pre-Christian wood constructed architecture from Heathen times, possibly part of a tradition going back thousands of years. As ancient European societies are acknowledged as being superb craftworkers in metal, it would be unrealistic to assume that they were living in primitive huts and dressed in rags and furs. The same level of artistic proficiency which is found in their metal and glasswork almost certainly was also applied to their wood-based architectural, as well as their textile designs.

(illustration: British Library Collection)

The Druid Code:
Magic, Megaliths and Mythology

The main method of dating these very early wood buildings such as the Stave chrurches of Norway is dendrochronology (analysing, rather than simply counting the tree rings). However, this method is flawed in that it overlooks the probablity that the wood could have been reused from an older structure(s). As a result, when the dates come back as being far older than expected, the results are generally discarded. The reason why dendrochronology and carbon dating is required to date these buildings reveals another story: that, like the mysterious Round Towers of Ireland (which we shall explore later), there are absolutely no Christian records of the structures being built.

Kilclooney Dolmen, in County Donegal, is a portal dolmen which sits amid a vast and wild landscape in Ireland's far northwest. The graceful and elegant tilted capstone of nearly six metres long makes it the longest in Ireland. The sense of stylised design is very apparent, and from certain angles can present an array of simulacra from birds to fish held within its overall shape.

Although the dating is speculative, some fragments of Neolithic pottery have been found nearby, but again, this may have been left there by a much later culture as Kilclooney Dolmen—more so than any other Irish dolmen—may be far older. Another interesting aspect is that the dolmen sits on top of an ancient asteroid impact site. Did the unusual geology of the region bring the Kilclooney Dolmen builders to this specific location?

(illustration: Thomas Sheridan Field Notes)

CHAPTER NINE

THE DEEPEST ROOTS

The Druid Code:
Magic, Megaliths and Mythology

The *Eo Mugna* was one of the five legendary trees of Ireland; a magical oak which bore apples, acorns and hazelnuts that is not only associated with the druids, but also with restoration, renewal and revival. Again, the symbolism is universal, but in this case, very specific. According to ancient Irish archives known as the *Metrical Dindshenchas*—itself a fascinating text which deals with the origins and topography of early Ireland explaining the origins of place-names, individuals/folklore associated with them, along with pagan rituals and festivals—the descriptions are conveyed in the form of bardic poetry, which would suggest that a druid either dictated them directly to early Christian monks, or Christianised druids wrote the verses down. The methodology of archiving the information is too artistically dynamic for Christian record, and demonstrated a completely different level of consciousness than had existed outside the 'celtic' fringe of the time.

Among the verses included in the *Metrical Dindshenchas* is this celebration concerning the glory of the oak tree, which could just as easily be considered a metaphorical satire on the delusions of Christian conversions:

"Eo Mugna, great was the fair tree, high its top above the rest; thirty cubits – it was no trifle – that was the measure of its girth.

Three hundred cubits was the height of the blameless tree, its shadow sheltered a thousand: in secrecy it remained in the north and east till the time of Conn of the Hundred Fights.

A hundred score of warriors – no empty tale – along with ten hundred and forty would that tree shelter – it was a fierce struggle – till it was overthrown by the poets."

The last line "till it was overthrown by the poets" describes the idea that a druid (or bard) can issue forth a verse of poety which contains an awesome power or psychic charge. So here we have documented proof of 'Drudic thinking' within the early Irish church. Practically a bardic satire mocking the false and fragile sancturary offered by the Christian church, it is indeed remarkable that a monotheistic faith from the Middle East, by way of Rome, would allow early Irish monks the blessing and resources to begin archiving vast numbers of Irish mythological texts, legends, bardic and Druidic poetry and philosophy (magic, obstensibly) within an administrative structure devoted entirely to the *Gosples* and the *one true god.*

FAR FROM ROME THE 'SNAKES' STILL ROAM

This leaves us with only two possible reasons for this tolerance of Irish mythology and committing so much of the Irish mythological record to writing in an era when the resources to do such were limited, expensive and time consuming: firstly, the Roman church needed to understand the Irish culture, folklore and mythology at the deepest levels of the psyche, in order to more effectively convert the population to Christianity, or secondly, the early Christian church in Ireland was filled with druids pretending to be, or at least philosophically wanting to become Christians while carrying the old faith into the new one. The transition was far more complex and profound than just adding the title 'St' to the name of a pagan god or goddess. There was also no guarantee that Christianity was going to survive in Ireland.

This, then, leads to another question: Why bother doing this at all, and why was it only the Irish monks and scribes who used the resources and opportunities created by wealthy monastic insititutions and other early Christian communities in order to essentially *re-paganise* Ireland (in a sense) by using the power and might of the Roman church in Ireland to do it? What was it they were trying to keep alive? What great stream of information and timeless resources and knowlege into far off antiquity was so important that it was recorded and kept safe for future generations?

In early Ireland, this concept of the power of language and myth possessing awesome and magical potential was taken very seriously indeed. Amergin Glúingel was reputed to be the most powerful druid of the Milesian Gaels, and who was one of the leaders in their war against the Tuatha Dé Danann. The conflict was a result of Amergin Glúingel seeking revenge for the murder of his

The Druid Code:
Magic, Megaliths and Mythology

great-uncle Íth by the Tuatha Dé Danann kings Mac Cuill, Mac Cecht and Mac Gréine. In one of the most spectacular and theatrical episodes conveyed within the Irish *Mythological Cycle*, Amergin issues a stunning declaration of his intent to the Tuatha Dé Danann with this epic poem:

> *I am a wind in the sea (for depth)*
> *I am a sea-wave upon the land (for heaviness)*
> *I am the sound of the sea (for fearsomeness)*
> *I am a stag of seven combats (for strength)*
> *I am a hawk upon a cliff (for agility)*
> *I am a tear-drop of the sun (for purity)*
> *I am fair (i.e. there is no plant fairer than I)*
> *I am a boar for valour (for harshness)*
> *I am a salmon in a pool (for swiftness)*
> *I am a lake in a plain (for size)*
> *I am the excellence of arts (for beauty)*
> *I am a spear that wages battle with plunder.*
> *I am a god who froms subjects for a ruler*
> *Who explains the stones of the mountains?*
> *Who invokes the ages of the moon?*
> *Where lies the setting fo the sun?*
> *Who bears cattle from the house of Tethra?*
> *Who are the cattle of Tethra who laugh?*
> *What man, what god forms weapons?*
> *Indeed, then;*
> *I invoked a satirist...*
> *a satirist of wind.*

Along with a druid being able to issue forth satires and poetry which could inspire one race and lead to the destruction of another, the retention of vast amounts of information could, and can only be undertaken by people of the most secure and highly tuned cognition. Druids who were devoted to learning the words which were the living repository of enormous archives of information were, therefore, the only ones who were the most trusted to safeguard it. According to *Classical* sources, the druid would spend twenty years memorising the poems, laws, family lineages and mythologies, while the Irish sources state that this period of initiation was twelve years.

In Ireland, Britain, Brittany and Celtiberia, the stories were passed down from generation to generation by druids/*filid* who were generally (though not always) in the service of chieftains and other important figures in society.

SECRETS AND SPIES: HOW THE 'DRUIDS' SURVIVED

"On the shore stood the opposing army with its dense array of armed warriors, while between the ranks dashed women, in black attire like the Furies, with hair dishevelled, waving brands. All around, the Druids, lifting up their hands to heaven, and pouring forth dreadful imprecations, scared our soldiers by the unfamiliar sight, so that, as if their limbs were paralysed, they stood motionless, and exposed to wounds. Then urged by their general's appeals and mutual encouragements not to quail before a troop of frenzied women, they bore the standards onwards, smote down all resistance, and wrapped the foe in the flames of his own brands. A force was next set over the conquered, and their groves, devoted to inhuman

superstitions, were destroyed. They deemed it indeed a duty to cover their altars with the blood of captives and to consult their deities through human entrails."—Tacitus

One of the great misconceptions of history is that the last of the druids died off, or were killed off, in one great and decisive event surrounding their absolute, ruthless final termination with the massacre of the British druids in 60AD on the island of Anglesey, off the coast of Wales, by the Roman army under the command of Suetonius Paulinus. With this massacre, Druidism ceased to be a force in the world. Reading between the lines of the *Classical* descriptions of the druids reveals something of a masked neurosis—if not outright envy—concerning their power and ability. Constant references are made by *Classical* authors to the 'superstitions' and savagery of societies under the stewardship of the druids. This is a tactic which has been used to disparage indigenous spiritual traditions all over the world until the mid twentieth century. We must understand that within Imperial Rome, the idea that a member of a priestly order possessing as much power within a society (or even more) than the king or chieftain would have been considered obscene. When one considers Julius Caesar's own writings on the druids, there is an element of almost envy, as he was aware that the very same 'superstitions' (magic) the Romans frowned upon, were also the same reasons why Druidic societies remained integrated and successful for time spans which even the Roman Empire would envy.

The druids and their people in Anglesey waiting for the Romans to arrive demonstrated absolutely no fear of death and dying as the Roman army crossed a body of water in order to exterminate them. From the viewpoint of the people on the 'druid side' of the *Afon Menai,* this would have only added to the magical charge of the combat, as their mythology would have been resplendent with tales of heroes meeting their (earthly) demise as a result of some manner of water crossing ritual. They showed no fear, because they knew, like their ancestors before them, that they would return from the otherworld when the dangers brought by the seas (once more) had passed. There was no death. Only temporary retreats from their earthly existence. They knew they would be back no matter what the outcome of their final, epic battle with the Romans.

When the army of Suetonius Paulinus crossed the *Menai Strait* and exterminated the last of the British druids, they wanted to put a line under the event as the final obliteration of not only the druids in Britain, but also the druids from Gaul and Ireland who were among their ranks. It was the final showdown, and the result was to be absolute as far as Rome was concerned. The druids were to be no more, being consigned to the Roman version of George Owell's 'unpersons'. Not only would they no longer exist, as far as the overall public consciousness was concerned, but the druids legacy, even in terms of the power and influence they commanded among their tribes, simply never existed. A minor footnote in official history of an obscure religious sect.

This very Anglo-centric viewpoint (by way of Roman indoctrination) disregards that not only did druids remain a powerful and potent force in Ireland (or *Hibernia*, 'the land of wind and cold'), but that the Druidic system was a central part of Irish life—and would remain so for many hundreds of years to come in the guise of the bardic *filid*—and until well into the *Renaissance* era. We can even indulge speculation here, and propose that if any *filid* had followed the last of the old Irish Gaelic lords to continental Europe during the *Flight of the Earls* (1607), they probably served this exiled Irish Gaelic community, taking with them an unknown 'sacred relic' which as we have seen, they claim to have lost in the most bizarre and purposely symbolic circumstances. We can only speculate on how many of the exiled old Gaelic lord's ninety followers were members of the *filid*. However, one thing is certain; that the power of the druids survived for centuries beyond Julius Caesar's famous 54BC record of their customs and practices:

> *"The Druids are in charge of all religious matters, superintending public and private sacrifices, and explaining superstitions. A large crowd of young men, who flock to them for schooling, hold the Druids in great respect. For they have opinions to give on almost all disputes involving tribes or individuals, and if any crime is committed, any murder done, or if there is contention about a will or the boundaries of some property, they are the people who investigate the matter and establish rewards and punishments. Any individual or community that refuses to abide by their decision is excluded from the sacrifices, which is held to be the most serious punishment possible. Those thus excommunicated are viewed as impious criminals, they are deserted by their friends and no one will visit them or talk to them to avoid the risk of contagion from them. They are deprived of all rights in court, and they forfeit all claim to honours."*

There is one arch-druid of supreme power. On his death, he is succeeded either by someone outstanding among his fellows, or, if there are several of equal calibre, the decision is reached by a vote of all the Druids, and the election is sometimes managed by force. At a fixed time of year they assemble at a holy place in the territory of the Carnutes, which is thought to be the centre of Gaul. Anyone with a grievance attends and obeys the decisions and judgments which the Druids give. The general view is that this religion originated in Britain and was imported into Gaul, which means that any keen student of Druidism now goes to

The Druid Code:
Magic, Megaliths and Mythology

Britain for information. . .

"The whole Gallic nation is virtually a prey to superstition, and this makes the serious invalids or those engaged in battle or dangerous exploits sacrifice men instead of animals. They even vow to immolate themselves, using the Druids as their ministers for this purpose. They feel that the spirit of the gods cannot be appeased unless a man's life is given for a life. Public sacrifices of the same sort are common. Another practice is to make images of enormous size, with the limbs woven from osiers [willows]. Living human beings are fitted into these, and, when they are set on fire, the men are engulfed in the flames and perish. The general feeling is that the immortal gods are better pleased with the sacrifice of those caught in theft, robbery or some other crime. But if a supply of such criminals is lacking, then they resort to the sacrifice of completely innocent victims. . ."

Firstly, let us consider where the school of Druidism Caesar tells us originated from. He clearly states that it is Britain. Not from the 'celtic' heart of central Europe, but from the most distant fringes of an archipelago jutting into the Atlantic. Did this school of Druidism reach Britain from the smaller island of wind and cold to the west of it? Taking this further, did the Druidism of Ireland arrive from now-submerged lands beyond the sea known as *Hy Brasil* and other names? Why did Caesar also report this unproven and unauthenticated story of mass sacrifice of people inside giant human-shaped cages? Was some druid 'pulling his leg' so to speak in order to make Rome fearful of druids as a whole?

Let us consider two factors: the first is that druids made their 'last' stand on the Welsh island of Anglesey. Ireland is visible across the Irish Sea and within relatively straightforward reach with any adequate sea-going vessel, and secondly, they not only knew this was not to be the day of their final extermination as they could, and it is possible many druids did, escape to Ireland. It would be inconceivable that their most highest arch-druids, with perhaps thousands of years of racial and cultural knowledge, would just simply sacrifice all this upon the thrusting blade of a Roman *Gladius* when a Roman-free large island under the control of druids was just over the sea.

Did the Romans lie about the British druids being fully exterminated? Almost certainly. It was a propaganda-driven imperative brought about as an attempt to restore social order in the wake of Boudica's—the leader of the Iceni tribe—uprising against the Roman Empire in Britain, in which tens of thousands of Romans had been killed while Suetonius Paulinus was busy exterminating the druids in Anglesey. When the revolt was crushed, the remaining Roman population of Britain needed all the psychological security it could get.

Within Julius Caesar's earlier depiction of the practices of the druids and the society they effectively ran, there is, not surprisingly, a healthy mixture of truth with propaganda. Certainly there is a genuine sense of some respect within the text, too. However, this account of the *Druids of Gaul* became—and remains to this day—the benchmark for any study into the druids and their beliefs. If we look at the records of the Irish *filid* quasi-druid class more than a thousand years after Julius Caesar's account, we begin to unravel a more complex and far more revealing picture. For example, a powerful individual living in the non-Romano world of Ireland would have a great respect for the poetry and oratory of a *filid*, for fear that a satire may be written about him or her, that would undo not only their social authority, but destroy their entire sense of self. The very concept to a Roman general, governor, or even Emperor considering that a mere holy man or woman could draft a worded spell which was more powerful than their own rank in society would have been both laughable and alien to the Roman mind. Yet this was how the bardic tradition functioned in Ireland and the other 'celtic' lands.

This reveals that the druids, and later the bards/*filid*, were, at their core, a type of proto-psychologists. They understood the complexities of the human condition. This was how they came to be. In the aftermath of the catastrophe(s) which devastated the coastlines of Atlantic Europe and the Mediterranean, the druids (in their earliest form, as possibly some kind of shaman), then took it upon themselves to restore the psychological health of the the post-Neolithic and later societies who experienced this disaster. Perhaps the Romans in Britain, following the wake of the Iceni revolt, learned a thing or two themselves about druid techniques relating to social trauma healing.

The healing power of mythology and ritual on one hand, and the power of words and linguistic mastery on the other. These societies had to be safeguarded, while social integration remained intact, in tandem with the psychological and cognitive tools of ongoing survival from any future catastrophe, be it environmental, economic or as a result of warfare.

THE SOCIAL ORDER OF THE MYTHOLOGICAL CYCLE

The stories and tales told by the druids or *filid* were part of a complex and powerful, supernaturally-driven ritual that were considered acts of magic in their own right. Everything—as inconceivable as this is to our modern thinking—had to be, and was, perfectly memorised and then repeated word for word—verbatim —as it was originally learnt perhaps many decades previously from an ongoing chain of memory, which was itself, incredibly ancient. The result was that ancient Ireland, and other places where a similar druid/*flid*/bardic oral transmission of knowledge was a defacto part of human existence, resulted in surprisingly successful societies which lasted for long historic periods, regardless of the exterior traumatic impacts foisted upon them by wars and so on. These cultures themselves demonstrated remarkable tenacity.

Along with the druids, in the emerging centuries from 2500BC onwards, Ireland was ruled by a warrior aristocracy which proved its worth and legitimacy on the battlefield, along with their wisdom, more so than by benefit of their inherited bloodlines. In tandem with the arch-druids, these kings or chieftains oversaw the other grades of society which went down through subordinated ranks from the military, noble families, crafts workers and then to the peasant classes. There were also slaves, with a male slaves known a *mug* and the female slaves called *cumhals,* who were generally concubines for the *falthi* (a Gaelic military elite similar to the Japanese Samurai) and other higher ranking members of society. Even today, in some parts of Ireland "cumhal" is still used as a slur term for a prostitute.

This system of hierarchy was commonly employed all over Heathen Europe at the time, and later mirrored in the Viking class system of the *Thrall* (slaves and concubines), the *Karl* (farmers and skilled tradesmen), and the *Jarl* (aristocrats). In both Irish and Norse society, a member of the (non slave) lower classes was in many cases entitled to try and take over the position of leadership, by either challenging the authority of the Chieftain directly, or by defeating them in combat should the situation arise. In some ways, a rather more egalitarian method of proving leadership qualities in an age before European royalty became an exclusive product of selective interbreeding.

The Druid Code:
Magic, Megaliths and Mythology

This system also ensured that the royal males, of both Gaelic and Norse, society were warriors capable of fighting alongside the men under their command, as well as being respected statesmen who oversaw the well-being of their tribe. This is why the mythology of Saint Patrick being a slave boy in Ireland (he was, in fact, a Romano-British aristocrat) who attempted to destroy the druids(snakes), can also be seen as something of a poor satire directed at the old Gaelic class system. Which, incidentally, lasted long after the arrival of Christianity. In time, the *cumhals* of the old Gaelic world would become the *nuns* who filled the Irish convents and became bound to Jesus, rather than to a warrior.

The druids and *filid* (similar to the Viking *Seiðr*) tended to operate somewhat outside these social classes, by performing a role of intermediary counsel between all segments of society, along with the more esoteric and spiritual—though no less important—stewardship of the community. Each druid or *filid* was something akin to a Natural Philosopher meets psychoanalyst meets wizard, in that they were expected to be adept in poetry, legal matters, history, magic and family lineages, (which is why Ireland became a land of 'O's and 'Mac's surnames denoting specific hereditary lines) and, in some cases, highly skilled artisans and gold/silversmiths.

In terms of the mythological record, the post-Druidic *filid* was considered to be primarily a crafts person of oratory and storytelling, and was responsible for dictating the mythology, which remains a part of Irish society to this day. Irish parents still 'christen' the children with the names of characters from the Irish *Annals,* such as Emer, Setanta and Finn. In recent decades, this trend has greatly increased, as more and more Irish parents have turned their backs on naming their children after Christian saints and biblical entities from the Middle East.

This situation has arisen due to the enduring legacy of the Irish mythological record which was carried by countless generations of druids and later, *filid*. From this, we have a remarkably comprehensive understanding of ancient Irish life, which goes way back into the far reaches of antiquity.

THE TRIBAL EXPERIENCE

We know that in ancient Ireland, family structures and local tribes were known as 'tuaths', and collections of these formed the five regional kingdoms. Each of these provinces were completely autonomous and generally separated by geographic features; mainly rivers, with the Shannon being the main frontier between Connacht and the other kingdoms. It is also worth noting that Ireland had no 'High King' as such, and that even Brian Boru, at best, could only declare himself the *High King of Ireland*, while the majority of the population ignored his self-appointed national leadership.

It was only by means of utilising the Christian/Roman system that someone of the nature of Brian Boru was ever going to be in a position to declare himself supreme leader of Ireland. The Irish term for High King is *Ard Rí,* and under the *Brehon Law* of ancient Ireland, the *Ard Rí* himself could be sacrificed to the land for failing his people. This insured that psychopathic types did not find it easy seeking to become a High King in pre-Christian Ireland. After Saint Patrick arrived, the megalomaniacs were safe to seek the title of *Ard Rí*.

That was until the *Battle of Clontarf,* when the Viking named Brodir decapitated Brian Boru while he was praying to the god of the *Bible*. However, there had already been a time when a less violent method of undermining the possibility of a Gaelic Caesar was undertaken, many hundreds of years prior to the rule of Brian Boru. Dynastic bloodlines can be put to the sword and ended. It is far more difficult to terminate the archetypes and collective experience contained within the repository of consciousness. Swords were also considered magical wands to the ancient Irish. In the tale where Ogma captures the sword of the war-god Tethra, the sword begins to recount its past deeds, speaking with a human voice. The early Christian scribes claimed that the swords were possessed by demons (similar to wands, and later witches brooms) for fear that the Irish would be worshipping their swords and other objects of false idolatry, when they should be worshipping a dying man from the Middle East nailed to two planks of wood.

If the Irish druids understood one thing, it was that open warfare with the new military and political superpower of Roman Christianity would result in such social and cultural suicide—of ferocious magnitude—beyond what had taken place in Anglesey in 60AD; as it would have resulted in the total loss of a legacy, culture, religion, magic and ancient identity. The druids of Ireland were not going to stand and fight, instead, they were going to eventually, in time, enter the Roman church and keep their world alive inside the safety of the new superpower from the east. Their weapons of choice? Mythology, artwork and language.

Such repositories of epics and sagas reveal secrets and hidden histories to the attentive reader. These are the colours and brushstrokes within mythology which give meaning to the often cold and monochrome official narratives regarding our ancient ancestors. We are exposed to their desires, fears and inclinations; and how these stories are so closely connected to the megalithic sites and other 'sacred sites' of the Irish landscape. This brings us to another reason why the druids, and later the *filid*, retained an oral record of Irish mythology: the ability to convey sometimes difficult and traumatic history and personal experiences in such a manner so that the listener could receive the powerful truths free from terrors which could manifest later on in social paranoia and neurosis, and which might undermine the integral structure of the society, leading to chaos and psychic implosion. Humans are more able to deal with the potential disasters of the future when they have the survival myths of their past deeply embedded within their subconscious.

The technique of using metaphor and allegory to convey dark and even very dangerous realities, as well as potential dark fates awaiting humanity, is a universal idea. Bruno Bettelheim, for example, in his 1976 book, *The Uses of Enchantment: The Meaning and Importance of Fairy Tales,* demonstrated how popular European folk tales (which we now know are incredibly ancient) were used to convey difficult topics about potential life-threatening facts to young children. It being far easier to warn young children of the dangers of everything from paedophiles to psychopaths in the guise of memorable, entertaining stories of evil old ladies and wolves in sheep's clothing, than to traumatise the children of the potential dangers which lurk in the world beyond the protection of their parents.

As a result, the metaphor creates a powerful charged repository of awareness and subliminal understanding within the subconscious of the child who is being told the story. Perhaps this is the real meaning of why the Tuatha Dé Danann wait inside the hills and fairy forts for the day when Ireland will face its greatest time of danger to ride out on their chariots and save us in our hour of need?

THE 'WONDER HILL' OF THE TUATHA DÉ DANANN

The mound at Newgrange, along with the extended megalithic complex of the Boyne Valley in County Meath, are within an hour's drive of Dublin city, and have always been at the centre of the ancient Irish identity. Having first visited, and entered the passageway, to be then excitably taken into the central chamber during a primary school trip when I was no more than eleven years old, the experience left an enormous impression upon me that was to last for the rest of my life. Although, at the time, not as deep an impression as viewing the decapitated head of the now Saint Oliver Plunkett, the last Irish Catholic martyr to die in England. His head was once a star exhibit on the sacred relics scene for decades, before ending up inside a glass box at *Saint Peter's Church* in Drogheda in 1921 after a successful world tour.

Following our school trip to Newgrange, we were paraded before the decapitated head of this 'great Irish hero' (who, incidentally, was born under the shadow of the Loughcrew megalithic complex) in order to show our respect and give our gratitude for him giving up his life for the Roman Catholic church. When we got back to our school, the teacher explained to us that Oliver Plunkett was a great man who died for the Catholic faith, and that Newgrange was just a place where the people were so backward at the time that they worshipped the dead. Irony, like sex on television, was an unknown concept in the Ireland of the 1970's.

Even today, the tour guides at the Newgrange site, tend to play down any connection the location has to Irish mythology, so as to keep the archaeology of the complex within the bounds of an ancient death cult. The official line is that a monument of the epic scale of Newgrange—which is a part of the larger *Brú na Bóinne* (an area of the Boyne River Valley which also contains the passage mounds of Knowth and Dowth)—was constructed and venerated by primitive savages wearing animal skins because they feared death. Essentially the same story applied to all major ancient megalithic sites in Europe.

How did the experts come to this conclusion? They made it all up, based on little or no evidence and agreed it was to become the official narrative. The Neolithic builders of Newgrange were simply a death cult, they tell us. They worshipped death because they, and their world, is dead to us now, and the evidence for this is that a few bones are found now and again, in or near some of the structures. The same official narrative also applies to Stonehenge to Carnac and all the other megalithic sites of western Europe, even though every last one of the Newgrange tour guides is fully aware that Newgrange is the repository of the soul of Aonghus Óg: the Tuatha Dé Danann god of sexual love and poetry.

If the visitor enters Newgrange aware of the mythological connections, rather than the cold, hard analytical archaeological narrative, they would find it a very different experience than it being a temple of death. I had the same experience when I visited the remarkable Ħal Saflieni Hypogeum in Malta in 2016, which, like Newgrange, is officially an underground prehistoric burial site composed of hard carved interconnecting rock-cut chambers dated at 4000BC. Yet, the last thing I saw or felt around me was a *necropolis* of the Neolithic era. It was a temple to life, not death. However, death and death rituals are constantly stressed by the tour guides as the exclusive reason for the Ħal Saflieni Hypogeum's only reason for existence. I found the my visit there to be deeply moving, and not in any way connected with the worship of death and loss. Like Newgrange, I instantly felt it to be a magical construction with a distinct, almost psychedelic sensation of other levels of consciousness, including, but not exclusively, the notion of a portal between this life and the otherworld. Rather than being terminal stations of the ancient human experience, I find such places to be the birth places of creativity and wonder.

Even the group of Vikings who were reported in the *Annals of the Four Masters* to have entered inside Newgrange in 861AD would have been more than aware of its supernatural importance. Did they merely go looking for plunder? Did they go looking for gods similar to their own? Perhaps both. The Neolithic chambered cairn in Orkney, known as Maeshowe, demonstrates the same complexity of construction prior to 2500BC. As with Newgrange, the *Winter Solstice* (this time with the sun setting) shines down the rather long entrance passage, filling the central chamber with light. Added to this, the inner chamber contains the largest collection of Viking runic inscriptions within a single location anywhere on earth. The runes themselves—amongst other things—speak of a mysterious hidden treasure to the northwest, and how some of the first Vikings who spent a night in the cairn went 'insane'. One wonders if the same insanity befell the Vikings who entered Newgrange looking for 'treasure' there? Was it mania, or was it similar to the near-psychedellic experience I underwent at the Ħal Saflieni Hypogeum?

When the sunlight of the *Winter Solstice* enters the central chamber at Newgrange—mythologically speaking—it is nothing less than the protector god the Dagda making love to the river goddess, the Boand, in order to resurrect the soul of Aonghus Óg, so that the long winter nights are filled with the warmth, love and poetry until the arrival of *Spring*. Certainly a far more appealing narrative than a place of human sacrifice and corpse veneration.

The question must then be asked as to how this supernatural legacy, of not only Newgrange, but just about every single other Irish megalithic site manage to survive at all? They survived because people with a vested interest in keeping their mythology alive made sure that very early on they would survive, even as Christianity was submerging the ancient gods and goddesses into their own aspirations for exclusive cultural legitimacy. It was a two-way race from the very start. An early Christian king of Meath—in order to appease the Christian power base in Ireland—attempted to rewrite the history of the *Hill of Knowth* as having been built by Nimrod himself as a tower to heaven.

This idiotic but purposeful legacy of disrespect is perhaps why Newgrange and many of the most well-known Irish megaliths often feel 'energetically dead' to many visitors, especially when compared to places such as Avebury in England, or the Callanish Stones on the island of Lewis in the Scottish Outer Hebrides. A notable exception is the previously mentioned large *Queen Meabh's Cairn* on the summit of Knocknarea in County Sligo. Each year, thousands of people make the long trek up the side of this impressive limestone mountain in order to experience what is believed to be the tomb of the legendary queen of Connacht. The visitors—as well as the locals in the nearby surfing community of Strandhill—have infused, or rather, reinforced the Queen Meabh narrative into the megalith itself, breathing some of the living experience into the structure. It has become a place of magic which communicates directly to the visitor, rather than a collection of stones placed there by ancient, godless peoples who are now represented exclusively by academics and government 'experts'.

This personal application of the magical narrative is what I believe brings the megaliths to 'life'. The megaliths require a 'charge'. When William Stukeley referred to Avebury as "A Temple of the British Druids", he was breathing a magical narrative into the location, which not only offset the attempts of the Puritan 'stone killers', but Stukeley himself was effectively charging the stones at

Avebury with his own romantic enchantments. This understanding almost certainly came about due to his own Freemasonic insights into such matters. The charge has held at Avebury, as it has at Knockarea, Tara and Callanish, because visitors continually keep these and many other megalithic locations 'alive' by encountering them not with a slide rule and a theodolite, but with a sense of myth and magic. Only then are their real secrets revealed to us.

The personal belief that one's own life is a monomyth of eventual heroism, and that all our individual triumphs and tragedies are part of the epic, is the most powerful message delivered by Irish mythology to the reader, as it was centuries later by Carl Jung, James Joyce, Joseph Campbell and others. This is what makes it so dangerous to any centralised power base that demands all humans must first cast off their personal understanding of themselves as being the hero or heroine of their own epic, in order for them to fit in with the prevailing dogma and social orders. The mythology becomes even more subversive as gods and goddesses are not only worshipped, but their divinity is challenged by mere mortals in many of these tales. This is something unimaginable in Abrahamic dogma. Remember what happened to Lucifer when he challenged the dictatorship of heaven? The wondrous chaos and earthly imperfection of the ancient Irish gods and goddesses creates dynamic energies and possibilities for both the gods and mortals.

GODS OF A COMMON KIND?

Considering the overall cohesiveness between narratives and tropes contained within the Irish and Norse mythologies, we can then assume that, if they both go back to the same deep ancient source, we can then also assume that there was almost certainly an Irish counterpart of *Muspell*, the place of fire and heat overseen by Surt at its entrance, holding his flaming sword awaiting the time when he burns all of creation back into the void. Perhaps the Irish version of Surt is an entity similar to Balor *of the Evil eye*. The symbolism of the eye in both Irish and Norse mythology is well worth considering in terms of what useful narratives and secrets it potentially can reveal to us about the very ancient past of Atlantic Europe.

How Odin came to lose his eye is told by Snorri Sturluson in his account of the land of *Gylfaginning*, by exchanging his eye for the gift of wisdom by placing it into the well of *Mimir* (again, sacrifice by water and loss in exchange for new knowledge): 'I know all, Odin: where your eye is hidden in the famous well of Mimir...'. Looking at the Irish mythology, the Irish goddess Brid removes one of her eyes to avoid being sold off in an arranged marriage. 'Here is that lovely eye for you,' said Brid . 'It seems to me,' she said, 'that no one will ask you for a blind girl.' Her brothers rush around her at once, but they have no water to wash the wound. 'Let my staff,' she said, 'be planted upon the sod before you.' With this act, Brid causes a well to burst forth from the earth. In both stories, we are confronted with the idea of a loss of an eye, for the gifts from a well.

The removal of the eye in Irish mythology does not stop there. The bard Aithirne Ailgesach demands the single eye of Eochaid mac Luchta, the King of Munster, and with this, the king then removes his own eye and hands it to the bard. 'Lead me, servant,' said the king, 'toward the stream, for the washing of my face.' Then he poured three waves of the water on his face. 'Is the eye plucked from my head, servant?' said the king. 'Woe is me!' said the servant. 'The hollow is red with your blood.' 'Be that its name forever,' said the king, 'namely, Dergderc.' Thus the king wrought generosity, namely, giving his only eye for the sake of honour'. Clearly we can see that a common theme in all these stories is a loss of normal vision in exchange for something of an *inner vision*. The symbolism of the well, or stream suggests a sense of stability and constant renewal; the sacrifice of part of the ego, in exchange for the knowledge and means of survival through intellectual and a deeper understanding.

THE LIMBS OF THE DISMEMBERED GODDESS

In the earliest of the *Brú na Bóinne* legends, we are also told that there is a hidden well inside a 'fairy mound' called *Segais*, guarded by Nechtan and his three cupbearers (Newgrange, Knowth and Dowth?). If any god or mortal dares to look into *Segais*' well, both of the eyes of whoever gazes into it will burst. Nechtan's wife, the Boand cow goddess, tempts fate by walking around the well three times. In response, three mighty waves spring from it, ripping away one of her feet, one of her hands and one of her eyes.

The Boand then attempts to flee from the waves, but the mighty waves follow her and push her into the Irish Sea. This results in the formation of the Boyne river. A very early poem describing the event entitled *Sid Nechtain Sund Forsin Tslei* states that two of the reaches of the Boyne are called 'the arm and calf of Nechtan's wife'. The sheer antiquity of the creation of the River Boyne from the limbs of a dismembered goddess has all the makings of another possible creation myth, as well as indicating some of the unstable and potentially dangerous nature of water if one chooses to defy its sanctity. Even a goddess is not safe from the wrath of its remorseless surge. The destruction of the Boand was also to serve as something of a *karmic debt* for her affair with the Dagda god and their illegitimate child Aonghus Og. Again, higher 'attributes' beyond basic survival results from this story. Wisdom through sacrifice are the end result.

The Boand mythology is also echoed in the story of how the river Shannon came to be. In this example, the goddess Sinann, as a beautiful virgin, approaches the well of *Segais* in order to procure the science and knowledge of the druids. In this case, the goddess is neither dismembered or mutilated. When we consider the allegory of sight in all these stories, we are talking about vision, both earthly and the vision of creativity, prophecy and intellect. This can also be seen as a kind of *Sympathetic Magic* and the transfer of one vital element in order to acquire a far greater result. The constant reminder of the power of rushing water, with its healing and destructive properties. Along with this motif appearing in both Norse and Irish mythology, there is a surviving *Brytonnic* parallel in that of Melorus, who has a right hand of silver (Nuada) and who causes a well to burst forth when his prosthetic limb comes to life, and this may be the origin of the Welsh proverb *Ilygadyffynnon*, which directly translates as the 'eye of the fountain'.

When one considers that the populations of Ireland and Orkney vanished for over half a millennia around 2500BC, and if we apply the speculation that this sudden depopulation was the result of a tsunami, then the very idea of water both as a villain and a means of salvation would be deeply entrenched within the subconscious minds of the people who survived the event. The loss of the old ways, and population loss (dismemberment), resulting in a changed landscape where the course of rivers are altered, and the social and cultural necessities which have to be redeveloped in order to begin again, while also applying healing from the enormous trauma to the survivors and their future generations.

The Druid Code:
Magic, Megaliths and Mythology

The mysterious and beautiful *Gallarus Oratory*, another interesting structure attributed to being Christian in origin, and which may well be an example of Heathen construction from a more ancient period. Located on the Dingle Peninsula, in County Kerry, Ireland, the building is built from dry stone techniques, and remains waterproof to this day, having never been repaired or restored. There are no other structures like it in Ireland, and it sits within a location rich in Neolithic and Bronze Age megaliths.

The main point of evidence used to claim that *Gallarus Oratory* being a Christian church, is that the entrance faces to the west. However, if the church is as old as has been claimed, the doorway should be facing towards the east. Early Christian churches were all built with the entrance to the east in the manner of the *Temple in Jerusalem*. It was not until the 8th or 9th century that the Roman Church enforced the building of churches with their entrances facing to the west; at least three hundred years after the building of the *Gallarus Oratory*. In practical terms, the building would be completely unsuited to Christian worship, and its tiny portal entrance is more indicative of the entrance to a Neolithic passage mound or cairn than that of a Christian church.

(illustration: Thomas Sheridan)

UNTOLD STORIES

Within the course of this book, I have attempted to demonstrate that all European magical traditions, as well as many religious and esoteric practices, found their origin in the magic of the druids of the Atlantic region—originally derived from a lost civilisation—which these present 'celtic' lands were once at the heart of. This magic was rooted in the far distant past among a proto-shamanic order which eventually gave rise to the megalithic builders until that all came to a sudden end around 2500BC. Out of this '*Ragnarök*', a new world of men, science and philosophies were required in order to heal and restore the survivors. These were to become the druids, and their powerful legacy is still with us to the present.

While the early proto-shamanic cultures of western Europe can be seen in terms of a culture who drank from the springs of magic and other states of *Super-Consciousness* which sprang from the ground, the druids were the first ones to 'hack' the operating system of the material and immaterial world by designing and building 'wells' into other spirit realms in order to actively search for the source of the magic of the phyche which connects the corporeal and incorporeal. Rather than waiting for the magic to unfold, they developed the arts and sciences in order to go and tap the unseen forces of the universe and actively control them with specific methods. Perhaps this is the idea of the *Holy Well* remaining so central to the Druidic principles for so long, as it could be hard to find a more fitting method to describe what was perhaps humanity's first foray into what we now call *Quantum Physics*.

The druids used nature and human consciousness as the primary tools of their laboratory. They tapped into the unseen states behind the human mind. Dreams became their research programmess. Humans have always known that the material world was not entirely material, but the druids were the first ones to figure out how to not only lift the veil between transcendental states of being, but also to hold the veil open and pass back and forth between this world and the otherworld. They use the pre-existing megalithic sites and monuments in order to harvest the psychic charge present within them, as did the later Christians who built their churches upon Druidic sacred sites in order to collect the same charge.

One of the more interesting, if not confusing, megalithic structures on the Isle of Man (Manx) is the unfortunately titled *King Orry's Grave*, named after one of earliest Viking leaders of the island. In reality, the structure has all the hallmarks of a Neolithic cairn. Excavated as late as the 1950s as a chambered long barrow with an open forecourt to the east.

(illustration: Thomas Sheridan)

CHAPTER TEN

Round Towers and Sacred Paths

The Druid Code:
Magic, Megaliths and Mythology

In May 2016, a vital piece in the puzzle of the *Druid Code* revealed iteself to me while travelling across the little known but highly significant megalithic landscape north of Killala in County Mayo. I was on a trip to photograph and measure a tall, thin standing stone facing out towards the north Atlantic next to the empty and picturesque golden sands of Lackan Bay at Carrowtrasna. Expecting to find yet another interesting standing stone, the journey to and from the charming fishing village of Killala turned into something of an adventure and a revelation at the same time. I was not expecting this to happen when I plotted out the route on the *Ordnance Survey* map. However, as with so many of my journeys to such places all over Europe, a sense of connected migration from this reality to *another* took place. I was being lured to the region. It was finding me; I did not find it.

The Druid Code:
Magic, Megaliths and Mythology

The standing stone itself is an impressive four metres high, and looks remarkably like petrified wood, as is common with several unusual looking stones found at certain locations all over the European megalithic arch. Local folklore claims that—yet, once again—Saint Patrick himself erected this stone. However, the earthworks around the megalith reveal a far more ancient landscape of great antiquity.

The menhir or standing stone at Carrowtrasna in County Mayo, which turned out to be something of a directional pointer across a megalithic landscape leading towards the solving of a mystery which had long wandered through my consciousness. I wanted to understand where the megaliths of antiquity ended, and when the later stone structures of Ireland, such as round towers, beehive cell houses and stone oratories of the Christian era began. What I discovered was, that they were all a continuum across the ages and built for the same reason. The Neolithic standing stones, Irish *High Crosses* and round towers all possess the same charge. They are, in effect, wands charging the landscape and the people who erected them with certain electromagnetic and plasma-based energies. A magical technology derived from a period far off in forgotten history.

(photo: Thomas Sheridan)

The Druid Code:
Magic, Megaliths and Mythology

As I looked around at the extremely fertile landscape immediately surrounding the standing stone, with its lush, almost luminous green grass—when compared to the wider surrounding landscape—my eye was constantly taken out to the great Atlantic beyond the mouth of Lackan Bay. The stone itself was—with its unusual tapered top—unifying land, sky and especially, the ocean beyond, as if pointing to a place of significance now lost beneath the turbulent waves.

The standing stone gestured to something 'out there' in the deep salty waters, rather than to the landscape surrounding it. As I took some measurements—as I usually do with megalithic stones—I could sense a distinct sensation of subtle pulsating waves of energy emitting from the rock face on the soft underskin of my arms. The only other location I have encountered such a perceptible sense of 'charge' was at West Kennet Long Barrow in England. Itself, sitting atop a hill among a rich, fertile landscape.

After leaving the standing stone at Carrowtrasna, we progressed southwards toward Killala, following a local narrow road which contained easy access to several other megaliths en route. The first of these was an exceptionally bulky Ogham Stone in the remote townland of Breastagh. Standing nearly three metres high and almost a metre thick, it is unusual for a number of reasons. The first is that the actual stone itself is much older than the usual time frame attributed to the use of Ogham script. It has been determined to be at least from the Bronze Age, and the general consensus is that the 'defaced' Ogham script on the stone itself was added later. Yet upon close examination, the weathering on the script and on the cut edges of the stone would appear to be contemporary with one another. Suggesting that either the stone is more recent than the Bronze Age, or more remarkably, that Ogham is far more ancient than the official early Christian era which it is attributed to. Again, when I placed my underarms on the surface of the Ogham Stone, I felt a distinct charge of energy pulsating from it. I had been long aware that specific detectable waves of energy have been discovered at megalithic sites, but never had I felt this almost 'daisy chain' sensation of charge from one megalith to the next across a landscape itself. And certainly not to the degree I was feeling it on this day.

Hardly the first time that this phenomena was noticed, in the January 1983 edition of none other than that vanguard of scientific orthodoxy, the *New Scientist* magazine, there was an article based on a major study of the Rollright Stones, one part of a complex of three Neolithic and Bronze Age monuments in the heart of the English Midlands. The objective of the initial study was to locate if there were any detectable magnetic forces at the Rollright Stone Circle itself. The research was conducted by an engineer by the name of Charles Brooker, by creating a magnetometer survey of the circle. What Brooker discovered, was how bands of magnetic force become attracted into the Rollright Stone Circle itself by means of a narrow gap at the entrance.

Incredibly, the measurements then demonstrated how these bands of detectable electromagnetic energy would form a spiral towards the centre of the circle, as if they were moving into another place. The bands were not dissipating or losing their charge as the spiralled towards the centre; they were literally curving into somewhere else, almost like vanishing into an invisible hole. Along with this, two of the stones of the west side of the stone circle pulsated with concentric rings of alternating current, creating a rippling polarity effect. This is precisely the sensation I was feeling coming from the megaliths in North Mayo on that sunny afternoon.

This was technology. This was Neolithic magic.

Nearby to the Breastagh Ogham stone—and still following the same north-to-south trajectory from the location of the Carrowtrasna standing stone—I came across a very interesting double wedge structure at Rathfranpark, constructed from large, smooth boulders of about two metres in diameter. There was also a stone circle at this location that has now vanished. If this was still present, there would be no doubt that we would be dealing with a highly significant Neolithic ritual landscape on par with the Coolera Peninsula in County Sligo.

At the rear of the Rathfranpark double wedge formation, I have identified a large stone laying on the ground made from the same geology as the Breastagh Ogham stone, and which apparently has escaped the attention of the archaeologists, in that its edges are clearly dressed and cut in a manner similar to stones I have seen in temples in both Malta and Sardinia. The stone had been worked, and was giving off the same rippling charge effect as the two previous stones examined in northeast County Mayo; although the larger round boulders which made up the main construction of the wedge enclosure had no detectable charge present.

It is also at Rathfranpark that the sight of the round tower at Killala comes into focus, acting as something of a bookend; beginning with the standing stone on the shores of Lackan Bay to the north, and ending at this mysterious, allegedly Christian structure which looms over the village to the south, as has done so for at least a thousand years.

Like the standing stone at Lackan Bay, the round tower at Killala looks out onto the ocean, not only to the mystery beyond the waves, but also across the bay, directly at the grave of the *Black Pig* in Enniscrone, of all places.

THE ROUND TOWER OF KILLALA

Ask any theologian or archaeologist if they can produce evidence—written or otherwise—to indicate that the mysterious round towers of Ireland were built by Christian monks, and you'll be presented with the same answer: there is no evidence that the Irish round towers have Christian origin. To add to this mystery even further, why were the round towers of Ireland not destroyed along with the other structures at Irish abbeys with the *Dissolution of the Monasteries*, started by Henry VIII in 1536?

If they were indeed ecclesiastical structures, surely they would have made an easy, if not highly symbolic target for demolition? The symbolic significance of tearing down the most impressive structure in a Christian abbey would have been too tempting *not* to do. Yet, they were left alone, while churches and other religious buildings adjacent to them were demolished or made unusable. Not a single round tower in Ireland was touched. Why?

The obvious answer is that they were not considered 'Christian' buildings, and therefore, were not targeted for destruction. The example in Killala offers much evidence that we are dealing with pre-Christian structures built for a very specific purpose which remains a profound mystery to this day.

They should really be called *Druid Towers*, as evidence suggests they were built long before Saint Patrick set foot in Ireland, and perhaps older than Christianity itself. Although Christian scholars will deny this, and then protest their antiquity, in reality, more hard evidence exists that the famous Irish round towers were built before Christianity arrived in Ireland, and not after.

The Druid Code:
Magic, Megaliths and Mythology

The impressive round tower at Killala in County Mayo, which looms over the village dominating the countryside for miles around, is not only a sublime piece of beautifully executed engineering, but also creates a distinct sensation from its stonework, as if the structure is acting as some form of antenna; an effect long known to Irish farmers who have grazed their livestock on the grass adjacent to round towers due to the high fertility and high yield of the surrounding agricultural land.

(photo: Thomas Sheridan)

The round tower at Killala stands in the centre of the village on top of a hill and, at over twenty five metres high, is clearly visible when approaching from all directions. The tower rests on a plinth-like structure of two dozen stones of varied sizes. The plinth is surprisingly modest in scale, considering the huge structural load it has to carry, with a circumference of just under sixteen metres and a south, southeast, facing entrance, approximately three metres off the ground. Interestingly, the four windows at the top are orientated just off the cardinal points, similar to sides of the standing stone at Lacken Bay. There is also a rather strange bulge in the structure about halfway way up which was a result of a direct lightning strike in 1779. Otherwise, the tower is perfectly straight from top to bottom along all exterior surfaces. This represents a very high-quality level of masonry for the period. There is no evidence that the internal part of the tower ever contained ladders, staircases or floors. Although this is difficult to fully determine, they may well have been interior wooden compartments connected to one another as part of the original construction.

The tower was located on the site of a monastery founded by Saint Patrick, who was believed to have been captured and held prisoner by druids there as a young man, before his release and his eventual return, to appoint Saint Muiredach as the first bishop of the abbey. The site was chosen because of a druid's H*oly Well* —which still exists—and which flows into the sea nearby. Among the legends pertaining to Saint Patrick at the first church of Killala is one claiming that, around 443AD, he raised a woman from the dead and baptised her.

The description of Saint Muiredach himself is interesting, as he was described as a elderly man, and also a hermit, who lived on the remote island of Inishmurray, off the coast of Sligo. Another interesting fact is that Saint Muiredach was a close family member of Lóegaire (who died in 462AD) and is generally recognised as one of the last powerful Heathen kings of Ireland at Tara. Considered to be a great enemy of Saint Patrick, Lóegaire's own story is resplendent with supernatural battles involving druids and Christians, as well as wars against rival kingdoms in Ireland. Clearly the influence of Heathen culture upon the round tower at Killala is far more significant than is generally accepted.

Nearby, in the church grounds at Killala, is a large *souterrain*—a type of underground man-made cave found all over Ireland and western France—and there is an entrance into this beehive-shaped structure. The *souterrain* is currently flooded and exploration is difficult, but there is a passage which leads in the direction of the round tower, and local folklore clearly states that the round tower itself can be entered by means of an underground passageway leading from the *souterrain* to the interior of the tower.

Early Victorian illustration of the round tower in Clondalkin in the suburbs of Dublin. Until the later nineteenth century, the origin of the famous Irish round towers remained an open question, and it was only in the last century or so thay they have been referred to as being Christian in origin. Yet, there is not one single record of any abbey or monastic institution which makes reference to the construction of round towers on ecclesiastical lands.

(illustration: The British Library Collection)

The round tower at Killala is, in every way, connected directly and symbolically with the Heathen ritual landscape around it—and remains so to this day—as it still stands long after the Christian abbey. which claims it was a part of its ecclesiastical infrastructure, has long since vanished.

OTHER ROUND TOWER MYSTERIES

There are approximately seventy round towers still standing in Ireland today. Their purpose has never been fully determined. Considering their antiquity at the time of their construction, they would have been considered among the tallest buildings erected in Europe, and their design and engineering would have been on par with the buildings of great Neolithic structures such as Stonehenge, in terms of procuring available resources and technology. Some round towers at well over thirty meters high, would have been the skyscrapers of Atlantic Europe, and all built far away from the main power base of Europe at the time: Rome.

One of the most distinctive design elements of round towers is that they all have an entrance door usually around four metres above the ground. The standard academic reason for this strange feature is that the Christian monks would use a ladder to escape into the tower—along with their valuables—during raids by the Vikings. This is clearly absurd, as the Viking raiders would have just lit a large fire at the base of the tower to both asphyxiate the monks inside, while undermining the exterior wall construction, bringing the entire structure crashing down. One of the reasons that makes the precise dating of the round towers so difficult—apart from the fact that they are not comparable to anything similar elsewhere in Europe—is continual and ongoing restorations, repairs and refinements which took place from the Middle Ages on. Details were later added which were clearly mediaeval in style and thus, has given a false impression of their actual antiquity

The round tower at Glendalough in County Wicklow is one of the most attractive and impressive round towers in all of Ireland. Peeping out above the tree line of a dense woodland among surrounding cliffs and mountains, it has been the subject of countless drawings, paintings, photographs, and been featured in numerous movies and television shows. Along with Cashel—which also has an impressive round tower amid a complex of ruined ecclesiastical buildings—the valley of Glendalough in Wicklow was considered a sacred landscape long before the arrival of Christianity; and when the Vikings arrived in Dublin, they chose the trees of Glendalough to build their longships from. They recognised the location as a place where the old gods of the forests, streams and mountains still dwelled.

Like all the round towers of Ireland, they conform within an almost rigid set of design specifications. As George Lennox Barrow (1921-1989) noted, "we may well conclude that most of the towers were the work of teams of builders who moved from one monastery to another using standard designs." In terms of defensive purposes, they were useless, and as bell towers, their small windows at the top would have muffled the sound of the bell rather than amplifying it. All the round towers were built initially as free standing structures, although later Christian buildings were grafted onto them. Over a dozen of the still surviving towers have a conical cap, and the logical assumption is that all the round towers once had the same capping, and which have subsequently been destroyed by perhaps lighning strikes and/or natural weathering over the many centuries they have stood standing in the Irish landscape.

The basic cement used to bond the granite blocks of the round towers contains a sand, lime, horse hair and ox blood mortar. This is one of the few pieces of evidence to suggest that the towers might be of Christian origin, as the same mortar was used in the construction of Roman buildings in Britain. The assumption being that British monks brought Roman construction techniques and engineering to Ireland. However, as there are no similar round towers anywhere else in Roman/Christian Europe from the same era, one could also suggest—if we dare to invoke William Price's assertion that the knowledge of the *Classical* world had been stolen from the druids—that the construction method of the round towers, the Romans had acquired from the Irish, who in turn had acquired it from a much older source.

Another anomaly is that while early Irish round towers were constructed from stone and highly engineered, early Irish churches were constructed from wood. There is no indication that these early wooden churches were as aesthetically glorious as the Norweigian *stave* churches (but this may still have been the case). This then begs the question: why would the most important structure of a Christian community take second place to a round tower?

Another matter is that an earthquake—which rocked Ireland in 448AD—caused damage to seventy five Irish round towers. This is mentioned in the *Annals,* and Christian scholars since have gone to great lengths to contradict this, saying that the *Annals* are in fact recording either the destruction of ring forts, or more bizarrely, the destruction of Constantinople by an earthquake in the same year. Yet the Irish *Annals* specifically mention towers, and make no reference to either ring forts or Constantinople. In 448AD, we are talking about a period in Ireland where the new religion of Christianity had barely made a dent, and yet there were dozens of round towers already in existence, according to a very specific citation within the *Annals*.

Almost certainly, these round towers were built long before Saint Patrick set foot in Ireland. This may well explain why there is absolutely no mention of them in the religious history of Ireland during the construction of the first monasteries, and would also explain why they were not targeted by Henry VIII for destruction along with all other religious buildings. They were pre-Christian in origin, and were probably considered secular buildings at the time of Henry VIII.

THE DRUID TOWERS

In *Round Towers of Ireland,* written by historian H. O'Brien in 1898, he goes as far as claiming that the Irish round towers were built by none other than the Tuatha Dé Danann, who brought their design, engineering and means of construction from their destroyed homeland from beyond the sea. The book is rather remarkable for its time, in that O'Brien's research was complex in scope and is well thought out and presented. He even gives special mention to the Irish druids —as being the origin of all the other druids—having a magic and level of skill that was far superior to other forms of Druidism around Europe. These magicians of the Tuatha Dé Danann oversaw the construction of the Irish round towers orientated to solar and lunar alignments, and were used on specific feast days such as *Bealtaine.*

Professor Philip Callahan, an American who spent many decades investigating the Irish round towers, noted that Irish farmers valued the land around the round towers for the fertility they generated in the soil. In one case, he discovered that farmers ferried their cows in row boats to Devenish Island, in Lower Lough Erne, County Fermanagh, so they could avail of the highly nutritious, lush and fast growing grass around the base of the round tower. Callahan's theory is that the towers are constructed of paramagnetic stone which contains a weak, but detectable magnetic field, and which, as we have seen, was independently and scientifically verified by Charles Brooker in 1983 at Neolithic and Bronze Age megalithic sites in the UK. This paramagnetic effect allows them to act as giant accumulators of some unknown energy—which may or may not be similar to Wilhelm Reich's theory of *Orgone* energy—and the charge created by the round towers energises the surrounding topsoil, resulting in increased yields and healthier livestock. As the Irish round towers are made from either granite or basalt, they are ideal for the purpose of collecting subtle energies in the atmosphere and charging them into the earth.

If Professor Callahan's theories are correct, and I believe that Charles Brooker's 1983 research proves that they are, then a complete reevaluation concerning all megalithic structures of ancient Europe—not just Ireland—would unleash a paradigm shift in terms of these sacred sites being no longer thought of as 'tombs' and places of 'pagan sacrifice'. That they are, in fact, locations and structures built with very specific scientific, artistic and 'magical' purposes developed by a truly ancient civilisation which has vanished from the historical record.

The achievements of this lost period of history was kept alive through magic, megaliths and mythology and lasted up until the arrival of Christianity in Europe, when the 'cradle of civilisation' was deemed to be the Babylonian civilizations which emerged between the Tigris and Euphrates rivers in Mesopotamia. As a result, the Atlantic and eastern Mediterranean megalithic regions, were reduced to the level of barbaric oddities on the edge of the civilised world. Atlantis had been completely submerged in every possible sense.

THE TOWER MUST FALL, THE TOWER MUST RISE AGAIN

If we look beyond the physical structure of the round towers themselves, and even the menhirs and standing stones of the megalithic world, and on towards what they can represent in terms of gaining an insight into the people who built them, perhaps we are looking at the very real embodiments of the archetypes contained within the *Tower Card* in the *Tarot*. In all depictions of the card, is a single, tall tower standing atop a rocky outcrop. Lightning is seen striking the top of the tower as it bursts into flames, sending the occupants crashing to the ground below. The *Tower Card* represents the destruction of what once seemed secure, and by violent means, so a new order can begin again. The lightning flash has been interpreted as *Mjölnir*, the hammer of Thor, or *Vajra*, the lightning thunderbolt of Indra, or even as the blinding flash of inescapable truths cast by the pure light of Lucifer. Regardless of the archetypal origin and significance of the symbology, the tower must fall! The old ways have ended and the new order has begun. Resistance to change will result in total destruction beyond the tower itself. **There is no escape.**

In the context of the Irish round towers, we are presented with an interesting psychological insight when one considers the time of their construction, as Ireland was moving from Heathenism to Christianity. The round towers being a symbolic reflection of the inner state of the people. Almost as if the Irish round towers were a gift of sorts to the new faith. Reminding them that eventually their own tower must fall in time. The figures represented in the *Tower Card* of a falling man and woman represent the two prisoners we see earlier in the *Major Arcana* shackled in the *Devil Card*. But to which Devil?

Further to this idea of the concept of a tower being an expression of necessary transformation through destructive forces, Carl Jung, within a decade of his traumatic break from his mentor Sigmund Freud, when he found himself in a state of professional and social isolation, eventually came to understand this traumatic experience was purposeful. His own psyche and professional tower had fallen, and beginning in 1922, he purchased land on the shores of Lake Zurich in order to create a "representation in stone" of his "innermost thoughts." During the initial construction phase, Jung had been delivered the wrong size stone blocks from a quarry.

Rather that rejecting them, he exclaimed "That is my stone; I must have it!" Eventually the tower that Jung built at Bollingen became a symbolic representation of his life and work, which he was to hand over as his own legacy to humanity as a whole. Concerning the building of his stone edifice, Jung came as close as anyone ever will to explaining the drive which led the builders of the megaliths of the Neolithic age, and later, the round towers and other structures of the *Druid Code* when he stated:

> "We have no symbolic life, and we are all badly in need of the symbolic life. Only the symbolic life can express the need of the soul – the daily need of the soul, mind you! And because people have no such thing, they can never step out of this mill – this awful, banal, grinding life in which they are nothing but."

> ...outside the Tower, and is like an explanation of it. It is a manifestation of the occupant."

CLOSING THE CIRCLE

I have come to the conclusion that the builders of the Neolithic European megaliths were unconscious humans—in that they operated in the context of what Jung called a 'Bush Soul' (in which they could unify their thoughts as a collective, and by free association), and that the development of the current human level of consciousness took thousands of years and was triggered into its present form as a result of recurring and ongoing trauma. This traumatic transformation from the 'Bush Soul' of the conscious human to the modern individual generated what Jung called 'complexes'. Yet the unconscious human still resides inside us, and it is to this, that the language of magic speaks loudest.

The two states of awareness inside every human being represent a schism of the psyche constantly attempting to reconcile the relationship between the conscious and unconscious states of being. At the same time, as a species, large parts and experiences of our collective and tribal human history is unknown to us, yet it ripples into our consciousness as mythological stories and mysterious stones across the landscape. The druids performed their self-appointed task well, and their code continues to be deciphered up to the very present, and no doubt will do so long into the future.

The majority of my own revelations regarding my many visits to megalithic sites around Europe were filled with intuitive and spontaneous realisations. Later on, I would discover that they were backed up by the work of other reseachers who were also pondering them at the same time. The proliferation of quartz seams in megalithic stones was something I had noted in my youth, but it was not until I made the connection through my hobby, and later, formal study of analog electronics, that my initial *eureka* moment made sense. Yet here I was communicating through the language of electronics with people who lived thousands of years ago. Tell me that is not a magical experience. At this stage in my life, it has gotten to the point when I am now aware that I am being lied to by the official narrative when it is presented to me. A recent visit to the Hypogeum of Ħal-Saflieni in Malta left me in no doubt that the official history of this astounding place is complete bunk, created by the usual suspects of Jesuit-trained historians and the 'all roads lead to Rome' propagandists. Yet, where does my restrained sense of arrogance to the lies of the official narrative come from? Certainly, I have spent decades doing my own research, being lucky to live in one of the megalithic epicentres of the world. My intuition is the key. It locks on to the sacred sites in the same way my psyche locks on to a beautiful painting inside an art gallery. The unbridled honesty of the artist and the creator is self-evident. It cannot be obscured with an official cover story.

The American writer Patricia Highsmith remarked that "conscious thinking is the weakest". Something which artists and occultists have known since the dawn of man. That, along with our everyday consciousness, below the surface is a kind of subliminal consciousness that is equally as rich, and which operates with breathtaking honesty in the background. It requires silence in order to optimally function. When one visits a megalithic site, they are often in rural areas, away from the sensory overloads of the twenty first century, and it is in this silence and sense of wonder that the subliminal consciousness works in tandem with the conscious mind. And from this, the revelations come forward, blooming like flowers of the psyche. The *Druid Code* then begins to move like a ticker-tape machine of insights and awareness through the mind of the experiencer.

In the Afro-Latin American magical tradition of *Santeria*, ceremonies—which I have personally been present at—are based on the invocation of non-material beings in order to gain information about the future. The effect of observing one of these entities entering a *Santeria* practitioner is both terrifying and startling. The entity will speak in obscure African or Portuguese dialects, and even the face of the person invoking the spirit occupying them will change. The entity will often demand large quantities of alcohol or marijuana, yet when the entity leaves the person's body, the *Santeria* practitioner is completely as sober and alert as they were before the ritual began. The impression one is left with is that there are most certainly layers of awareness beyond the normal human consciousness level, and that among these other layers, all manner of other personalities, entities and beings can emerge.

In Vivekananda's 1896 book entitled *Raja Yoga*, there is a state described as *Samadhi,* which is similar to *Super-Consciousness,* and is considered the ultimate goal of all yoga. What Aleister Crowley wrote as "employing the methods of yoga to produce genius at will." Such states of awareness serve to illustrate the underlying ethos of this book: that my own journey into and out of the *Druid Code* has left me in no doubt that, above and beyond the hard research and other data I have collected over the years, the most important tool of all was the unseen hand which has led me to believe that the *Atlantis* of Plato was based on a very real place, and that the megalithic arc from Malta to Orkney is what remains of this lost civilisation. That the development of what we call 'magic' was to compensate for the loss of the sciences and arts of this perished world. That the racial memory was collected within mythology, and that the druids played a huge part in guiding the survivors through the centuries, and perhaps even into the present, until a *New Atlantis* returns, and the *Druid Code* shall be completed. Until that ultimate votive hoard is finally uncovered, we can still fill our lives with magic, megaliths and mythology.

Index

Aberdeenshire	139
Ailill	101
Ancient Order of Druids	47
Anglesey	91, 234
Annals of the Four Masters	247
Aonghus Óg	246
Ard Rí	242
Arjuna	208
Ark of the Covenant	90
astral light	108
Atharvaveda	42
Atlantis	27, 113, 152, 216
Autonomous Complexes	133
Avebury	108, 181
Badb	147
Balor of the Evil Eye	71, 211
Banba	164
Barrow, George Lennox	269
baseline of human consciousness	75
Bealtaine	32
Beauty And The Beast (Shamanic Origin)	65
Bedd Taliesin	99
Ben Bulben	173
Berserkers	145
Bhagavad Gita	208
Bicameral Mind	111
black magic	82
Black Pig	201p.
Blake, William	213
Blavatsky, Helena	49
Boand	247, 252
Bohea Stone	41, 87
Book of Ballymote	67
Book of Dun Cow	40, 140
Boudica	238
Brân the Blessed	220
Breastagh Ogham Stone	263
Brennan, Martin	29, 144
Brian Boru	242
British Israelism	90
Broighter Hoard	18, 211
Broken Menhir of Er Grah	190
Brooker, Charles	262, 272
Brú na Bóinne	61, 251
Bruniquel Cave	50
Bryn Celli Ddu	91
Bush Soul	275
Cairn	144
Callahan, Professor Philip	271
Callanish Stones	248
Campbell, Joseph	147, 150
Carnac	217
Carrowmore	177, 185, 196
Carrowtrasna Standing Stone	259p.
Cashel	40
Cathars	121
Cauldron of the Dagda	34
Caves of Kesh	130
Celtic Church	120
Cernunnos	219
Cessair	137
Chaos Magic	114
Children of Lir	119
Clondalkin	267
Clonehenges	215
Cloverhill	184, 197
Collective Unconscious	16, 158
Conchobar	102
Conn of the Hundred Fights	230
Cope, Julian	139
Croagh Patrick	87
Crom Cruach	88
Cromlech	159
Cromlech of the Almendres	52
Crowley, Aleister	277
Cú Chulainn	99, 147p., 150, 165, 200, 208
cumhals	240
Cursed by removing megalith	110
Cursed by the Sidhe	110
Dagda	247
Danu	34, 61
daylight atheism	131
Dee, John	172
Demiurge	213
demons	118, 132
Devil Card	273
Devil's Arrows at Boroughbridge	218
Devil's Bridge (Gotthard Pass)	37
Diarmuid and Gráinne	71, 202
Dissolution of the Monasteries	264
djinn	65
DMT-Dimethyltryptamine	148
Doggerland	25
Dolmen	159, 226
Domsteinane	24
Donar	222

Douglas, Alfred	35
Dún Ailinne	39
Durrington Walls	115
Eddas	92
Elcmar	59
electromagnetic energy of megaliths	91, 107, 262
elementals	133
Enochian	171p.
Eo Mugna	229
Eochaid	102
Eogan, Professor George	60
Erne	49, 271
Étaín	102
Eternal Recurrence	213
Évora, Portugal	52
excarnation	146
Fairy Folklore in Ireland	167
fairy fort	109
Fairy Tales	64
fairy tunes	167
falthi	240
familiars	133
female druids	99
Fenian Cycle	38
filid	37, 69
Fir Bolg ('men of the bag')	198
Four Functions of the Psyche (Jung)	43
Four Treasures of Ireland	33
Freemasonry	45, 48
Gaelic Revival	61, 100
Gallarus Oratory	253
Gamla Uppsala	122
Geoffrey of Monmouth	32
Giants	28
glamour (in magic)	147
Glendalough	268
Gnostics	213
Göbekli Tepe	178
Goblins	126
Golden Dawn	170
Grail Hallows	35
Grand Orient Lodge	47
Grianan of Aileach	186
Gulf of Morbihan	203
Gundestrup Cauldron	219
Gylfaginning	250
Harrying of the North	214
Häxan magic	35
Hebrew	140
High Cross	38, 41, 107, 144
Highsmith, Patricia	276
Hill of Tara	207
Hill of Torah	90
Hollow Earth theory	130
Holy Grail	35
Holy Lance	35
Holy Well	254
Hrungnir	102
Huginn and Muninn	114
Huxley, Aldous	57
Hvergelmir	163
Hy Brasil	27
Hypogeum of Hal-Saflieni	276
Iceni	238p.
Ilygadyffynnon	252
Individuation	52
Indra	273
Inishmurray	266
Ireland's Lost Stonehenge	89
James Joyce	249
Jung, Carl Gustav	16, 52, 125, 157p., 164, 206, 274p.
Kelley, Edward	172
Killala	266
King Orry's Grave	255
kingfisher	73
Knocknashee (Hill of the Fairies)	197
Knowth	60
Krishna	208
La Tène	184
Lascaux	30
Lebor Gabála Érenn	33
Leprechaun	67
Lesser Arcana	34
Levi, Eliphas	132
Lia Fáil	34
Lóegaire	266
Loki	101, 210
Long Meg and Her Daughters	52
Lost Treasure of the St Gotthard Pass	37
Lost Tribes of Israel	151
Lough Gur	162
Loughcrew	29, 41
Louth	89, 207
Lovecraftian	21
Lucifer	273
Lugh	90, 207p.
Lugh as a possible comet	211
Lughnasadh	207

Lusitania	89, 207
MacGregor Mathers	172
Macha	38
Maeshowe,	247
magical circle	41
magnetic field	271
Mahabharata	62
Malta	28, 246
Manannán mac Lir	203
Manx	203, 255
Masonic Annals of the Grand Lodge	46
Mata	20
Matasovic, Ranko	221
Melorus	252
Mên-an-Tol	161
Merlin	113, 116, 207
Mesopotamia	272
Metrical Dindshencha	229
Midgard Serpent	101
Milesian Gaels	110, 168
Mímisbrunnr	163
Modern Pathological Magic	143
monomyth	249
Morrígna	141
mug	240
Mythological Cycle	38
Nechtan	251
negative spaces (trilithons)	95
Nemed	38
Nemedians	186
New Scientist	262
Newgrange	59, 247
Noah's Ark	151
Normans	35
Norns	158
Nuada	34
O'Neill, Cormac	59, 215
oak	221, 229
Oak Men	222
Odin	203, 206
Ogham	31, 62, 64, 140
Ogma	243
Orgone	272
Origin of Freemasonry	46
Oscar Wilde	167
Oweynagat Cave	129, 198
ox blood mortar	269
Paine, Thomas	46
Palmer, Samuel	214
paramagnetic effect	272
People of Partholón	38
petrified wood inside cairns	156
phosphene	21
Pi	106
Picardy Stone	72
Piskie (fairy)	161
polymathēs	27
Pontypridd	48
Porcupine Bank,	152
portals to another reality	172
Pranu Mutteddu	51
Price, William	48
Puranas	164
Quantum Physics	254
quartz	275
Queen Meabh	39, 129, 198p.
Queen Meabh's Cairn	248
Ragnarök	15, 101, 254
Ráith na Ríogh (the Fort of the Kings)	40
Raja Yoga	277
Ramayana	62
Rath	109
Rathcroghan-Cruachán	39, 124, 129p., 198
raven	146
ravens	114
Rigveda	42
Ritual Sacrifice	17, 60, 82, 88, 99, 123, 163, 272
Roberts, Jack	29, 144
Rollright Stones	262
Romantic Movement	214
Round Towers	257, 264, 268
sacred sites and personal healing	160
Saint Ciarán of Clonmacnoise	39
Saint Cyprian	81
Saint Muiredach	266
Saint Patrick	87, 260, 266
Salmon of Knowledge	73
Samaveda	42
Samhain	170
Santeria	277
Sardinia	51, 106, 181
satire	66
Second Battle of Moytura	209
Senex	206
Shadow (Jung)	210
Shadow Beings	131
shape-shifters	145
Shiva	52, 99
Sicily	25

Sidhe	109p., 132, 161, 166pp.
sigil	30
Silbury Hill	181
simulacra	61
Skara Brae	177
Skellig Michael, an	138
Sligo	197
Society of the Rocking Stone	48
Somhlth	99, 102
souterrain	266
Spare, Austin Osman	133
Spear of Lugh	34
stage-Druidism	219
Stave Church	225
stone killers	139
Stone of Benn	20
Stone of the Divisions	32
Stonehenge	94, 216
Stonehenge (as a sacred landscape)	94
Stonehenge Two	112
Stukeley, William	215
Sword of the Spirit	35
Sympathetic Magic	252
Synod of Whitby	120
Táin Bó Cúailnge	39, 165
Taliesin	98p.
Tanderagee Idol	49
Tannenbaum	221
Tarot	34, 42, 273
Temple of Ġgantija	28
Tetragrammaton	42
The Children of Lir	18
The Golden Bough	221
The Golden Dawn	171
The Land of Heart's Desire	173
The Stone of Fál	34
The Stone of the Tree	162
The Uses of Enchantment	244
Theosophy	133
Thor	101, 152, 273
Thunar:	222
Tibetan mandala	52
Tir Na Nog	27
Treatise of Human Nature (1789),	166
Tsunami	185, 200
Tuan macCairill	99
Tuatha Dé Danann	34, 45, 49, 59, 111, 166, 246
Uisneach	32
Ulaid	39
Ulster Cycle	38, 208
Unconscious Celebration	132
Urðarbrunnr	158
Ure-Swale	218
Valkyrie	145
Vedas	164
Veles (Volos)	211
Vikings	67, 144, 247, 268
Vikings (TV Show)	92
Vivekananda's 1896 book	277
von Franz, Marie-Louise	206
walwōn	139
Wayland the Smith	220
Wcelceasig "the slain-choosing one"	142
weather magic	74
West Kennet Long Barrow	108, 143, 261
Williams, David Lewis-	155
Wirth, Oswald	42
Woodhenge	93
worded spell	239
Wordsworth, William	98
Y Maen Chwyf	48
Yajurveda	42
Yeats (on fairies)	126
Yeats on 'Magic'	171
Yeats, William Butler	100, 195
Yggdrasil	158, 163
York Rite	47
younger futhark runic text	101
Yule Log	222
zoomorphic war goddess	141
	191p.
Earth	130
Manannán mac Lir	18
('men of the bag'),	198
Æsir	210
Šetek (Slavic entity)	131